ARAB MEDIA
AND
POLITICAL
RENEWAL

Community, Legitimacy and Public Life

Edited by
Naomi Sakr

I.B. TAURIS
LONDON · NEW YORK

Published in 2007 by I.B.Tauris & Co. Ltd
6 Salem Road, London W2 4BU
175 Fifth Avenue, New York NY 10010
www.ibtauris.com

In the United States and Canada distributed by Palgrave Macmillan,
a division of St. Martin's Press, 175 Fifth Avenue, New York NY 10010

Library of Modern Middle East Studies 68

ISBN (Hb) 978 1 84511 433 6
ISBN (Pb) 978 1 84511 327 8

A full CIP record for this book is available from the British Library
A full CIP record for this book is available from the Library of Congress
Library of Congress catalog card: available

Typeset in Minion by Dexter Haven Associates Ltd, London
Printed and bound in Great Britain by TJ International Ltd, Padstow, Cornwall

CONTENTS

LIST OF TABLES
AND FIGURES

TABLES

FIGURES

NOTE ON SOURCES, CITATIONS AND TRANSLITERATION

Two methods have been adopted for citing sources, depending on their type. Primary sources, such as interviews, internal reports, newspaper or magazine articles, press releases, speeches and conference presentations, are cited in full in the endnotes but not the bibliography. Books, monographs, journal articles, academic theses and published reports are cited in both the endnotes and the bibliography. Arabic words and names are mostly transliterated following an informal and flexible method that generally omits diacritical marks, except in the notes to Chapter 5, where the transliteration system identifies the *ain* and the *hamza*. Where the *jeem* appears in Egyptian names it is represented with a hard 'g', as in Gamal, in accordance with Egyptian pronunciation. In certain cases, authors' names follow the Roman spellings they have adopted for themselves. Where copyright material has been reproduced, every effort has been made to obtain permission from copyright holders.

ACKNOWLEDGEMENTS

This volume grew out of a series of six one-day seminars on Arab media, organised by the Communication and Media Research Institute (CAMRI) at the University of Westminster, between December 2003 and June 2005. The series, entitled 'Towards an Arab Public Sphere? The Impact of New Media Technologies on Public Life in the Arab World', was funded by the Research Seminars programme of the UK's Economic and Social Research Council. These facts alone are indicative of the large number of people whose hard work and cooperation ensured that the project was conceived, the funding proposal was drafted and approved, and the seminars were organised and held. Colin Sparks, CAMRI's director, is first on this list. Thanks are due to him, to Tarik Sabry, and to the 30 other speakers who agreed to share their research and experience with a lively audience of more than 35 specialists over the six events. Based on the success of the seminars, CAMRI has formed an Arab Media Centre.

The contributors to this collection are to be thanked for their help and patience during the compilation and editing process. As editor I also wish to record my personal appreciation of the encouragement provided by Philippa Brewster at I.B.Tauris and the unfailing technical and moral support of my husband Ahmad.

NOTES ON
CONTRIBUTORS

Oliver Hahn is Professor of Journalism at the Business and Information Technology School (BiTS), University of Applied Sciences, Iserlohn, Germany. He is also Research Fellow at the Centre for Advanced Study in International Journalism (Erich Brost Institute), University of Dortmund, and a consultant to various international media and European bodies. His PhD thesis investigated the European cultural television channel ARTE.

Albrecht Hofheinz is Associate Professor of Modern Arabic Language and Culture at the University of Oslo, Norway. After receiving his doctorate from the University of Bergen he worked for three years in humanitarian and development aid, particularly in the West Bank and Gaza and Sudan. From 1999 to 2004 he held positions at the Institute for Advanced Study and the Centre for Modern Oriental Studies in Berlin, where he began field-based and online research on the use of the Internet in the Arab world.

Imad Karam is a Visiting Lecturer in the Department of Sociology at City University, London, where he has been completing a doctoral thesis on Identity Construction among Youth Audiences of Arab Satellite Television. Born in 1976, he graduated from Al-Azhar University in Gaza and has an MA in Media and Communications from Goldsmiths College, University of London. He worked as a journalist in Palestine before undertaking postgraduate studies.

Lina Khatib is a lecturer at the Department of Media Arts at Royal Holloway, University of London, where she teaches media theory, non-Western cinemas and international television. Her research interests include the relationship between media (film, television, Internet) representations and politics in the Middle East. She is the author of *Filming the Modern Middle East: Politics in the Cinemas of Hollywood and the Arab World* (I.B.Tauris 2006) and is currently writing *Lebanese Cinema: Imagining the Civil War and Beyond* (I.B.Tauris 2008).

Marwan M. Kraidy is Assistant Professor of International Relations and International Communication at the American University in Washington, DC and director of the Arab Media in Public Life (AMPLE) project. He is the author of *Hybridity, or The Cultural Logic of Globalization* (2005), and co-editor of *Global Media Studies: Ethnographic Perspectives* (2003). A former Fellow at the Woodrow Wilson International Center for Scholars, he is completing a new book on the social and political impact of Arab reality television as a Scholar-in-Residence at the Annenberg School of Communication, University of Pennsylvania.

Giovanna Maiola is a media research analyst at the Osservatorio di Pavia who has worked as a member of election observation missions to Uzbekistan (1999), Albania (2001 and 2003), Congo (2002), Sri Lanka (2004), Tunisia (2004) and Palestine (2004-5). She graduated in Political Sciences from Pavia University and gained an LLM in Media Law at the School of Oriental and African Studies, University of London.

Dina Matar teaches in the Media and Film Studies Centre at the School of Oriental and African Studies, University of London. Her research interests are diasporic politics and identities; Middle East politics; communication and culture; media audiences; political communication and journalism studies. Her published work has appeared in the *Journal of Ethnic and Migration Studies*, the *International Journal of Media and Cultural Politics* and *Westminster Papers in Communication and Culture*. She previously worked as a journalist and editor covering Europe, the Middle East and Africa.

Tarik Sabry is Senior Lecturer in the School of Media, Arts and Design at the University of Westminster, where he also edits the journal *Westminster Papers in Communication and Culture*. His research interests include globalisation, media audiences and Arab cultural studies, and his published work has appeared in the *European Journal of Cultural Studies*, *Transnational Broadcasting Studies* and *Journal of Global Media and Communication*.

Naomi Sakr is Reader in Communication in the School of Media, Arts and Design at the University of Westminster. She is the author of the prize-winning book *Satellite Realms: Transnational Television, Globalization and the Middle East* and editor of *Women and Media in the Middle East: Power through Self-Expression*, both published by I.B.Tauris. Her work has also appeared in books on Al-Jazeera, television policy, transnational television, international news and media reform.

Bruce Stanley is Provost and Professor of International Relations at Huron University in London, where he teaches courses on the Middle East and runs the MA in Conflict Resolution. He has been a consultant for the EU, National Democratic Institute and American Friends Service Committee on issues of conflict resolution and civil society in Israel/Palestine, served as Director of Amideast in the West Bank and Gaza, and is currently a Research Fellow in the Department of Politics at the University of Exeter.

David Ward combines work in international development with an academic interest in media policy and law, both in transitional democracies and Western Europe. He has worked as a media consultant for several governmental and non-governmental organisations including the European Commission and UN. The latest of his three books is an edited collection, *Television and Public Policy: Change and Continuity in an Era of Liberalization* (2006).

- I -

Approaches to Exploring Media–Politics Connections in the Arab World

Naomi Sakr

Political leaders continue to ascribe considerable influence to television news. Despite the proliferation of digital media outlets and the accompanying fragmentation of audiences that characterised the early years of the twenty-first century, this was also a period when governments of leading world powers deemed it worthwhile to channel more state funds into overseas broadcasting, not less. By end-2006 France was due to have launched a joint public–private television news network called France 24, aimed at helping to express French views and values to an international audience. Russia Today, a state-funded television channel, went on air in English in December 2005 to broadcast news from a Russian perspective around the world. In the preceding months the BBC World Service, funded by the British Foreign and Commonwealth Office, had announced its intention to launch a television channel in Arabic during 2007, thereby entering a market where the US-backed Al-Hurra TV and the German public broadcaster Deutsche Welle were already active. Chief among the declared motives behind these initiatives was the desire to counter the influence of existing channels (CNN and BBC World in the case of France 24; Al-Jazeera Satellite Channel in the case of Al-Hurra) or maintain a key position in world media (in the case of the BBC). Al-Jazeera, itself a trigger for new US and European television programming in Arabic, responded in kind with Al-Jazeera English, which underwent prolonged and costly preparations for start-up during 2005–6.

Ultimately, the rationale that motivates governments to use media as an arm of foreign policy shares some of the same assumptions that they rely on to rationalise censorship. The idea that 'hearts and minds' can be won by providing television coverage of certain issues in one case, or silencing coverage of certain issues in the other, downplays the extent to which individuals and communities form opinions and prioritise issues based on their own lived experience, cultural knowledge, expectations and interpretive frames of reference.[1] When viewers' lived reality includes personal experience, even at second hand, of foreign policy or military measures that directly contradict media messages from the same source, the messages are inevitably undermined. The credibility problem that 'attends the US as a promoter of democracy in the [Middle East] region' is a case in point,[2] with negative implications for the potential influence of Al-Hurra TV. Jacques Chirac, as French president, suggested in 2005 that France 24 would place France at the forefront of a 'global battle of images'.[3] Yet no struggle for influence and impact can be conducted at the level of images alone. Even those who argue strongly that media influence matters, and is traceable, also acknowledge the relevance of viewers' personal experience and the need to be aware of diversity and 'resistance' in audience responses.[4] Moreover, television viewing is essentially voluntary. The more choice viewers have, the more they are able to switch to programmes that they find least objectionable in terms of their own politics and priorities. Indeed, according to one survey of several decades of research, the accumulated findings confirmed that the average audience member 'pays relatively little attention, retains only a small fraction, and is not the slightest bit overloaded by the flow of information or the choices available among the media and messages'.[5]

Long-standing arguments highlighting audience resistance to the intended messages of audiovisual texts suggest that persuasion via television is likely to have mixed results. It may carry more weight with viewers when media accounts of distant happenings cannot be checked against the immediate environment, but even then the risk of dissonance is ever present.[6] By the same token, however, evidence that audiences retain little of what they watch implies that it does matter what they see. This book starts from the premise that the processes involved in media influence are complex and that the volume of scholarly research into the influence of television and the Internet in Arab countries is still very limited by comparison with that on Europe and the US. While the book's authors are keenly interested in the link between media and participatory politics, their research findings illuminate the complexities of that relationship in the Arab context, especially in the field of transnational media. It was, for example, never to be expected that a small margin of freedom of expression, when limited solely to satellite television and the Internet, would simply trigger political reform. Thus it was no surprise that political liberalisation in Arab states was still fragile and faltering nearly a decade after some observers started to celebrate the supposedly democratising potential of new media in the Arab world. Yet nor was it possible to analyse notable political events of 2005 – including Egyptian, Iraqi, Lebanese, Palestinian or Saudi elections for various tiers of government, or protest demonstrations in Cairo or Beirut – without invoking references to Arab media coverage as integral to an understanding of how and why the events took place. In other words, as the coming chapters will show, there is plenty to be said about ways in which changes in the Arab media are related to political change. Where differences arise is over how that relationship is perceived, interpreted and understood.

CAUTIONARY RESULTS OF AUDIENCE RESEARCH

Perceptions of the media–politics link have been hampered to date by a paucity of research data on audience responses to overtly political content. Some detailed studies, such as those by Lila Abu-Lughod, Christa Salamandra and others, have provided insights mainly into the reception of drama series, including examples of viewers rejecting didacticism and misrepresentation.[7] These insights notwithstanding, Jon Alterman was justified in writing, in an afterword to a book of essays dealing with most aspects of Al-Jazeera other than its viewership, that 'we know shockingly little about what the people of the Middle East watch, and how they interpret that information'.[8] Advertisers, who have long bemoaned an absence of credible ratings for channels and programmes, voiced their dissatisfaction again at the Arab and World Media conference organised by the Arab Thought Forum and Dubai Press Club in December 2005.[9] But, as indicated by Alterman and by the richness of findings by Abu-Lughod and others, numbers alone would not fill the knowledge gap. The expansion of political content in Arabic on television and the Internet during the late 1990s and early 2000s was not matched by a corresponding volume of ethnographic studies of relevant user responses, perhaps because of the same combination of official and informal constraints that held back most types of public opinion polling until the early 2000s.[10] Difficulties encountered by the authors of the 2003 and 2004 editions of the *Arab Human Development Report* (AHDR) illustrate the general problem. For the 2003 edition the AHDR team tried to gather data about knowledge acquisition from fellow academics; they received answers from just seven Arab countries, with the requisite number of respondents taking part in only three.[11] For the 2004 edition the team tried to commission opinion polls on issues related to freedom of opinion, expression and association in seven countries, but were eventually able to do so in only five.[12] With the voices of ordinary television audiences still barely audible, and with only a relatively short time having elapsed since satellite broadcasting and the Internet became prominent elements in Arab politics, pronouncements about new media influence have too often been limited to observations about causality that are broadly positivist in character but without being grounded in empirical research.

Where satellite television is concerned, these observations sometimes view its contribution in terms that can be reduced to either 'good' or 'bad'. A United States Institute of Peace (USIP) study, published in 2005, opted for an assessment in the latter category, based on a notion of objective 'reality' that the study's authors seemed to present as fixed and unquestionable, not something that depends on who you are and how things appear to you. They wrote:

> Arab audiences watch the news through a prism of individual and collective humiliation and resentment. To cater to those audiences, media portray the distorted reality created by this prism; and to compete with each other, they exaggerate the distortion. [...] To ignore or somehow justify their [i.e. the new satellite channels'] lies and inflammatory reporting as incidental to doing business in their political environment amounts to gross relativism.[13]

While such a judgement may suit certain political purposes, its notions of 'distortion' and 'exaggeration' close off the avenues to understanding that would be opened up by 'thick description', of the kind envisaged by Clifford Geertz. For Geertz, 'culture is not...something to which social events, behaviours, institutions or processes can be causally attributed; it is a context, something within which they can be intelligibly – that is thickly – described'.[14] Far from dismissing the task of deconstructing the 'prism' through which audiences watch television news as misguided relativism, researchers interested in Arabic-speaking audiences would see this as part of their work. Geertz proposed that 'understanding a people's culture exposes their normalness without reducing their particularity'.[15]

Marc Lynch makes more of a concession to the need for thick description in his assessment of what he calls the Arab satellite channels' 'democratizing power'. Unlike USIP, Lynch is optimistic about these channels' influence on Arab politics. Despite warning that television talk shows alone cannot produce 'democratic transformations', because they cannot substitute for the hard work of political organisation and negotiation, he nevertheless argues strongly that political talk shows have had two beneficial long-term 'transformative effects': they have helped to build 'the foundations for a pluralistic political culture by affirming and demonstrating the legitimacy of disagreement' while also 'eviscerat[ing] the legitimacy of the Arab status quo'.[16] Referring to thoughtful panel debates, rather than the stormy head-to-head confrontations which initially attracted attention to Al-Jazeera, Lynch suggests that these are helping Arab satellite television to 'refashion the political terrain' in a way that should be the focus of more research.[17] Here again, however, sustained audience narratives remain conspicuous by their absence, replaced by the assumption that voices heard in public represent those that remain unheard. Bold assessments of a causal link between television content and public opinion[18] would be more convincing if backed by evidence that opinion polls alone are unable to capture – about how diverse groups in Arab countries really regard such matters as pluralism, legitimacy, political reform and media representations of dissent.

Indeed, the audience research work in the present volume raises serious doubts about the kinds of generalisation that can be made regarding television programming as either a reflection of, or an influence on, what large sections of the population think. Imad Karam's path-breaking study of youth audiences reveals just how marginalised members of this age group still feel. Bombarded with music channels and generous helpings of adult advice, young people in Arab countries are little closer to finding a voice either in public or in private in the age of satellite television than they were before. Dina Matar's chapter on Palestinians in the diaspora shows how members of this community feel different from other Arabs. Participants in her research include some who turn to news for confirmation of their identity, but others who harbour strong suspicions about possible covert political and economic agendas of Arab television channels. Matar discovers that, where media create polarised contexts of 'us' and 'them', her respondents tend towards defensive and essentialising reactions. Importantly, however, they turn to a wide range of sources for news. This choice of viewing offers alternatives to polarised media contexts, with the result that members of the diasporic audience seem to move continuously between essentialising and more open positions. Matar states that 'that movement challenges assumptions about the emergence of particularistic identities that are increasingly common' in popular media and political discourse.

The rarity of studies like those of Matar and Karam is highlighted in Tarik Sabry's chapter, which peers into the void where a nascent project of Arab cultural studies should be. Sabry probes a possible set of explanations for why it is that Arab scholars currently take cultural imperialism simply as a given, discerning no need for empirical enquiry into the ways in which imperialism and its aftermath have affected the contemporary 'ordinary' and 'everyday'. He finds that intellectuals tend to conflate past and present, leading to disdain for the culture of the tellingly named 'Arab street' and blindness to the need for a coherent field of cultural studies that engages with lived experience today. In the absence of a legitimated space for the study of contemporary culture, Sabry warns that current modes of thinking risk 'masking the very dynamics of imperialism' that an effective anti-imperialist project would want to understand.

MEDIA, POLICY-MAKING AND VESTED INTERESTS

Ideas about media influence are sometimes framed in terms of the so-called 'CNN effect'. In this approach, the spotlight switches away from media influence on the general public, towards policy-makers and their responsiveness to media accounts of situations and events, such as those provided by the Atlanta-based satellite channel CNN during and after the 1991 Gulf War. Precisely speaking, the core of the debate around the CNN effect relates to whether the media are able to 'influence governments to pursue military intervention during humanitarian crises', thereby overriding long-standing principles of non-intervention and state sovereignty.[19] More loosely, the implication is that, whatever their influence on public opinion, the media can bring pressure to bear on those in power to change their policies. The authors who coined the term 'Al-Jazeera effect' did not use it to probe the precise dynamics of media and high-level policy-making in the Middle East.[20] Nevertheless, the potential for representations via the Arab media to influence the decisions of Arab political leaders is an important issue to be addressed. If it could be shown that the existence of media narratives and images of war, conflict, angry crowds, or even just some forms of media discourse, had an identifiable impact on policy in their own right, then some of the grander claims made for new Arab media might carry weight. Dale Eickelman, for example, has written that new communications media are 'turning the Arab street into a public sphere in which greater numbers of people, and not just a political and economic elite, will have a say in governance and public issues'.[21] The point about an observation such as this lies in the fact that its author refers to 'a say in governance', not 'a say about governance'. The distinction is important, because most evidence suggests that the alliances and priorities of Arab ruling elites influence the shape and orientation of the Arab media, so that editorial content is ultimately attributable not to people outside the elite but to political agendas that reflect patterns of elite ownership and control. Thus the argument can be made that it is change caused by divisions and realignments among ruling elites that surfaces via the Arab media landscape, rather than media content that triggers political change.[22]

The question of how far media practitioners work – knowingly or not – to the agenda of governments and politicians, rather than in the service of the electorate, is a perennial subject of investigation in the general field of political communication. Studies over many years pointed to the importance of elites as dominant media sources in Western contexts, and thus as 'primary definers' of news agendas,[23] which is why the notion of the CNN effect and its suggestion of a shift in this balance was so significant. For example, Daniel Hallin's research on the allegedly oppositional media coverage of the Vietnam War had seemed to show that this coverage essentially reflected little more than widening differences over the war among the political elite. Hallin concluded that

> the media, as institutions, … reflect the prevailing pattern of political debate: when consensus is strong, they tend to stay within the limits of the political discussion it defines; when it begins to break down, coverage becomes increasingly critical and diverse … and increasingly difficult for officials to control.[24]

As Piers Robinson has pointed out, evidence exists to shed more light on aspects of this interpretation and capture more precisely the process whereby media criticism of government, instead of being brushed aside or resisted, may actually become instrumental in bringing about policy shifts. At the time of the Vietnam War, certain political actors who were looking to justify a change of US policy were able to find that justification in visual evidence supplied by journalists.[25] Picking up on the twin ideas implicit in this scenario – namely elite dissensus and policy uncertainty within the executive branch of government – Robinson suggests that media criticism of government is only rarely influential in policy-making in Western contexts because a combination of elite dissensus and acute policy uncertainty within government is also rare. In the theoretical model he proposes, it is only in such a situation that the media may start to operate outside what Hallin called the 'sphere of legitimate controversy',[26] thereby becoming active participants influencing elite debate. That is partly because political actors seeking a change in policy can use critical media coverage, which may reflect non-elite concerns, to gain bargaining power vis-à-vis other members of the elite.[27]

It is important to remember that Robinson's own research focuses specifically on the role played by news reporting of humanitarian crises. Nevertheless, the extent of elite dissensus and policy uncertainty at the heart of certain Arab governments, which are under intense internal and external pressure to adopt new policies, suggests striking parallels with aspects of a theoretical model in which highly placed, but competing, political forces deploy critical media content to create additional pressure for policy change.

Saudi Arabia's ruling family has many branches, whose leading figures occupy key government positions but also hold different visions for their country's future. In the absence of channels for legitimising their policy preferences through the ballot box, they have invested in media operations at home and abroad in order to ensure favourable publicity for these preferences at both the national and regional levels.[28] Press reports that Saudi Arabia's King Abdullah is accustomed to have 32 small television screens and one large flat-screen television in his office, and another television in his car, suggest a more intense interest in television news reporting at the highest levels of Saudi policy-making than might be the case if government members had to deal daily with an elected legislature, party political debate and continuous opinion polls. A key question posed by the dissensus–uncertainty model of media influence, however, is whether people from outside the ruling political and business elites ever get a chance to see their critical views not only represented in the media but also seized upon as compelling evidence of the urgency of a policy shift. In her chapter for the present volume, Lina Khatib examines the interaction of media, public and policy-makers after the assassination of Lebanon's prime minister, Rafiq Hariri, in 2005. With Lebanese television stations in the hands of political leaders with diverse agendas, television became a symbolic battlefield during this period, between stations that stood opposed to the Syrian military presence in Lebanon and those that did not. Khatib recounts the calculated steps that stations took to mobilise their audiences. She also shows that, for a brief period, audiences in turn mobilised the medium to serve their own ends. But, as her analysis reveals, the moment soon passed, reinstating the gap between images of public action and behind-the-scenes political reality.

In theory, election campaigns offer the public a chance to be heard in political debates more directly than is usually the case. Media coverage is supposed to reflect this, which is why the chapter by Giovanna Maiola and David Ward, based on media monitoring during the 2005 Palestinian presidential election campaign, can also help to answer questions about where media outlets stand relative to voters and political elites. Here a comparison of Palestinian and pan-Arab television stations proves illuminating, not least because Palestinians tend to watch the latter in preference to local and national alternatives, despite the fact that pan-Arab channels devote less time overall to Palestinian affairs than local Palestinian channels can. Maiola and Ward note the devastating impact on the Palestinian economy of conflict arising from the Israeli occupation and the effect of consequent dangers and restrictions on local journalism. Against this backdrop, their examination of television coverage demonstrates that the spectrum of active Palestinian political forces was better reflected on

Al-Jazeera than on the Palestinian national channel, PBC TV. In particular, the two stations adopted different approaches to Hamas, which boycotted the presidential race but still, in the words of Maiola and Ward, represented a 'crucial interlocutor' and a 'main referent' for election debates. Hamas was relatively prominent on Al-Jazeera, where it received coverage roughly equal to that of Fatah. Its virtual absence from PBC TV, on the other hand, testified to a national media system whereby the ability to reflect views is 'dictated by factors' outside journalists' control. It follows from this that, if factors external to journalism shape editorial decisions, efforts to promote a peace agenda solely through journalism training may be misplaced. Yet, as copiously documented by Bruce Stanley in his chapter on aid for peace-building through the Arab media, US and European donors have spent millions on media intervention programmes that talk peace and democratisation with journalists but fail to consider either the structural underpinnings of conflict or media structures. Stanley's work, in uncovering how and why donors have shown such limited concern with the complex and problematic processes of conflict transformation, also explains the backlash among Arab civil society groups against projects that promoted dialogue in a way that was decontextualised and oblivious to hard political realities.

SEEING THINGS IN A DIFFERENT LIGHT

In contrast to the sparse evidence of critical media content forcing Arab governments to change policy or respond seriously to inconvenient public concerns, examples are plentiful of government figures appearing to adopt television-friendly modes of conduct that were unfamiliar before access to satellite television and the Internet spread through the Arab world. Such examples include simple things, such as answering media requests that would once have been ignored. Hala Gorani, a Syrian-American anchor for CNN, told *The Daily Star* in March 2006: 'I have found that even in Syria I can get a governmental reaction in five minutes.' 'Ten years ago', she said, 'it would take you a week to get one.'[29] Other examples may be more elaborate, such as the unprecedented invitation to a private sector media personality to stage a three-part televised interview with the Egyptian president, Hosni Mubarak, months ahead of the country's first multi-candidate presidential election campaign in 2005. Since the speeded-up Syrian government reaction to a media query is still likely to be a 'stock answer',[30] and since there was never any chance of Mubarak losing the election, or even of other presidential candidates gaining equivalent airtime on state television,[31] it is reasonable to ask why political leaders should feel any greater need to play the media game today than they did beforehand. In the old days they were content for television news to consist of a 'seemingly endless and substance-free listing of the doings of the head of state'.[32] If government opponents are still effectively crushed today, by laws and intimidation, what exactly is it about the new media that prompts those in power to adjust to more demanding media conventions and routines?

A possible answer might be similar to the one Joshua Meyrowitz produced in the 1980s to explain why electronic media, especially television, differ so strikingly from print media in their effect on social behaviour. He argued that it was not the power of any particular television message that accounted for change, but the way the whole medium of television physically reorganised the social settings within which people interact.[33] Instead of media content and its influence, Meyrowitz focused on the possibility that 'new media transform the home and other social spheres into new social environments', making private behaviours public, and private places accessible to the outside world, thus leading to forms of interaction that were once exclusive to situations of immediate physical proximity.[34] They do not just give us 'quicker or more thorough access to events and behaviors',[35] Meyrowitz wrote; they give us, instead, 'new events and new behaviors'. Little wonder then, he suggested, that 'widespread rejection' of traditional roles and hierarchies began in the late 1960s 'among the first generation of Americans to have been exposed to television before learning to read'.[36] Meyrowitz's approach came in for criticism for being media-centric and technologically deterministic,[37] in attributing change to media technology rather than seeing the adoption of technology as bound up with relations of power. Such criticism might seem justified by the fact that television, both public and private, was around in the Arab countries from the 1950s and 1960s without apparently triggering new behaviours; instead it suffered from a lack of credibility among viewers, who perceived broadcasting as a 'mere propaganda machine for the ruling elite'.[38] Nevertheless, Meyrowitz himself argued that societies change in their patterns of access to, and exclusion from, certain situations and social information, and that these patterns are linked to media use.[39] Patterns of access changed in Arab society with the injection of credibility delivered by satellite channels that broke taboos, which not only encouraged people to gain access to new media but also – crucially – ensured that awareness about access also increased.[40] The significance of that awareness for public behaviour was illustrated by a Lebanese protest organiser in Martyrs' Square in March 2005, who said: 'Why should we be afraid of Syria now? The world is watching us on television.'[41]

The logic of this analysis is not that leaders will be forced to act more democratically if their actions are exposed to public view. On the contrary, violence against demonstrators captured on camera in Cairo, Damascus and elsewhere proves that to be untrue. It is simply that people gain a different sense of their own potential when they can use electronic media to overcome restrictions on social interaction that are imposed by physical space. In the case of Internet users, as Albrecht Hofheinz shows in his chapter for this book, the socialisation process online is quite different from the one that takes place in ordered, close-knit, offline communities, where traditional world-views and power hierarchies may be considered self-evident. Online, individuals are faced with never-ending choice. They become more conscious of their individuality and 'more distinctly aware of the role of choice in creating social communities, knowledge and values' – a process that Hofheinz associates with a growing assertion of the self through blogging and through personal interpretations of Islam. In the case of television, Marwan Kraidy finds that audiences' interaction with each other and with programme makers, through the weekly voting routines of reality TV entertainment, has led to the development of a new political vocabulary. His chapter, on the singing competition, *Star Academy*, highlights ways in which Lebanese viewers translated their personal participation and the programme's reliance on audience interactivity into references for communicating ideas about political and sociocultural change. Meanwhile, as Kraidy demonstrates, Kuwaiti Islamists strongly resisted plans to translate the social interaction offered by the television show into physical access for audience and singers at a *Star Academy* concert staged in Kuwait.

TOWARDS A PUBLIC SPHERE?

Intrinsic to any discussion of media and politics is the notion of the public sphere, which has been widely evoked in the growing literature on new Arab media as a rubric for discussion of news journalism and current affairs debates. Dale Eickelman's observation about people having a 'say in governance', quoted above, is fairly typical in this respect. Lately, however, there has been some scholarly agonising over the degree to which the public sphere concept fits new phenomena emerging in the Arab media landscape. Since public sphere theory directs us to consider how far critical-rational and inclusive public argumentation supersedes status and tradition in defining the public interest and driving political action, recent research has tended to focus on questions about access, and about boundaries between 'public' and 'private' or between secular and religious discourse. For Marc Lynch, in his recent work on pan-Arab television talk shows, a public sphere consists of 'routine, ongoing, unscripted arguments before a [participating] audience about issues relevant to many'.[42] For Dyala Hamzah, focusing on Egyptian media, the 'existence of layers of public discourse that never intersect with each other'[43] leads to the conclusion that Arab public opinion, and thus an Arab transnational public sphere, are absent.[44] For Armando Salvatore and Mark LeVine, a 'central problem' is that the 'idea of the public is culturally embedded'.[45] They revert to the 'discourse of the common good', whose long genealogy cuts across East–West divides, seeing this as the guiding approach for a 'broad, transcultural understanding of the public sphere as the communicative and legitimizing basis of potentially democratic political systems'.[46]

An important aspect of public sphere theory that has so far tended to receive less attention in research on Arab media is regulation. This is puzzling since, as Nicholas Garnham has pointed out, part of the 'attraction of the public sphere approach' lies in its 'stress on the necessary institutional foundations' for the realisation of 'citizen rights to free expression and debate'. It addresses the 'problem of constructing the institutions and practices of democracy at the level of both state and civil society' in countries where these have been eroded or are lacking.[47] Oliver Hahn, in the chapter immediately following this introduction, takes account of how institutions affect transcultural communication. He draws on research into changes in communicative space across Eastern and Western Europe to assess how the concept of the public sphere may help as a tool for analysing developments not only in Arab media but in Arab–European exchanges in times of crisis. On the way, he notes the significance of the journalist's potential role as interpreter and the dominant influence of wider political systems and relations of power on the functioning of the media as intermediaries for public communication.

Both reminders serve well when we consider changes in media regulation in some Arab countries, including those under foreign occupation, and their impact on the security of journalists. The hazards of journalism have been underlined by events in Iraq, where Reuters reported more than 70 journalists killed in three years after the US-led invasion,[48] with many more injured or detained without trial. Jail sentences for journalists continued in Egypt into 2006, despite earlier presidential promises to end them. A 'new' press law in Kuwait in 2006 imposed jail sentences for religious offences and fines for criticising the ruler. In Morocco, at the same time as licences were being issued for new private broadcasters in spring 2006, independent print media were struggling to survive in the face of steep fines. The list of contradictions could go on. As to the political configurations that produce them, and the strategies media entities and citizens adopt to overcome them, a range of thoughtful insights are contained in this book.

- 2 -

Cultures of TV News Journalism and Prospects for a Transcultural Public Sphere

Oliver Hahn

Since the suicide attacks on US targets on 11 September 2001 and the subsequent US-led campaigns against so-called rogue states in a context of asymmetric conflict, it has been possible to observe a structural transformation in the communication of crises by the globally networked mass media. Particularly in the field of satellite television, Western market leaders such as BBC World and CNN International have been joined in Arab markets by locally based competitors, notably Al-Arabiya in Dubai (United Arab Emirates) and Al-Jazeera Satellite Channel in Doha (Qatar). Al-Jazeera in particular indicated its intention to compete directly with CNN International and others by launching an English-language satellite television news channel, Al-Jazeera English, in 2006. Since the US-led invasion of Iraq in 2003, when Al-Arabiya joined Al-Jazeera in the marketplace, Western news organisations have come to consider some of the young generation of Arab satellite broadcasters as reliable and credible external sources. This is apparent from the extent to which they quote such broadcasters and reuse footage obtained from them. It is also implicit in the cooperation agreements, both formal and informal, that exist between Western and Arab broadcasters. These developments suggest that inroads are being made into the global monopoly that US and European broadcasters previously enjoyed in reporting on conflicts in the Middle East. Such a change could have a considerable impact on the public in matters of international relations.

Many observers have been tempted to conceptualise changes in the global television news landscape in terms of a transnational and/or trans-cultural public sphere.[1] New media in the Muslim world, and especially the Internet, have been presented as promoters of a public sphere.[2] A growing body of academic literature on Al-Jazeera likewise refers to theories of the public sphere.[3] Such a conceptualisation maintains that, alongside ongoing structural change in the global media market, cultures of Arab news journalism on satellite television are also playing a part in the emergence of a single or multiple public sphere(s) in the Arab world. It also presupposes that Jürgen Habermas's concept of the public sphere is applicable, or directly transferable, to the authoritarian politics of the Arab world. To assess whether this supposition is correct, it is important to re-examine both the concept itself and the way it has been used in European research, including research conducted in German – the original language in which Habermas wrote about the public sphere – and in other languages. This chapter begins by considering three different conceptualisations of the public sphere that are discernible in research into the notion of a transnational European public sphere or spheres, abbreviated here to EPS(s) in line with existing UK research on the subject.[4] It goes on to look more closely at developments in Arab news journalism to discover whether, or how far, any of these conceptualisations can be applied transculturally to encompass media developments in the Arab region as well as in Europe. It ends by drawing conclusions about the application of theories of the public sphere to transnational structural changes in the Arab and global media landscapes.

'GLOCALISATION' AND PUBLIC SPHERE THEORY

Television news companies that operate globally in both the West and the Arab world seek to conquer new markets and acquire new audiences beyond the boundaries of their own cultural and linguistic spaces. To this end they embark on a management strategy of programme adaptation captured in the term 'glocalisation'. This neologism, although combining two seeming opposites, 'globalisation' and 'localisation', is only superficially contradictory. It is in fact translated from the Japanese word *dochaduka*, meaning 'global localisation'.[5] Roland Robertson defines glocalisation as

> a term which was developed in particular reference to marketing issues, as Japan became more concerned with and successful in the global economy, against the background [...] of much experience with the general problem of the relationship between the universal and the particular.[6]

In order to maintain a dominant presence in world media, certain television news stations have opted for a policy of glocalisation, whereby they disseminate content in other languages besides that of their home base. BBC World, CNN International and Al-Jazeera have all followed this strategy. BBC World has operated an Arabic-language website since 1999, which it revamped in 2003, and CNN has done likewise since 2002. Al-Jazeera added an English-language website to its existing Arabic-language website in 2003. As already noted, Al-Jazeera English started in 2006. In October 2005 the BBC decided to introduce an Arabic-language satellite TV news channel starting in 2007, to be based in London with an operating cost of £19 million a year.[7] This was not the BBC's first entry into the market for Arabic-language television news. Between 1994 and 1996 it produced such a service under contract with the satellite broadcasting platform Orbit Television and Radio Network in Rome, financed by the Saudi Arabian investor Mawarid Group. Following a dispute between the British broadcaster and the Arab financier over editorial independence, BBC Arabic TV was shut down and many of its journalists moved to Qatar, in order to help build up Al-Jazeera, launched in 1996.

According to several Arab media commentators, including on Al-Jazeera,[8] the planned new BBC Arabic TV runs the risk of being considered a copy of Al-Hurra, the Arabic-language satellite TV news channel financed by the US State Department, which started in February 2004 from a base in Springfield, Virginia. But Al-Hurra was not the only other Western television station to broadcast in Arabic by this stage. Germany's international broadcaster Deutsche Welle (DW), based in Bonn and Berlin, started Arabic subtitling of its programming in 2002 and moved to broadcasting three hours per day of television news programming in Arabic in February 2005. Arabic was also one of six pilot languages for DW websites from the beginning of 2005. Whereas BBC World Service radio included Arabic from 1938, DW had followed suit in 1959, choosing Arabic as the first non-European language for its radio broadcasts. Nearly half a century later DW's Arabic radio service was on air for five hours a day. In light of US, British and German funding for Arabic-language broadcasting, it should also be noted that French plans for a TV project, under the name France 24, envisaged Arabic as potentially one of the new channel's languages, alongside French, English and Spanish. Dubbed 'CNN à la française' by observers, France 24 was planned to involve a joint venture between France's national commercial television channel TF1 (which runs its own French-language satellite news channel, La Chaîne Info) and the public service broadcasting group France Télévisions. Initiated by the French president, Jacques Chirac, and approved by the European Commission in Brussels in June 2005 as not contravening European Union rules on state aid, France 24 was given Euros 30 million of French government funding for 2005 and another Euros 65 million for 2006.[9]

Projects such as these assume that a certain level of transcultural communication and cooperation is possible. One example of such cooperation exists in ARTE, the cultural television channel formed through Franco-German collaboration. ARTE represents a joint cross-border effort based on parity of input from both sides and programming from different points of view, aimed at audiences from both language areas at the same time. But this is not the same as saying that ARTE reflects or contributes to something that could be described as a common Franco-German public sphere.[10] That is a separate question and some analysts think it does not. Barbara Thomaß states that it has been a mistake made by previous 'European media' to 'anticipate the emergence' of a public sphere or spheres. She writes that such media 'suppose an audience which does not yet exist'.[11] If it is premature to think of European public spheres in respect of European broadcasting, the public sphere concept in an Arab-European context may be even more problematic.

Indeed, attempts to apply the notion of the public sphere trans-culturally raise many questions.[12] As introduced by Habermas in his normative meta-theoretical study of communication in Western-style democracy, a public sphere is created through dialogic critical-rational discourse.[13] Although the much-repeated terminology associated with Habermas's approach is specific to the histories and political developments of certain nation states such as Germany, France and the UK, today it is increasingly adopted in discussions about the transnational arena. According to Hans Kleinsteuber, Habermas's study is itself a textbook example of transcultural scientific 'communication', having been published originally in German in 1962 and translated into English in 1989, more than a quarter of a century later.[14] Yet there is a central obstacle to this supposed transcultural communication in that there is no direct translational equivalent of the Germanic term *Öffentlichkeit* (or *offen*) in other European languages whose vocabulary is limited to derivates of the Latin word 'public'. Hence Kleinsteuber proposed coining the term 'openicity' as a more suitable equivalent to *Öffentlichkeit*.[15] Translations that rely on terms related to the word 'public' bring in connotations that were not there in the original.[16] Thus *Öffentlichkeit* has been roughly translated to the English phrase 'public sphere' or to the French term *sphère/espace public*. According to Peter Uwe Hohendahl, these are both 'downright artificial terms'.[17] The translation 'public sphere' added a spatial dimension to the concept,[18] even though such a dimension was missing from the original.

Another problem inherent in transcultural application of the term arises from the history of how Habermas's study was received in the German and extra-German contexts. During the first years after its release the original publication was exhaustively discussed only within the German-language scholarly community of disciplines such as philosophy, humanities and social sciences, but without serious international feedback. Indeed, the work initially had a relatively low profile in German-language communication and media studies. In recent times discussions in those fields have died down. Following its English translation, the so-called 'Habermasian approach' has enjoyed a renaissance within the international academic world, which continues until today. Its eager reception has 'long gained a life of its own'.[19] In UK media studies, for instance, debates about a flourishing public sphere have been linked to arguments in favour of adequately funded public service broadcasting.[20] At the same time, anglophone academics have discussed the media's ability to mediate a public sphere.[21] Outside Germany there has also been a booming debate on chances for the emergence of EPS(s).[22] As noted previously, new media in the Arab and Muslim worlds are discussed in similar terms.[23] To recapitulate, the international scholarly community has furthered the Habermasian approach as a research paradigm. Naturally, this has had repercussions on German-language public sphere research.

Over the past few years German-language EPS(s) research has gained momentum, leading to more heterogeneity and differentiation than consistency. Indeed, it is possible, from within the German-language humanities and social sciences, including communication and media studies, to set out a typology of models of the public sphere(s) which take account of feedback from international usage of the concept. Three different conceptualisations of the public sphere(s) can be sketched out: the traditional-sceptical model, the liberal-representative model and the deliberative-discursive model.[24] Proponents of the traditional-sceptical model follow a homogeneous approach, have high normative expectations, and consequently discount the existence of a pan-European public sphere.[25] According to this conceptualisation, the EU and Europe lack a non-elite collective identity. They do not constitute a communication community because there is no common media system and no common language.[26] For them, the alleged deficits of public sphere and democracy are interdependent.

As for the liberal-representative model, this stands in contrast to the previous one in the sense that it makes fewer normative demands. Its demands, or expectations, are limited to transparency and the development of national public spheres in democratic systems with a view to the eventual Europeanisation of national public spheres.[27] In a national public sphere, citizens' interests and will should be strongly related to political decisions, particularly through elections. The media are thus understood to be the most important information source to serve as intermediary institutions between politics and citizens. The tasks of the media include projecting and controlling political accountability as well as helping citizens to form their opinions. In the liberal-representative model, the building of EPS(s) takes place through media coverage of EU and European issues and actors, as well as their evaluation through an EU and European perspective. This model allows for incongruence between the Europeanisation of economic and political processes on the one hand and media coverage of EU and European issues on the other. The alleged deficit with regard to a public sphere or spheres is regarded as a consequence of the alleged deficit of democracy at the EU and European level. While the requirements of the first model are too idealistic to (ever) be reached, the second model is less distinctive, but also less utopian and more realistic. It is appropriate for, and tailor-made to, the EU and European context.

The third model can be described as deliberative-discursive. Underlying it are low normative demands and an acknowledgement of the existence within Europe of partial, segmented, public spheres.[28] This conceptualisation assumes a broader definition of EPS(s), symbolised through arenas of public communication, including day-to-day communication and communication by civil society actors, as well as mass communication. It regards public spheres as being shaped by thematic relations between national media arenas through common topics. This assumption is rooted in Habermas's concept of the public sphere emerging through dialogic critical-rational discourse to which everybody has access and in which everyone can participate, so that opinions are formed by collective processes. Although pinpointing the importance of an EU and European media agenda, including equivalent interpretations and opinions with regard to the various issues, the third model does not regard a common language as a precondition. Instead, cohesion develops through issue-specific communication communities above the nation state. Thus, public spheres are considered as intermediate spaces between governmental structures and society. Communication is not limited to taking place only within different national public spheres but can be transnational. Its processes can be characterised by conflict and dissent, which are not seen as hurdles but as proof that communication is taking place. According to this model, there is no public sphere deficit in the EU and Europe.

Reviewing these three models, my co-authors, Julia Lönnendonker, Karen Rosenwerth and Roland Schröder, and I concluded that they basically show contradictory conclusions regarding the question of the existence of EPS/s. It seems that this is due to the underlying level of normative demands. One hypothesis is that high normative demands inevitably lead to the denial of EPS/s, whereas low normative demands permit the understanding of the emergence or pre-existence of EPS/s.[29]

In considering Europe as a whole, meanwhile, it is also necessary to take account of experiences and research findings related to the transformation of media in post-communist countries of Central and Eastern Europe. These emphasise that the media are in no way solely responsible for allowing a public sphere or spheres to emerge, since concerted action is also called for from civil society actors. Leonidas Donskis, a Lithuanian professor[30] and host of the talk show *Be Pykčio* (English: *Without Anger*) on Lithuania's public service television station, notes the emergence in the former Soviet bloc countries of what he calls a 'new kind of historical, political interpreter'. Based on his analysis of European travel literature and novels, Donskis argues that Central and Eastern Europe was, in a way, 'invented by Western Europe', which is why it suffers from 'gaps of identity, self-perception, and self-comprehension'. Nevertheless, he says, the period since the collapse of the Soviet Union has witnessed 'the emergence of the new kind of journalism, [...] the emergence of critical social and political thought, [...] the emergence of media persons'. The latter, being able to 'bridge' national sensibilities, are, according to Donskis, 'absolutely indispensable to a European public sphere'.[31] It may be that elements of his analysis have parallels in recent developments in Arab television journalism.

CULTURAL COMMITMENT AND INTERCULTURAL FRICTION

The conceptualisations of the public sphere(s) outlined above provide a framework against which to consider the realities of Western and Arab television news journalism. Despite all the tendencies towards the globalisation of journalism, the geography of news broadcasting remains decisive in the sphere of crisis communication. It therefore seems useful to investigate the politico-cultural foundations for different conflict perspectives and their influence on the selection and presentation of news.

According to Rami Khoury, editor-in-chief of the Lebanese English-language newspaper *The Daily Star*, '[t]he electronic mass media are the only sector in which a balance of forces between the USA and the Arab world exists'.[32] This balance of forces results from a kind of 'arms race' between the contemporary globally networked Arab and Western media worlds, both sides mobilising satellite television channels as 'weapons of mass communication'. Each side conveys its own perspective on conflicts in the Middle East against the backdrop of its own politico-cultural baggage. Instead of concealing their significantly different viewpoints, the two sides both use them for self-promotion. For example, during the US-led invasion of Iraq in 2003, Al-Jazeera courted its audience by promising to report on the targets hit by US bombs and accusing CNN International of simply showing the aircraft from which US forces dropped bombs. The competition for higher audience ratings led to a commercialisation of the war victims' perspective and to a kind of television that seemed to demonise offenders.[33] The result was a 'cold media war'[34] waged by Arab and Western satellite newscasters. On the one hand, both are committed to their own respective (political) cultures, societal values and communication systems which they share with their respective target audiences. On the other hand, both also define their respective (political) cultures, societal values and communication systems.

In order to emit and receive, to explain and make sense of an information item coming from media in foreign cultural and linguistic systems and contexts, one has to know the latter exactly. According to early anthropological findings on cross-cultural communication by Edward Hall,[35] cultures (civilisations) across the world tend to differ in their communication systems even though they are constantly in contact with each other. Thus, any item of information in both individual and mass communication is culturally conditioned and coded. An information item is not unequivocal per se; it acquires meaning only within its cultural context. Consequently, the meaning of the same information item could be different and varying from one cultural context to another. Different politico-cultural contexts and communication systems lay down different sets of parameters within which their respective media operate. Contemporary Arab and Western satellite newscasters do not operate within hermetically sealed spaces but within their respective politico-cultural contexts, and within the communication systems of their respective target audiences. That is one reason why reporting perspectives on the same conflicts can be extremely different. The journalistic objectivity demanded from both sides can only be evaluated against the backdrop of their respective politico-cultural commitments or contexts.

Mohammed El-Nawawy and Adel Iskandar have suggested that news values and selection criteria are conditioned by 'contextual objectivity'. They describe their perhaps somewhat controversial theory as follows:

> The journalistic standard applied here required some form of contextual objectivity, because the medium should reflect all sides of any story

while retaining the values, beliefs, and sentiments of the target audience. [...] This dual relationship underscores the conundrum of modern media. [...] It would seem that the theory of contextual objectivity – the necessity of television and media to present stories in a fashion that is both somewhat impartial yet sensitive to local sensibilities – is at work. [...] Although this appears to be an oxymoron, it is not. It expresses the inherent contradiction between attaining objectivity in news coverage and appealing to a specific audience. This is one of the great struggles among networks today, especially during times of war. Contextual objectivity can be seen in every broadcast in every media outlet in the world, not just Al-Jazeera and the US networks.[36]

For El-Nawawy and Iskandar, 'contextual objectivity' is like the Minotaur, the Cretan mythological character that bore the head of a bull and body of a man. It reflects, they say, 'the instinctive and the rational, the relativist and the positivist'. It is an attempt to 'articulate and capture the eclectic discursive and epistemological tensions between the relativism of the message receivers and empirical positivism of message builders'.[37]

The collision of different viewpoints or contextual objectivities by representatives of different mass media or journalism cultures can lead to intercultural friction. A clear example was provided by the clash in early 2006 over the decision by some European media to reprint offensive caricatures of the Prophet Mohammed, previously published in the Danish daily *Jyllands-Posten*, in the face of intense indignation about the publication expressed in the media of Arab countries. Whereas many European outlets joined in denouncing theocratic censorship and *France Soir* claimed the right to caricature not only the Prophet but also God, the majority of Arab news anchors referring to the controversy used phrases such as *al-nabi al-karim* (English: the dear Prophet) or added 'peace be upon him' after the Prophet's name. Meanwhile, problems of understanding arise from inexact translation equivalents from one language to another, or one culture to another. For example, many Arab media have in the past used the same Arabic word for Palestinian suicide bombers in Israel as for the victims of violent conflicts, namely *shahid* (singular) or *shuhada* (plural). The word derives from the verb 'to witness' and also means 'passed away', but it is often translated as 'martyr', a term that is understood in the West as taking sides with the Palestinian cause. By the same token, some Western news outlets use euphemisms adopted by military forces when referring to the Arab–Israeli conflict. They refer to the Israeli army's operations against alleged Palestinian terrorists as 'targeted killings', instead of the more correct designation 'assassinations'. As these examples demonstrate, intercultural friction results from cultural and political power relations in international relations and their implications for communication.[38] One dilemma for news organisations relates to the question of who holds the power to decide which acts of extreme violence are described as terrorism. What one side condemns as 'terrorism' is legitimated on the other side as 'freedom fighting'. What Western, especially US, media call the 'war on terror' is referred to in Arab media, roughly translated, as the 'US war against so-called terrorism'. In Western news reports the US-led invasion of Iraq in 2003 was sometimes described as a 'war of liberation', whereas the more frequently used term in Arab reports was 'war of occupation'.[39]

PUBLIC DIPLOMACY AND MEDIA DIPLOMACY

Arab and Western satellite newscasters often accuse each other of allowing themselves to be manipulated by their respective governments into churning out anything from political public relations (PR) to state propaganda. All over the world, governments in both democratic and non-democratic systems are able to produce and launch disinformation. Politically motivated communication focuses on the management of information, news or perception. Strategies of politically motivated communication are described by the concept of public diplomacy, meaning governmental PR institutions and instruments targeted at audiences abroad. After its introduction in the USA in the mid-1960s, several Washington administrations applied public diplomacy to stress what they considered to be the superiority of Western capitalism over Eastern communism until the end of the Cold War. After the 9/11 suicide attacks in the US the concept of public diplomacy was reformed. Its funds were increased, new institutions were founded and more specialised personnel were hired. The National Security Strategy (NSS), published by the US government in 2002, considered public diplomacy to be a mass communication 'weapon against international terrorism', targeting an 'anti-Americanism' which it suspected to be widespread in the Arab and Islamic worlds. Based on their assumptions about a lack of accurate and balanced information about the US and its values of freedom and democracy, political institutions in Washington invested huge amounts of money in what they saw as winning the hearts and minds of people living in the Arab and Muslim worlds. One principal medium for this was international satellite broadcasting.[40]

Between 2002 and 2004 the US Broadcasting Board of Governors (BBG) set up three special media organisations aimed at Arab and Muslim audiences. In March 2002 it outsourced a former department of Voice of America (VOA) to build up Radio Sawa (*sawa* being Arabic for 'together'), targeted at Arabic speakers aged under 30. Radio Sawa broadcasts a mixture of pop music in English and Arabic along with Western-style news. In December 2002 the BBG followed the same formula of pop propaganda to found Radio Farda (English: tomorrow) to reach young listeners in the Farsi-speaking world. In February 2004, with finance approved by the US Congress, the BBG launched a satellite television channel called Al-Hurra (English: The Free One), devoted primarily to news but also to discussion programmes and entertainment. US President George W. Bush suggested Al-Hurra was intended to serve as a counterbalance to Al-Jazeera.[41] Yet few Arab viewers and journalists regard Al-Hurra as a reliable source of information. The station discredited itself with Arab audiences in its early weeks with items that appeared not to meet international norms of journalism. When the channel interviewed Bush about allegations that US soldiers had tortured detainees at Abu Ghraib prison near Baghdad, Bush ended the interview by complimenting the journalist for doing his job well.

Particularly in times of acute crises, Arab and Western satellite newscasters are disposed to open their programmes to governmental PR, apparently considering it a valid journalistic source. Mohammed El-Nawawy and Leo Gher recommend that high-ranking political officials should take advantage of such openings to public diplomacy in order to appear in television programmes of the other party to the conflict. They call this communication strategy 'media diplomacy'.[42] Their concept paraphrases Eytan Gilboa's concept of 'telediplomacy', which envisages the use of 'mass media to communicate with state and non-state actors, to build confidence and advance negotiations, as well as to mobilise the public support for agreements'.[43] However, this strategy can be counterproductive. Particularly during acute crises, Arab and Western satellite newscasters have shown themselves prone to anticipatory obedience to political decisions made by their governments. In the case of such behaviour, according to Kai Hafez, the media play the roles of a 'co-party in conflict' or of a 'third party in conflict', the latter status reflecting only commercial interest in reporting on the conflict.[44] At these times, self-censorship by the mass media often seems to be more effective than censorship by state authorities.

This phenomenon is compounded by difficulties over what both sides understand by terms such as 'public' or 'public opinion'. Mohammed Zayani, discussing the intercultural pitfalls of translating such words or phrases, argues that even the word 'censorship' does not have the same resonance in Arabic as it has in Western languages, because, in Arab society, 'censorship emanates out of a feeling [...] that information is dangerous and has to be monitored or controlled'.[45] For Zayani, the media's role in the Arab world cannot be described as primarily 'public', because even viable channels that have emerged in the past few years are 'not a bottom-up phenomenon, but a top-down development [...] created and sponsored by governments'.[46] He maintains that, whereas opinion polls have risen in political importance in 'the West', polls are much less common in the Arab world and do not have the same potency or effect. Zayani goes so far as to describe the 'whole concept of public opinion' as 'alien to the region'.[47]

In the structural transformation of the global media landscape, brought about through the communication of crises on the global mass media market, one can also observe an aesthetic of dramatisation on Western and Arab screens. As a consequence of the global competition, television aesthetics are characterised by a normative approach to reporting that takes place under extreme pressure of topicality. In this context, Western and Arab news media often appear simply to indulge an obsession with up-to-the-minute reporting, instead of choosing to grapple with the backdrop of long-standing structural problems in international relations as the real causes of conflicts and human suffering.[48] An obvious example lies in a comparison of coverage of the US-led invasion of Iraq in 2003 with coverage of the 12 years of UN sanctions on Iraq that preceded it. Event-centred reports at the peak of the conflict in 2003 vastly outnumbered the few process-centred reports on the consequences for the Iraqi people of the long-running economic sanctions against Iraq, which followed the Iraqi invasion of Kuwait in 1990. An obsession with up-to-the-minute reporting tends to produce mostly 'snack news journalism', lacking in coverage of causes or structures. Crisis communication needs sustainability, in the sense that the public needs to be informed about circumstances likely to produce crises before they happen. Likewise, information is needed not only on the day of an attack but years later, about its aftermath and consequences.

Competition between broadcasters seeking to break the latest news gives a false impression of sustainability. In comparison, features, doc-umentaries and reports that provide background are rare and, being broadcast mostly outside peak viewing times, do not reach mass audiences. The dramatisation aesthetic favours events happening live and in real time. It makes media consumers believe they are physically close to and psychologically concerned with events and discourses, even though these may in fact be very distant. According to Gilboa, the impression of continuing proximity and concern is strengthened by redundant audiovisual loops and special logos.[49] He warns against overestimating the so-called CNN effect[50] or newly envisaged Al-Jazeera effect.[51] He argues that global television news coverage, rather than taking over the task of devising policy, creates pressure on primary political actors to act more quickly and pushes them 'to produce instant policy'.[52] Furthermore, televisual dramatisation of crises uses programme formats drawn from sports coverage and hi-tech action movies. For example, shortly before the US-led invasion of Iraq in 2003 started, most of the news television channels broadcast dramatised trailers and started a countdown to the expected beginning of military operations.

TELEVISION TALK SHOWS

One further editorial practice to be considered in the light of public sphere theory is the broadcasting of political debate. Jon Anderson prejudged the history of political debate in Arabic when he declared Al-Jazeera's controversial talk shows to be the end of a 'migration of debate-and-discussion formats from salons to the air'.[53] Close scrutiny of these shows provides evidence to refute both the proposition that television talk shows involve open, rational dialogue and the claim that salon-style discussion has 'migrated' to the airwaves. Political talk shows, an innovation in Arab media, were conceived as flagship programmes for Al-Jazeera. In practice, according to both Western and Arab critics, they have often been characterised more by emotion and a lack of rationality than by rationality. Where interactive television disputes dominate the schedules they indicate tendencies towards extreme politicisation, polarisation, personalisation and emotionalisation. Because these multiple 'boxing rings'[54] often finish in verbal affray among the invitees,[55] Al-Jazeera has been accused of populism, sensationalism and one-sidedness.[56] One of the best-known talk shows on Arab television is Al-Jazeera's *Al-Ittijah al-Muaakis* (English: *The Opposite Direction*) presented by Faisal Al Kasim.[57] Open to categorisation as 'politainment',[58] this weekly talk show, modelled on the format of CNN's *Crossfire*, brings together two guests with diametrically opposing views to debate contentious topics with viewers calling in. Comparing Qasim's talk show to a 'fighting arena', Muhammad Ayish interestingly concludes that *The Opposite Direction* lends itself more to what he calls 'media brinkmanship' than to 'rational media discussion'.[59] Furthermore, the participatory character of any television discussion involving live phone-ins has to be questioned, given that editorial staff in the newsroom decide which callers go on air.

CONCLUSION

Editorial and journalistic practices such as those discussed in this chapter raise fundamental questions about whether Habermas's concept, expressed as 'openicity' by Kleinsteuber, involving dialogic critical-rational discourse open to all, is applicable or directly transferable to crisis communication, including crisis communication to and from the Arab world or, as discussed by Mehdi Abedi and Michael Fischer, the Muslim Middle East.[60] El-Nawawy and Gher argue that it can be transferred.[61] Yet evidence suggests that much television news journalism to and from the region, far from fostering the emergence of critical-rational dialogue, actually hinders it. Assessed against the backdrop of the three-way public sphere typology set out earlier, the global media landscape that now includes pan-Arab media seems not to fulfil the necessary criteria in any convincing way.

If the existence of a pan-European public sphere has to be ruled out under the traditional-sceptical model, then the same would clearly be true of a pan-Arab, and therefore an Arab–Western, public sphere. Although pan-Arab media do exist and enjoy the major advantage of a shared language for pan-Arab political discourse, there is no common media system shared by all Arab countries, just as there is none in Europe. Meanwhile, the liberal-representative model, being tailored to the EU and European context, foresees the eventual transnationalisation and regionalisation of national public spheres in democratic systems. Under this scenario, national public spheres develop when citizens' interests, expressed in elections or opinion polls, are mirrored in political decisions and when the media serve as intermediaries between politics and citizens, having informational (coverage-related), controlling (evaluation-related) and opinion-building functions. These functions have to be contrasted with assessments of the performance of Arab media. In his analysis of newly emerging satellite channels, Zayani suggests that '[a]rguments over politics and life, while an essential part of daily life for the people of the Middle East, are expected to be harmless by the time they hit the mass media – these are the informal restrictions under which the mass media operate in the Arab world'.[62]

As for the deliberative-discursive model of the public sphere, even here there are few matches with what is emerging in the Arab world or in the global media landscape that includes pan-Arab media. The most important characteristic of this model is its acknowledgement of partial, segmented, public spheres through arenas of public communication on interpersonal, intersocietal or mass communication levels, which the model sees as interrelated through common topics. Common topics may include a particular crisis. It has been observed that, particularly in times of acute crises, some pan-Arab media engage in what Mueller calls moments of 'rally-round-the-flag'.[63] That is to say, some pan-Arab media may have occasion to construct a certain would-be collective Arab position, trying to form opinions by collective processes. In this case, public spheres emerge on the basis of cohesion developed through issue-specific communication communities within the nation state and/or transnationally above it. However, the third model's assumption that public spheres are present as intermediate spaces between governmental structures and society is controversial in the EU and European context for which it was devised, as is its denial of an alleged public sphere deficit. In the context of crisis communication to and from Arab countries, a characterisation of the media as open intermediaries between politics and citizens scarcely holds true.

Nevertheless, if public sphere theory is to serve a purpose in analysing change in a media landscape that includes the Arab world, it seems there may be benefits from exploring the emergence of national or transnational issue-specific communication communities, as well as the new kind of 'interpreter' identified by Donskis. This would anyway be more productive than suggesting that anything approaching a public sphere is already in place. Indeed, the main attribute emerging so far in pan-Arab media, and in the global media landscape to which they belong, seems to be heterogeneity. Zayani sees heterogeneity linked to transparency and suggests that one should try to 'tease out' a 'transparency model' of the way Arab media work.[64] But any study of the media has also to acknowledge that the media alone cannot produce a public sphere.

- 3 -

Television and Public Action in the Beirut Spring

Lina Khatib[1]

In February 2005 Lebanon's prime minister, Rafiq al-Hariri, was killed by a bomb targeting his motorcade. Hariri's death catalysed an unexpected popular uprising in Lebanon, in which protestors insisted on knowing the truth behind his assassination and, blaming Syria as the culprit, demanded the withdrawal of Syrian troops from Lebanon. It also resulted in the formation of a coalition of Muslim and Christian factions, which declared themselves the 'opposition' to the government and eventually played an active role in steering the uprising that they came to term the 'Cedar Revolution'. The uprising brought together Muslim and Christian Lebanese citizens, who converged on downtown Beirut in a series of demonstrations between February and April 2005. That period of public action is referred to in this chapter as the Beirut Spring. Coverage of the demonstrations and other incidents of public protest related to Hariri's death dominated the airwaves of Lebanese television.

Television in Lebanon remains in the hands of political figures with diverse agendas. All television stations other than the state-owned Télé-Liban are commercial and privately owned. Terrestrial channels in operation during the period in question were: LBCI (Lebanese Broadcasting Corporation International), affiliated to the Christian Maronites; Future TV, owned by the family and associates of Rafiq Hariri and second only to LBCI in terms of audience reach; NBN (National Broadcasting Network), a channel affiliated to Nabih Birri, the Shiite speaker of the Lebanese parliament; New TV, run by opponents of the Hariri government; Télé Lumière, a Christian religious channel; and Al-Manar, the commercial channel owned by Hizbullah. All the channels, apart from Télé Lumière, offer mixed programming, presenting news and current affairs as well as talk shows and entertainment programmes, from live entertainment to soap operas. Television is Lebanon's most popular medium; almost every house in the country has a TV set.[2] The chain of public protests that the country witnessed marked a transformation in the role of television, and the media in general, in Lebanon. For the first time television spoke for the Lebanese public, and the public was able to speak through television. This chapter charts and analyses this change in the relationship between television and the public in Lebanon during the events of the Beirut Spring.

Nabil Dajani's work on the state of the Lebanese media just after the end of the 1975–1990 civil war reveals how much room there was for this relationship to change. In a work published in 1992, Dajani wrote:

> The Lebanese media ... have contributed to the alienation of the citizenry by not helping them participate in the affairs of their society. This alienation takes place by making the citizenry feel that they are distant and separate from the political process in society. The common Lebanese citizen cannot find in the content of the mass media any relationship to real life problems. He/she realises that what the media tell them about what is happening in their country is beyond their reach.[3]

When Dajani revisited this study a decade later he reached a similar conclusion. He wrote that television still did not address the need for different sectarian groups in Lebanon to unite. The media, he argued, still focused on the 'disorienting views of the different political, sectarian, and ethnic groups ... and consequently ... failed to bring about national accord'.[4] While this chapter does not argue that a media revolution took place in Lebanon in 2005, it does identify the Beirut Spring as a media landmark that challenged what Dajani had only recently described as the status quo. The chapter starts with a brief exploration of theories about the role of visual media in social change and goes on to examine the Beirut Spring as an event in which both television and the public took an active role. It shows how television was used as a symbolic battlefield between the different actors in the protests, and how the Beirut Spring, as a television event, calls for some refinement of our understanding of media events and their relation to physical public space. The chapter concludes with an assessment of the uprising and its aftermath, and considers the nature of the relationship between these events and the democratising potential of the media.

THE POWER TO SHOW

Jürgen Habermas defines the public sphere as 'a sphere which mediates between society and state, in which the public organizes itself as the bearer of public opinion'.[5] Monroe Price elaborates that the public sphere is 'a zone for discourse which serves as a locus for the exploration of ideas and the crystallization of a public view'.[6] He agrees with Habermas that the public sphere should have a 'limiting effect on the state'.[7] In other words, the public sphere is seen as a space where people may organise themselves into a counter-hegemonic force,[8] and where 'access is guaranteed to all citizens' so they may 'confer in an unrestricted fashion'.[9] An idealised public sphere thus ensures the availability of undistorted information to all citizens, enabling them to communicate and engage in political decision-making.[10] This is why it is regarded as an essential requirement 'for the conduct of a democratic polity'.[11] Democracy here is defined as those 'procedures for arriving at collective decisions in a way which secures the possible and qualitatively best participation of interested parties'.[12]

John Hartley writes: 'The public domain is in modern times an abstraction; its realm is that of representation and discourse, it is graphic and photographic but not geographic.'[13] In this sense, the public sphere, as a representative space, is 'literally made of pictures'.[14] Media institutions and media representation are, meanwhile, seen as forming important dimensions of the public sphere,[15] insofar as they are able to contribute to democratic practice by informing the public about the political structure and enabling them to engage with this structure. Democratic practice makes a number of demands on the media: surveillance of the socio-political environment; agenda-setting of key issues; platforms for expression by politicians and interest groups; space for dialogue between power holders and the public; a watchdog over the performance of officials; involving citizens and ensuring their activity; upholding their independence; and respecting their audience.[16] The visual media are seen as having the potential to play a crucial role in sustaining democracy, and even in creating social and political change.[17] Television, in particular, has been identified as the primary medium in such a process. For example, Pierre Bourdieu argues that television's visual nature marks its uniqueness in creating social change.[18] As he puts it, the 'power to show is also a power to mobilize'.[19]

One way in which mobilisation can take place is through what Nicholas Mirzoeff terms the 'visual-popular', meaning the way people are brought together by shared images.[20] Mirzoeff's term is based on Antonio Gramsci's concept of the national-popular, which refers to how popular culture brings together disparate groups in a nation.[21] Daniel Dayan and

Elihu Katz have also shown how television serves as a medium of national integration. They have coined the term 'media event' to refer to televised happenings that have an assimilating impact on the nation, because they interrupt routine and are broadcast live by all television channels simultaneously.[22] Such events, although organised by the establishment, have the unpredictability that goes with live broadcasts. Yet Thomas Meyer prefers the term 'pseudo-events',[23] to emphasise the artificial nature of events that are politically staged. In view of such potential contradictions, Margaret Morse's concept of 'televisual event' is useful,[24] since it distinguishes between the staged media event and and the televisual event, which is spontaneous. Morse argues that televisual events occur when a media event is disrupted. In this sense, the Olympics are a media event but the Romanian Revolution of 1989 was a televisual event due to its spontaneous domination of the Romanian television broadcasts. In the televisual event, the underlying assumption is that the camera can be used as a weapon, that

> the camera as an *active* mass tool of representation is a vehicle for documenting one's conditions…; for creating alternative representations of oneself…; of gaining power (and the power of analysis and visual literacy) over one's image; of presenting arguments and demands; of stimulating action; of experiencing visual pleasure as a producer, not consumer, of images; of relating to, by objectifying, one's personal and political environment.[25]

What these theories have in common is the challenge they present to arguments such as those of Jean Baudrillard, that today we live in a world saturated by images that have no resemblance to any outside reality.[26] Similarly, they challenge Meyer's view that the visualisation of culture has resulted in viewers' unquestioning acceptance of images and paralysis of their 'critical faculties'.[27]

THE ACTIVE ROLE OF TELEVISION

Several local commentators' instinctive response to Lebanese television's extensive coverage of the rallies in downtown Beirut in March 2005 echoed Bourdieu's argument about television's power to mobilise and Hartley's comments about the role of journalism being to visualise the 'truth'.[28] Ghassan bin Jeddou, chief of Al-Jazeera's Beirut bureau, said on 1 March that the Lebanese 'intifada' (uprising) had used the Ukranian Orange Revolution as a template, and he praised the opposition for being media-savvy.[29] On 4 March *Al-Safir* journalist Zainab Yaghi highlighted the changing role of television by arguing that the Lebanese audience wanted to 'see' to believe. In her opinion, in today's visually saturated world, 'history is seen, not told'.[30] Evidence also suggests that the Lebanese media, and television in particular, not only enjoyed the power to mobilise but actively used this power.

The protests in downtown Beirut created a convergence between public space and media space in the sense that television gave the public access to salient political issues. For a whole week after Hariri's assassination the leading Lebanese channel, LBCI, focused on the crime and related issues, including the protests in downtown Beirut. It continued to devote a significant portion of its airtime to this coverage during the Beirut Spring. Hariri-owned Future TV went even further. Almost all its airtime was used to cover Hariri's killing and its aftermath for a full 40 days after it happened. After that the issue continued to dominate the station's schedules. Both LBCI and Future appealed to the audience not only through news reports and political programming but also through popular culture products specifically aimed at mobilising the public behind the protest at Hariri's assassination. Contestants on LBCI's reality TV show *Star Academy* gathered together to sing a song specially commissioned as a tribute to Hariri. Future TV gave significant airtime to video clips devoted to Hariri, with a number of songs sung by former contestants on its own reality television show, *Super Star*, such as singer Ranin al-Shaar.

Both stations deliberately contributed to a new public discourse in which Martyrs' Square, where the protests at Hariri's killing took place, became known as Freedom Square. In place of their usual practice of referring to downtown Beirut as 'Beirut Central District', they started to call it *al-balad* (city centre), which was the area's colloquial name before the civil war.[31] Ever since the post-civil-war reconstruction of downtown Beirut the area had come to be popularly known as either 'Downtown' (in English) or 'Solidère', after the name of the company (largely owned by Hariri) that rebuilt the centre. By resurrecting the term *al-balad*, television stations seemed to be trying to reconnect with the public, invoking a lost language relating to a shared experience of a time before the civil war. At the same time, television played a role in mobilisation through its dominant images, which were those of the Martyrs' Square protestors. The images were often panoramic ones taken from high-rise buildings surrounding the area, and therefore dramatised the events by showing the vastness of the demonstrations. They became a symbol for the ability of the crowd to say things an individual cannot say,[32] and therefore to create a change in the political landscape.

There was also an element of calculated mobilisation in the way television stations sought to bring audiences together and create a sense of collectivity among them. Because of what was being shown live on television, politicians and people relied on the medium to create a sense of connectedness. Live television connected the public to events and fulfilled the need felt by members of the public to connect themselves with others through those events. Television's creation of collectivity manifested itself in two ways: a focus on religious togetherness through the representation of Lebanon's diverse religious symbols, and an emphasis on national unity through the representation of national symbols. The first method was seen as early as Hariri's funeral on 16 February, which was a public, not a state, funeral and drew thousands of mourners. Hariri was buried next to Al-Amin mosque, which he was building near Martyrs' Square. Television images included that of a nun and a Muslim sheikh praying side by side at Hariri's grave. Pictures of the gathering at Hariri's grave a week after his death showed a man carrying a cross, a Quran and a Druze skullcap. In the coverage of later protests, people who had painted a crescent and a cross on their faces became a familiar sight on television screens. This marked a significant departure from custom and practice on Lebanese television during the years since the civil war, when media personnel shied away from alluding to the country's different religious affiliations in the same report. As Dajani had noted, television previously never represented a Christian and a Muslim together in the same programme.[33]

National togetherness was, meanwhile, portrayed visually through the striking imagery of the Lebanese flag. After Hariri's funeral the Lebanese flag started to have a prominent presence in the downtown Beirut protests. Protestors would carry the flag or even wear it on their heads. The flag dominated the space of downtown Beirut and beyond, being hung from buildings and perched on car aerials. Again, this was in stark contrast to norms during and after the Lebanese civil war, when Lebanese people had been alienated from their flag and their nation. With the country fragmented, the flag was a marginalised and empty symbol, seen only inside government buildings and at official ceremonies. Like the lost moniker *al-balad*, the Lebanese flag was resurrected during the Beirut Spring as a symbol of the pre-war nation. It finally gained acceptance as a sign of national unity, its presence symbolising the need for the Lebanese to come together at a time of national crisis. Television camera crews clearly contributed to this as they picked up on the imagery in covering the events.

Television, through its persistent and blanket coverage, also played an indirect role in connecting the Lebanese people. Viewing live television is partially motivated by the 'need to know others are watching at the same time'.[34] Or, as Claus-Dieter Rath puts it, 'The experience of watching television may...be described not so much by the words "I see", as by the words

"I am among those who will have seen".[35] In contrast to Dajani's assessments of the Lebanese media in the early 1990s and early 2000s as being party to a process of fragmentation,[36] television's representations of the crowds, the religious symbols and the flag in the Beirut Spring played a key role in creating a sense of community.

THE ACTIVE ROLE OF THE PUBLIC

What is significant about the role of television during the Beirut Spring events is not only its reflection of the events, or even its attempt at mobilisation of the people, but also its use by the people themselves. In other words, not only did the media seek to mobilise the audience but the process also worked in reverse, in that the audience mobilised the media. Much has been written on the role of the public in the creation of mass media messages. Such writings tend to converge on the idea that the public plays a limited role in this context, which in turn has serious implications for the role of the media in creating a public sphere. For example, Price argues:

> Broadcasting often creates the illusion of a public sphere…[I]n the ideal public sphere the reader or viewer is an engaged participant; in the simulated model, the audience takes part in the debate only vicariously, only as spectators.[37]

Others agree, saying that people 'mainly figure…as the recipients and users of visual culture'.[38] Members of the public are defined as being an audience as well as citizens, with a separation between each status.[39] It is their *response* to media messages that is seen as determining the extent of their participation in making political judgements.[40] What those arguments imply is that, first, the public are consumers of media messages rather than creators. Second, there is a distinction between media consumption and citizenship. And, third , the public's role is limited.[41] As Michael Gurevitch and Jay Blumler argue, 'Of the three main elements in a political communication system – politicians, journalists, and audience members – it is the audience that…is least powerful.'[42] In other words, at best, the public's role is seen as merely to receive media messages, whereas the role of agenda-setting falls to the media, since theirs are the frames that 'define problems…diagnose causes, make moral judgements and suggest remedies'.[43] By presenting their own frames of events, the media not only 'have the power to be selective about what is covered but also the power to interpret events and issues' for the audience.[44]

The Beirut Spring events and their interaction with the media complicate the above arguments. The events marked a challenge to the idea that the media always have their own separate role in framing events, because the Lebanese protestors participated in framing the events by communicating directly with the audience through the television cameras. The public/audience acted as a creator of media messages. Direct audience participation in the media events meant the audience was not just 'active', but also 'acting'.[45] This activity blurs the lines between spectatorship, consumption and citizenship. The protestors used text to address both other citizens and the state through the media. The use of text was through the carrying of placards and the posting of signs carrying written statements. The earliest attempt by the public to send messages intended for television (and press) cameras took place on the day after Hariri's funeral. Television stations showed a young man carrying a sign in English saying 'Enough' at Saint George, the site of Hariri's assassination. Soon similar textual messages would spread across the demonstrations and the public spaces in downtown Beirut. Large black and white posters were stuck around the statue in Martyrs' Square, spelling out 'The Truth' in Arabic and English. The use of Arabic and English continued during the demonstrations, signifying not only Lebanon's linguistic hybridity but also the intention of protestors to communicate through television with an audience beyond the Arab world.

The proactive use of text was coupled with the proactive use of images, which reached a climax on 14 March. Following a pro-Syrian demonstration in Riad al-Solh Square on 8 March, opposition leaders called for an even bigger one on 14 March, one month after Hariri's assassination. That demonstration was the climax of the events of the Beirut Spring. The heavy reliance on and use of media messages by protestors on 14 March illustrate Bourdieu's argument that demonstrations have to be produced for television in order to be effective.[46] The 14 March demonstration presented the protestors as having a high degree of media literacy. They appropriated familiar media discourse and used it in a new context. Texts from popular advertisements were used to comment on the political situation. The slogan 'Keep walking' from a television advertisement for Johnny Walker whisky was used on a placard, on which the map of Lebanon was drawn, with the Syrian map to its right blacked out and an arrow pointing in the direction of Syria, signalling to Syrian troops to withdraw from Lebanon. An advertisement for the fabric detergent Persil was used for the same purpose. A placard carrying the picture of what looked like a box of Persil declared '1559 removes them from the Beqaa, all the Beqaa'. This play on the slogan about Persil's power to remove stains alluded to UN Security Council Resolution 1559, which demanded the withdrawal of Syrian troops from Lebanon. But it also contained a pun on the name of Lebanon's Beqaa Valley, with its significant Syrian military presence, and the Arabic word *boqaa*, meaning stains.

Popular culture also provided a reference for the slogans. A line from a song by Madonna, 'Papa don't preach, I'm in trouble deep', was written on a placard carrying the photographs of Syrian president, Bashar al-Assad and his late father Hafez, the former president. The words 'We surprised you, mooo?' ('mooo?' is colloquial Syrian Arabic for 'no?') were written in black and white on several placards, using the punch line in a popular joke to refer to the Lebanese people's defiance of Syrian dominance. The use of posters carrying pictures of wanted criminals, familiar from the film genre known as westerns, also provided an inspiration. Some demonstrators carried a photo of the then Lebanese minister of justice, Adnan Addoum, seen as collaborating with Syria, captioned with the word 'Wanted'. Some also carried photos of Lebanese president, Emile Lahoud and of Assad with the caption 'Sign Out.net', a phrase familiar to the millions of users of Microsoft's e-mail facility, Hotmail. The images, beamed across the Arab world through LBCI and Future TV's satellite channels, as well as through pan-Arab channels such as Al-Jazeera and Al-Arabiya, were striking in their 'peaceful' nature. As Ghassan Rizk commented, the public protests were a first for the Arab world; by the end of February 100,000 people were demonstrating without any confrontation with the state.[47] The power of the people was hailed at the time as having a great impact on democratisation. Satellite television was regarded as a facilitator for this phenomenon to spread across the Arab world.[48]

THE 'TELEVISION-SCAPE' AS A FIELD OF BATTLE

The television-scape during the Beirut Spring was used as a symbolic field of battle: between the opposition leaders and the public; between the opposition on the one hand and supporters of the Syrian presence on the other; and between television stations that backed the opposition (Future Television and LBCI) and those that did not (NBN, New TV and al-Manar). Opposition leaders and the public battled over the steering of the Beirut Spring events. Dissatisfied with the spontaneous public protests, political leaders actively tried to direct the mass gatherings. On 26 February they organised the formation of a human chain composed of 30,000 people carrying the Lebanese flag, which extended from Saint George to Martyrs' Square. Future TV covered this event, and aired a speech by MP Ghinwa Jalloul in which she proposed that the protestors needed new slogans to chant. In this way the slogan 'Freedom, Sovereignty, Independence', which opposition leaders had initially taught to the protestors on 18 February, turned into 'Truth, Freedom, National Unity'. On 12 March opposition leaders organised the formation of a human mosaic in the shape of the Lebanese flag near Martyrs' Square. Politicians also used television to send other non-verbal messages. Rafiq Hariri's sister, MP Bahia Hariri, started wearing a blue badge signifying 'the truth' during her television appearances. All presenters on Future TV later started to wear the badge too. In an episode of LBCI's talk show *Kalam El-Nas [People's Talk]* on 28 February, politician Samir Frangieh waited until he was live on air to carefully wind a scarf in the colours of the Lebanese flag around his neck.[49]

The beginning of March marked a media contest between pro- and anti-Syrian demonstrators over the same symbols and issues. The saturation television coverage of anti-Syrian demonstrators did not go unnoticed by Syrian president, Bashar al-Assad, who announced that he was well versed in camera techniques. He accused Lebanese television of zooming their cameras in on the Martyrs' Square crowd of protestors to make the crowd look bigger than it actually was. On 8 March Hizbullah took part in organising a pro-Syrian demonstration, which was given as much airtime by Lebanese stations as the anti-Syrian protests in downtown Beirut. The pro-Syrian demonstration utilised the same symbols as the anti-Syrian protestors. Religious symbols were deployed to signify the agreement of all Lebanese factions on their loyalty to Syria. A number of demonstrators were shown carrying a Quran and a cross at the same time. And, although the demonstration saw a lesser presence of the Lebanese flag than in the opposition gatherings, the flag was still used as a background in signs carrying slogans such as 'No for [sic] the Foreign Interference' and 'Thank you Syria'.

The Lebanese flag had also been invoked just two days earlier, when Hizbullah's Sheikh Hassan Nasrallah was seen speaking on television with the Lebanese flag as a background. Instead of the usual Hizbullah flag, which was this time placed marginally to the right of the Lebanese flag and was barely visible on the screen,[50] the Lebanese flag was taken to signify the national loyalty of the pro-Syrian Hizbullah. Placards carried by the 8 March demonstrators reinforced the meaning of this symbolic message when they declared 'No to divisions among the Lebanese'. To refute the accusation that Syria was responsible for Hariri's assassination, the 8 March demonstrators carried placards demanding 'We want to know the truth'. They likewise emphasised Lebanon's and Syria's affinity against outsiders through placards stating 'No to American intervention'. Perhaps most interestingly, the demonstrators carried signs saying 'Zoom out USA (camera)', in a direct reference to Bashar al-Assad's comment on camera 'bias'. The opposition's response to the 8 March event was to organise the 14 March demonstration, in which participants responded directly to Assad's allegation about camera angles and the use of 'Zoom out' signs by the pro-Syrian demonstrations.

Some placards instructed the television cameras to 'Zoom out and count'. One placard commented directly on the demonstration itself as a television event, carrying the Arabic words 'isn't the demonstration obvious [a phenomenon]?' (the words for 'phenomenon' and 'obvious' are the same in Arabic).

Lastly, there was a symbolic battle between different Lebanese television stations. The Beirut Spring events were significant in their interaction with Lebanese television because, although the channels remained faithful to the ideologies they represent, the events were something they could not ignore. With the exception of Télé Lumière, all channels took part in covering the protests in downtown Beirut and related issues, and interrupted their normal schedules to air live footage of the protestors in downtown Beirut on 14 March. Differences in coverage, between Al-Manar, NBN and New TV on the one hand and LBCI and Future TV on the other, were seen most clearly in the reporting of the pro-Syrian demonstration on 8 March. LBCI and Future Television, which supported the opposition, focused their cameras on Syrian nationals in the crowd, implying that Lebanese people generally were not participating in this event. In contrast, New TV seemed to be trying to present a progressive image of Syria's supporters by singling out attractive women demonstrators to interview. The opposing television stations offered wildly different estimates of the number of demonstrators on 8 March; estimates reported by LBCI and Future ranged around 235,000 whereas Al-Manar, NBN and New TV put the number at 1.6 million.[51] It was later confirmed that there were some 300,000 people on the 8 March demonstration, compared with around a million on 14 March.[52]

THE 'TRUTH CAMP' AS A PUBLIC–PRIVATE SPACE

By bringing about a convergence between media space and public space, the Beirut Spring events highlighted the importance of physical space to public action. Hartley has argued that democracy 'is conducted through representations circulated in public, even though no public…assembles in one place to constitute and govern itself'.[53] Yet what happened in Beirut relied on virtual (media) space and physical space being closely linked. Downtown Beirut became a space open to citizens from all factions, who could congregate there to air their views and exchange ideas with others about salient political issues. This was not the first time that downtown Beirut had functioned as a physical public sphere. Samir Khalaf maintains that the events of the Beirut Spring were only the latest in a series of incidents in the history of downtown Beirut in which it functioned as a forum for public action. From the anti-Ottoman national struggle between 1880 and 1908 to the struggle for independence in 1930s, to the student movement demonstrations in the 1970s, downtown Beirut has acted as a host for public protests.[54] The significance of the Beirut Spring was the return of the space of downtown Beirut to this role after 15 dormant years during the civil war and the 15 years that followed.

Also significant, however, was the way in which the Martyrs' Square 'Truth Camp' challenged established ideas about boundaries between the public and the private and about the *'place of citizenship'*[55] as shifting from public space to the family home in modern times. On 27 February the Lebanese government declared Martyrs' Square a no-go area as a general strike was announced. The army erected barriers around the square, allegedly to prevent people from gathering there. But a number of soldiers moved the barriers slightly, deliberately creating gaps that allowed people to 'sneak' inside. A planned demonstration was cancelled, but students decided to stay in Martyrs' Square and the Truth Camp was born. The next few days would see the erection of tents in the square, where demonstrators decided to stay until all Syrian troops would be withdrawn from Lebanon. Television cameras covered daily life in the camp as students and young people from different political parties in the opposition moved in. *Al-Safir* newspaper commented that it was as if the squares of downtown Beirut (Martyrs' Square and Riad al-Solh Square) had been transformed into television studios.[56] The camp protestors lived there 24 hours per day, transforming the site into one that was simultaneously private and public. This blurring of the lines between private and public prompted Rasha al-Atrash to refer to the television coverage of life in the camps as being similar to reality television.[57] Reality television combines drama with the voyeuristic pleasures of watching the 'real'. Arguably, television 'calls for *dramatization*'.[58] Drama in turn calls for '[p]rofound emotions about human triumph and defeat', following 'archetypal narratives' that present binaries such as friends and enemies, powerful and powerless.[59] The camp protestors in particular and the Beirut Spring protestors in general became protagonists in a classical narrative of good and evil. They were an illustration of Hartley's argument that today we see the drama of democracy only at times of social and political crisis.[60] The camp gave shelter to people from different political parties, and therefore functioned as a democratic public sphere because the citizens within it were equal in their representation of political interests and in their expression of opinions.[61] The camp also acted as a tool of material expression. It was used both functionally and symbolically, acting as a concrete expression of dissent that goes beyond the fleeting nature of speech.[62]

AFTERMATH OF THE BEIRUT SPRING

By the end of March the protests in downtown Beirut lessened and became more fragmented. Television's coverage of the events followed the same path. The beginning of April saw Future TV create another media campaign, this time aimed at reviving the ailing Lebanese economy that had suffered under the strain of the political crisis in the country. The campaign included the airing of short videos urging the public to visit downtown Beirut not as protestors but as consumers. As Bradley Butterfield put it in an article on the aftermath of 9/11, the 'implicit promise ... is that to consume is to live'.[63] At the same time, Bahia Hariri launched a campaign to mark the thirtieth anniversary of the outbreak of the Lebanese civil war in 1975. Up to that point, ignoring the civil war had been a defining feature of post-war Lebanese society – a feature which seems to validate the thesis that, in the creation of national memory, people 'are bound together as much by forgetting as by remembering'.[64] Bahia Hariri's campaign was considered crucial as the country was seen as being at risk of disintegration; the act of commemorating the start of war was presented as a warning against repeating past mistakes.

Future TV was the mouthpiece for this campaign. Instead of images of protestors carrying Lebanese flags, the channel used the flag as a motif in advertisements that it aired for a week-long commemoration to take place in downtown Beirut. This new project included sports, music and arts events as well as food and flower markets. A concert by Lebanese singer Majida al-Roumi took place on 13 April, the precise anniversary of the start of war, and was broadcast live on Future TV. The jubilant nature of the concert, which took place a few metres away from Martyrs' Square, was in striking contrast to the solemnity surrounding Hariri's grave and the Truth Camp nearby. LBCI chose to mark the anniversary on 13 April by airing a game show entitled *See the Difference and Do Not Discriminate*, in which questions revolved around the theme of Lebanon's confessional diversity. The spontaneity of the Beirut Spring came to an end. Television time was devoted to politicians once again. While some engaged in giving familiar ideological speeches, others supplemented their words by performing symbolic acts. Thus Bahia Hariri was shown releasing a white dove during the commemoration week. Pop stars also benefited from the media exposure, and singers such as Nancy Ajram and Haifa Wehbeh were shown reading to children in downtown Beirut. People were still seen wearing the Lebanese flag as a scarf or a hat, but the flag was also used in advertisements for products ranging from banking services to cosmetics. The flag ceased to be a national symbol per se; it also became a fashion item and even a brand.

In the months that followed the Beirut Spring, Lebanon was to witness a series of assassinations of politicians and journalists that triggered a proliferation of smaller, short-lived 'Beirut Springs'. For short periods of time television schedules would be interrupted so as to cover the funerals of Samir Kassir (*Al-Nahar* columnist), George Hawi (former leader of the Lebanese Communist Party) and Gibran Tueni (editor of *Al-Nahar*), as well as the public tribute to May Chidiac, a LBCI journalist and presenter who was severely injured in an attempt on her life. The funerals resembled the Beirut Spring protests in their public nature, but the Lebanese flag was by then slowly being dwarfed by the flags of different political factions, which used the occasions to get media coverage. Downtown Beirut gradually lost its role as a homogenising space and instead became a source for 'reawakening segmented and parochial identities'.[65] A new government was elected in Lebanon and the United Nations released a report on the investigation into Hariri's murder, but without thereby ending the dispute between pro- and anti-Syrian officials and their followers. Television, meanwhile, continued to try to mobilise people. An episode of the colloquially named talk show *Sireh w'infatahit*, aired by Future TV on 19 December 2005, had the presenter Zaven Kouyoumdjian offer to bring members of the opposition and Hizbullah to the studio to air their views and reach a common ground. In instances such as these, television tried to perform the democratic role still missing from the political realm, albeit to little or no effect.

CONCLUSION

It can be argued that the Beirut Spring protests would not have had the impact they did had it not been for the media. Unlike state-sponsored media events, the Beirut Spring protests were controlled by the people and opposition leaders, not the government. They were important for the impact they had on the Lebanese government, in that they led to the resignation of members of parliament and the prime minister, and the withdrawal of Syrian troops from Lebanon after three decades of occupation.

The Beirut Spring protests have elements of both 'media events' and 'televisual events'. Dayan and Katz argue that media events are the interruption of routine. They are live and unpredictable but monopolistic, as all television channels cover them simultaneously.[66] The Beirut Spring protests, as illustrated above, had all those elements. Dayan and Katz also find that, where media events invite a 're-examination of the status quo', they can be liberating for the people.[67] Their findings shed light on what happened during the Beirut Spring protests, except that in this case the protests themselves constituted a re-examination of the status quo. The reception of the coverage of the protests in people's homes also conformed to Dayan's and Katz's view that media events transform the home into a public space.[68] By the same token, the Beirut Spring events illustrated Margaret Morse's argument that the televisual event can turn viewers into 'on-screen protagonists'.[69] But, given the relationship of mutual dependency and symbolic exchange between television and the protests in this case, it is perhaps more accurate to dub the Beirut Spring a 'television event'. A television event may be seen as sharing elements of both the media event and the televisual event, while at the same time differing from both. The Beirut Spring was staged not by the establishment but by the opposition. Whereas television was mobilised almost accidentally by protagonists in the Romanian Revolution, in Lebanon the mobilisation was direct, calculated and deliberate. In this sense, the suicide attacks of 11 September 2001, including specifically the televised collapse of the World Trade Center's twin towers, were also arguably a television event. In sharp contrast, the Beirut Spring protestors were peaceful. But they were notable for the degree to which they capitalised on television's power to show and mobilise.

Television contributed to the short-lived existence of a democratic public sphere during the Beirut Spring. Yet it is crucial not to overestimate the role of Lebanese television in the process of democratisation, since prominent television images of protest do not in themselves bring about political transition. Images can perform a significant role in mobilising people and providing means of expression, but they can also be seen as filling the gap left when major questions remain unanswered. White refers to the explosion of the Challenger space shuttle in 1986 as an occasion when images were relied on as substitutes for answers.[70] He quotes the news commentator Tom Brokaw, who explained why television stations repeatedly showed the same image of the shuttle exploding by saying simply: 'What else could we do? People wanted answers.'[71] As Dayan and Katz have shown, images can act as catharsis for viewers.[72] In Lebanon, with no closure in the search for those who assassinated Hariri, Kassir, Hawi and Tueni (killing many others in the process), and with the internal clash of political ideologies unresolved, television images of a proactive public provided a glimmer of hope to the Lebanese audience and a chance for emotional release after the many years during which they were publicly mute.[73]

However, we cannot disregard the importance of the mediation of the Beirut Spring. Although the protests were an act of resistance in themselves, it is their mediation through television that became the focus of attention, making the narrative of the protests an event in its own right. This follows Jean-François Lyotard's argument that stories neither follow the axis 'real history→narration→'narrative' nor 'narrative'→narration→referential history', but rather that there is a 'synchrony or total achrony of the story, the narration and the narrative'.[74] As a television event, the Beirut Spring protests carved a space in Lebanon's national memory. They acted not just as protests against the past and the present but also as an example of the writing of history. The Beirut Spring was a television event that served as an 'electronic monument'. As such, it has an effect on public memory, transforming what has been and what will come.[75] 'The event is the occurrence after which nothing will ever be the same again. The event, that is, happens in excess of the referential frame within which it might be understood, disrupting or displacing that frame.'[76] In this way, the Beirut Spring confirms Walter Benjamin's statement: 'History does not break down into stories but into images.'[77]

- 4 -

Idioms of Contention: *Star Academy* in Lebanon and Kuwait

Marwan M. Kraidy

Within weeks of its launch by LBCI in December 2003, *Star Academy* became the most popular and most controversial programme in the history of Arab satellite television. Broadcast via satellite to Arab audiences between Morocco and Iraq, as well as Arabic-speaking communities outside the Arab world, this singing competition and reality television show, adapted from an international format, became the subject of everyday gossip, media commentary and, as this chapter will demonstrate, political debate. In effect, as a publicly disseminated cultural commodity subjected to intense interest, scrutiny and debate, *Star Academy* was a pan-Arab media event. As such, the programme compelled several social, political and religious players from across the Arab world to debate its implications for Arab societies. Building on previous research, in which I conducted a comparative analysis of public discourse surrounding three Arab reality television programmes, *Super Star, Al Rais* and *Star Academy*,[1] this chapter takes a closer look at *Star Academy* as a political space, focusing on Lebanon and Kuwait as case studies. In it, I draw on the results of extensive fieldwork conducted in 2004 and 2005, in Lebanon, Kuwait and Dubai, to address questions about the competing political discourses that *Star Academy* brought to the centre of public discourse at the pan-Arab level. What were the issues that motivated various groups to participate in the debate about *Star Academy*? What does the controversy surrounding this programme reveal about the dynamics of public debate in the Arab world?

Clearly, turbulent events unfolding in the Arab world, from the protracted conflict in Iraq to the festering crisis between Israelis and Palestinians, constituted the backdrop to the *Star Academy* event. Without in any way diminishing the importance of these fraught and intractable pan-Arab issues, this chapter seeks to understand how the controversy surrounding a pan-Arab programme, *Star Academy*, took different shapes as it was drawn into various episodes of contentious politics that were nationally distinct. Notably, it focuses on how the *Star Academy* controversy was simultaneously incorporated into specific political issues while also becoming a force animating these issues. *Star Academy* is explored as a political space, using the Lebanese–Syrian conflict in the wake of the assassination of Rafiq al-Hariri, and the interrogation and sacking of government ministers in Kuwait, as two case studies.

The chapter opens with a general discussion of the links between entertainment and politics, which then narrows to consider connections between reality television and politics. From there the study proceeds to provide a brief analytical description of the transnational Arab television industry. Production practices and programming strategies shape the contexts of the production, distribution and consumption of *Star Academy*, in addition to the reproduction of the programme in public discourse – the ways in which it is discussed, analysed, protested against and incorporated into other issues and debates. This process of cultural reproduction is central to analysing the political impact of reality television, because it concerns the everyday 'uptake' of the programme by viewers and activists. The chapter ends with some preliminary conclusions about what the cases of Lebanon and Kuwait may reveal about the broader pan-Arab public sphere.

POLITICS AND TELEVISION ENTERTAINMENT

'Public and academic debate,' writes Dutch media scholar Liesbet van Zoonen, 'maintains that television entertainment and politics are separate spheres whose requirements and qualities do not travel well.'[2] In the rare instances when a connection between politics and entertainment is acknowledged, it is usually in a way that expresses concern about the putatively negative effects of the latter on the former. With its simplistic slogans, slick packaging, promises of fast gratification and grounding in consumerist imperatives, entertainment is often described as having a corrupting impact on politics. Yet, despite this widely shared belief, several 'entertainers' have successfully crossed the bridge towards politics. In the US, Jesse 'The Body' Ventura, former *enfant terrible* of the World Wide Wrestling federation, was elected governor of Minnesota as a third-party candidate. His friend, one-time action movie collaborator, former Mister Universe and Hollywood star Arnold Schwarzenegger, was elected governor of California, the United States' wealthiest and most populous state. Particularities of public culture in the US make it a particularly fertile ground for crossing over from entertainment to politics, but examples of this phenomenon can also be found elsewhere, including in Italy, India and some Latin American countries.[3] These examples give some credence to van Zoonen's statement that the role of entertainment in politics is 'not...detrimental to democracy but...necessary and useful in contemporary culture'.[4] While this statement is open to qualification, it nonetheless opens a space for considering the entertainment–politics nexus beyond the thesis that 'entertainment corrupts politics'.

Although historically the Arab world has been the scene of many connections between entertainment and politics, such overlaps have become more frequent with the rapid growth of commercial media industries, especially the satellite television sector, since the early 1990s. Academic studies focusing on these overlaps are rare and usually tackle the subject indirectly.[5] The Arab press, however, including the pan-Arab dailies *Al-Hayat*, *Asharq Al-Awsat* and *Al-Quds Al-Arabi*, reflects a growing awareness of the connections between entertainment and politics. 'Stars return to politics...a job or a search for the audience?' asked a relatively lengthy August 2005 article in *Asharq-Al-Awsat*.[6] Filed from Cairo, the story commented on historical examples, such as Abdel-Halim Hafez becoming a spokesperson for the Egyptian Revolution and Umm Kulthum raising funds for Arab war efforts against Israel. It then posed a question:

> What is the relation between entertainment and politics? Is it necessary for the entertainer to have a well-defined political stand or to belong to a political party? Do entertainers accept roles with political themes that are not compatible with their tendencies and desires and political orientation?[7]

The article went on to interview several Arab entertainers and media critics, most of whom declared it to be natural for public figures, including entertainers, to be politically engaged. Other headlines, such as 'Fifi Abdo confronts corruption and smuggling of antiquities',[8] or even 'Because of their political activities, Israel considers Nancy and Maria and Haifa to pose a danger',[9] indicate that the entertainment–politics nexus is part of Arab public discourse. The overlap is mostly understood to involve celebrities who use their status to promote political causes to which they are sympathetic.

It is, however, the advent of reality television and the controversies it has elicited in Arab societies that have placed the entertainment–politics nexus at the centre of Arab public discourse. Elsewhere in the world, some reality television programmes were unequivocally political in the narrowest sense of the word. In 2002 *El Candidato de la Gente* (*The People's Candidate*) was broadcast by a television channel in Buenos Aires to enable viewers to select their candidate for the then forthcoming legislative elections in Argentina. In the US, the Fox network received intense publicity when it prepared to launch a similar show, *American Candidate*, on its FX cable channel. The project, involving viewers voting weekly to disqualify all but one of 100 hopefuls, was proposed by a documentary film-maker who had previously made *The War Room*, a political documentary about Bill Clinton's successful media strategy for winning the 1992 US presidential election.[10] Both these cases caused public commentary that was brief and confined to the media and perhaps an intellectual elite. In other words, as we shall see, public discourse surrounding these two cases was qualitatively and quantitatively less important than the debate surrounding all forms of reality television in the Arab world.

Indeed, the intensity and scope of the controversy surrounding Arab reality television suggests that the genre touched a raw nerve in Arab societies. As I have explained elsewhere, several Arab reality television shows have been controversial: they have either articulated inter-Arab rivalries and nurtured nationalistic discourse, or served as a platform for discussing socio-economic issues.[11] It is *Star Academy*'s combination of unprecedented popularity and intense controversy that makes it a particularly rich case study of the entertainment–politics nexus in Arab countries. As media events, reality television broadcasts act like magnets, attracting various groups to participate in public contention about socio-cultural change. The debate around *Star Academy* is thus a useful analytical field, giving us a view of the social and political fault lines in Arab societies. To understand the role of the mass media in making these divisions and points of contention visible, the next section includes brief descriptions of the Arab satellite television industry and of *Star Academy* itself.

SATELLITE CHANNELS' SEARCH FOR COMMERCIAL SUCCESS

The so-called Arab 'information revolution' in the 1990s initiated a process of transnationalisation that was initially regionwide. While this process can be characterised by the term 'regionalisation',[12] referring to expansion within the Arab countries' shared geo-linguistic sphere, the term 'transnationalisation' takes into account Arab diasporic communities in the Americas, Europe and Australia. Features of this process of transnationalisation include the growth of a simplified and media-compatible version of Arabic and the rise of journalists, anchors, singers and directors with pan-Arab fame and star appeal, in addition to an increased standardisation of production and distribution in Beirut, Cairo and Dubai.[13] Broadcasts are also increasingly tailored for the globally dispersed Arabic-speaking audience, with programming schedules, promotions and trailers referring to time zones around the world, including Greenwich Mean Time, US Eastern Standard Time or Pacific Time as well as the time in the Muslim holy city of Makkah in Saudi Arabia. Some Arab satellite broadcasters, such as the Lebanese National Broadcasting Network or Egypt's Nile International, also offer programmes in languages other than Arabic, notably English and French.

Transnationalisation also entails a growing synchronisation of the Arab television sector with the global television industry, characterised by what I have referred to elsewhere as 'post-Fordist practices' such as co-productions and format adaptations.[14] While co-productions have not been widely used in Arab media production, format adaptation has hit the industry like a craze since the major success of *Man Sa Yarbah al-Malyoun*, the Arabic version of *Who Wants to Be a Millionaire?*, broadcast on the Dubai-based Middle East Broadcasting Centre (MBC) in 2000 and still running in 2005.[15] Since then there has been flurry of format adaptations by several Arab satellite channels. Even news and talk shows can be said to reflect format adaptation, albeit indirectly. For example, Al-Jazeera's flagship programme *Al-Ittijah al-Muaakis* (*The Opposite Direction*) is widely acknowledged to have been modelled on CNN's *Crossfire*, and MBC's all-female-hosted *Kalam Nawa'em* was clearly inspired by ABC's *The View*.

The rise of entertainment as a staple in pan-Arab satellite television broadcasting is a story of competition among three networks. The first of these is the Saudi-owned MBC, based in London during the 1990s before it moved to Dubai. The second is LBCI, once the platform of the Lebanese Forces militia and then a shareholding corporation. The third is Future TV, owned by the family and associates of Lebanon's former prime minister, Rafiq al-Hariri. At its launch in 1991 MBC was initially seen primarily as a news broadcaster, a 'CNN in Arabic'. This worked well until LBCI and Future TV started their own satellite operations in the mid-1990s. With their slick production values, depictions of flashy and stylish Lebanese lifestyles, and reliance on attractive and alluringly dressed female anchors and programme hosts, LBCI and Future TV forced MBC to reconsider its strategy. This led to the launch of the Arabic version of *Who Wants to Be a Millionaire?* by MBC. That set the stage for Future TV's launch of *Super Star*, adapted from the format *Pop Idol* and aired in 2003, with the first season's finale taking place in August that year. LBCI's answer came in the form of *Star Academy*. All three programmes are watershed events in the history of Arab satellite television broadcasting, both because all three were unprecedented commercial successes and also because they influenced production and programming practices throughout the industry. Of the three, *Star Academy* is undoubtedly the most controversial.

Indeed, *Star Academy* is probably the most (in)famous Arabic-language format adaptation. The programme already had francophone French, Belgian and Canadian versions, in addition to the UK's *Fame Academy*, when it was first broadcast to the Arab world from Lebanon in December 2003. LBCI, a private company with a terrestrial channel registered in Lebanon and a satellite channel registered in the Cayman Islands, began a vast recruitment campaign across the Arab region in the summer of 2003, using television, radio, print and outdoor billboards. These efforts, which effectively operated as a pre-broadcast marketing campaign for *Star Academy*, attracted some 3000 applicants. Through auditions, this number was reduced to 16 finalists from various Arab countries, including Egypt, Kuwait, Lebanon, Morocco, Saudi Arabia and Tunisia,[16] who became 'students' at the eponymous 'Academy'. Beginning in December 2003, Arab viewers could watch the contestants 24 hours a day for four months on LBC Reality, a satellite channel that usually broadcasts music videos under the name 'Nagham'. For this purpose the channel was redirected to transmit live footage captured by 60 cameras positioned inside the four-storey building of the Academy, in addition to a nightly 'access' show and a weekly Friday evening 'prime'. One out of two contestants nominated on a weekly basis by a jury of experts was voted out of the Academy; this continued every week until the winner of the finale was crowned with the *Star Academy* title in April 2004.

Star Academy met unprecedented success and controversy throughout the Arab world. Its popularity prompted Lebanese restaurant owners to complain about decreased dinner business, Saudi clerics to issue religious rulings enjoining Muslims to boycott it, Kuwaiti politicians to launch parliamentary inquiries into media policies that allowed *Star Academy* broadcasts, and fans and detractors to set up websites about the programme. Myriad columns in Arab newspapers such as *Al-Riyadh* in Saudi Arabia and *Al-Watan* in Kuwait, and pan-Arab dailies such as *Al-Hayat*, *Asharq Al-Awsat* and *Al-Quds Al-Arabi*, commented on the show, displaying various levels of criticism and approval, triggering a massive volume of readers' letters stating their agreement or disagreement with the columnist in question. While some of the political activities triggered by *Star Academy* aimed at repressing it,[17] it is important to point out that many saw it as indicative of an alternative future. Arab columnists linked *Star Academy* to political issues such as voting, elections and due process, often using their commentary about the programme as a platform from which to mount critiques of Arab politics. This, in addition to other characteristics, made *Star Academy* a political media event.

THE POLITICS OF *STAR ACADEMY*

In what ways can *Star Academy* be described as 'political'? First, the programme triggered widespread controversy and fuelled heated regionwide debates. Clerics, intellectuals, artists, journalists, psychologists, advertising executives and politicians all participated in these debates, waged in the pages of daily newspapers, on television talk shows, during Friday sermons, on cassette tapes, in public colloquia and in cyberspace. These debates were invariably contentious and involved actors articulating normative claims about the public good, advocating policies they deemed capable of promoting desirable social values. As they formulated their arguments, these claimants appealed to the 'hearts and minds' of their readers, listeners or viewers, attempting to rally people to their views. These debates were, in other words, political.

Second, *Star Academy* is political in the sense that it articulated an alternative view of public participation in a public process. The programme stages an apparently 'fair' competition where contestants win to the extent that they can woo the viewing public with their creativity and competence. This, as some columnists in the Arab press noted, is discordant with how many young Arabs experience politics, an avenue of participation that is often blocked. A correlative of this is that decision-making in *Star Academy* is ostensibly determined by the voting public. Unlike in Arab politics, the programme organisers, the contestants and the audience must respect the results of the vote, where winning is often by a narrow margin, as opposed to Arab politics and the infamous 99 per cent election 'victories' according to which Arab rulers wield power.[18] In other words, *Star Academy* illustrates how, as the media scholars Daniel Dayan and Elihu Katz have argued, media events 'invoke subjunctive thoughts of alternative social order'.[19]

Third, *Star Academy*'s theme song, *Jayee al Haqiqa* (*Truth is on the Way*), is melodically an Arabic version of *Let the Sunshine In*. Although the lyrics are different, it draws on the soundtrack of *Hair*, the famous film about the American counter-culture in the 1960s, itself a political text. The song's lyrics criticise, albeit indirectly, the status of Arab societies, using words such as 'darkness' and 'cold', and they proclaim that the forthcoming truth will change the situation for the better. Visually, the music video has strong political connotations.[20] Directed by Nadine Labaki, a star in her own right who was made famous by the music videos she directed for

Lebanese singer and pan-Arab superstar Nancy Ajram, *Star Academy*'s music video is dominated by hues of blue, grey and black. *Star Academy* contestants are pictured marching through streets, shaking their fists and waving Arab national flags. Towards the end of the video the marchers are joined by children, an all-too-symbolic gesture about future Arab generations. Most intriguingly, the video's depiction of young demonstrators bears a resemblance to the 2005 'Cedar Revolution' that, in hindsight is almost prophetic. In fact, as the forthcoming analysis demonstrates, *Star Academy* was directly and transparently appropriated for political purposes.

STAR ACADEMY AND LEBANON'S 'CEDAR REVOLUTION'

In fact, the Beirut demonstrations following Hariri's assassination, dubbed the 'Cedar Revolution' in the West, provided the context for the explicit politicisation of *Star Academy* in its second season (referred to as *Star Academy 2*). Soon after the car bomb in Beirut that killed Rafiq al-Hariri, prime minister of Lebanon and leader of a parliamentary bloc, a curt announcement was made on the screen indicating that 'Lebanon was mourning', and heralding a ten-day hiatus in *Star Academy* broadcasts. The show resumed at prime time on Friday 25 February, subsequently referred to by the press as 'a patriotic evening'. The 'prime' opened with *Star Academy* contestants, including some contestants from the programme's first season brought back specially for the occasion, dressed head to toe in black, singing patriotic songs with a long and large Lebanese flag hanging in the background. Most importantly, by the end of the evening the Syrian contestant Joey had been voted out by viewers.[21] The political connotations of that incident are clear and were noted in the Arab press, which was relatively friendly to the Lebanese in a context in which Syria's responsibility in Hariri's assassination was widely assumed. On 14 March 2005 a massive demonstration was organised by diverse 'opposition' forces, including Hariri's own Future Movement, the Lebanese Forces, the Progressive Socialist Party, the Free Patriotic Movement, the Democratic Left Gathering and others, united by their opposition to what they termed the 'Lebanese–Syrian Security Apparatus'. The demonstration in Martyrs' Square, by some accounts the largest demonstration in Lebanese history, was itself a response to another demonstration organised by Hizbullah and its allies on 8 March in Al-Solh Square, a few blocks from Martyrs' Square, which was also massive.

In the 14 March demonstration and others, demonstrators carried a variety of signs asking for 'The Truth', which became the slogan of Hariri's supporters, calling on Syria to withdraw its troops from Lebanon, and calling on Emile Lahoud, the Lebanese president, and leaders of various security and intelligence services to resign. Several demonstrators brandished signs using the language of reality television, specifically that of *Star Academy*. These signs typically carried a portrait of the person whose resignation was called for, with the word 'nominee' written under his name. In *Star Academy*, there were two weekly nominees, one of whom would be voted out during the Friday prime. One sign was particularly interesting in the way it encapsulated a political agenda. It carried the picture of President Lahoud, with the word 'nominee' written above the picture and the exhortation 'Call 1559' written under the picture. In *Star Academy*, viewers are given four-digit mobile phone numbers to call in and vote for the nominee they want to continue in the show. In the poster, however, the number '1559' referred to United Nations Security Council Resolution 1559, which called for the withdrawal of Syrian troops from Lebanon and the cessation of Syrian intervention in Lebanese affairs. A political agenda was thus articulated using a few words and a picture, relying on viewers to understand its tenor because of their assumed familiarity with the procedures and vocabulary of reality television.

STAR ACADEMY, PUBLIC MORALITY AND DISMISSAL OF MINISTERS IN KUWAIT

As in the Lebanese–Syrian political struggle following Hariri's assassination in Lebanon, *Star Academy* was drawn into raging political struggles in other Arab countries, notably Kuwait.[22] The *Star Academy* debate in Kuwait is best understood as a continuation of the Islamists' strategy to mobilise public opinion by launching campaigns against the putatively corrupting influence of popular culture. Led by a member of parliament, Walid al-Tabtabai, the 18-member Sunni Islamist bloc in Kuwait's National Assembly was highly critical of *Star Academy* from the beginning of the broadcast. *Star Academy*'s enormous popularity in Kuwait was due in large part to the participation in the programme of Bashar al-Shatti, a charismatic young Kuwaiti who lost the *Star Academy* title to Egypt's Mohammed Attiyeh.[23] Because Kuwaitis were able to receive the programme on satellite that the government is unable (and probably unwilling) to control, the Islamist bloc was incapable of mounting an effective attack during the broadcasts.

However, when the *Star Academy* finalists visited Kuwait to give a concert in late spring 2004, Tabtabai and his associates launched a parliamentary debate about *Star Academy*. In addition to its claims about the immorality of the programme, the Sunni Islamist bloc had a basis for its campaign in Kuwait's past laws banning public concerts. In early May 2004, about a month after the first season of *Star Academy* ended, the Islamist bloc began publicising the issue and threatened to hold hearings about it, with the minister of information in the hot seat. After the concert was held, with tight police security and a demonstration opposing it, a statement by a leading bloc member, MP Faisal Al-Muslim, summarised the block's perspective on *Star Academy*: '[T]his program is silly and indecent. It promotes corrupt values that undermine the family and Islamic morals.'[24] Threats to call the information minister for questioning were taken seriously, because Kuwaiti MPs are not only authorised to question ministers but have often exercised that right in recent years, sometimes precipitating ministerial resignations. In 1999 the grilling of Ahmed al-Kulaib, then minister of justice, led to a major political crisis in the country.

Two weeks later the Kuwaiti Ministry of Islamic Affairs issued a religious opinion, known as a *fatwa*, stipulating that '[I]t is not allowed for any side to organize a concert by *Star Academy*, or under any other name, as long as they include practices forbidden by Islam'.[25] While singing and dancing are frowned upon by the strictest Islamic interpretations, the burning issue raised by *Star Academy* was the social mixing of unmarried men and women, which the programme displayed 24 hours a day through its satellite channel, in spite of LBCI's efforts to keep the most controversial types of scenes – in bedrooms, for example – off the air. It was this issue that was the focus of the Islamist bloc's official request in November 2004 to 'grill' the minister of information, Mohammed Abul-Hassan. Tabtabai said at the time: 'There is a defect in the ministry's performance in protecting morality and the minister's supervision over the media is lacking and negative.'[26] In the event, the minister did lose his job, and one of the first decisions of his successor, in March 2005, was to announce the creation of a Committee to Monitor Video Clips, another controversial genre of popular culture.[27]

The full dynamics and details of *Star Academy*'s life in Kuwaiti politics will be unravelled elsewhere.[28] In this context, it suffices to remark that changing political and sociocultural norms, in addition to the Islamists' strategy of focusing on popular culture, explain the scope and consequences of the controversy, which essentially pitted elements of the executive and legislative branches of the Kuwaiti polity against each other. The increasingly open media environment is fertile ground for such controversies. Al-Rai TV, Kuwait's first private television channel, plunged into the fray by showing, among other things, a programme featuring a transsexual man claiming affairs with male members of Kuwait's highest social and political echelons.[29] The reception of such material is facilitated by the spread of portable media technologies that are hard to control.

Arguably, *Star Academy*'s political resonance in Kuwait also extended to the decades-long struggle for women's political rights in that country, which concluded in May 2005 with the Kuwaiti government using suddenly adroit methods to persuade the all-male National Assembly to agree that Kuwaiti women should have the right to vote and run for office. Portrayals of women in the television programme cannot be separated from the warnings of Islamists, who, for so long, have opposed changing the electoral law on the grounds that women's political participation would endanger family values. In a speech reported first by the Kuwaiti daily *Al-Watan* and later by another daily, *Al-Siyassa*, Tabtabai allegedly said that those who force women to enter political life seek to increase the number of orphans, spread homosexuality and destroy family life. He was sued for these remarks by Shaikha Hamoud al-Nusuf, head of the Kuwaiti Women's Cultural Society, and fined the equivalent of more than $17,000.[30] Articulations between political episodes such as these and the *Star Academy* controversy remain to be fully explored.

CONCLUSION

Star Academy created a pan-Arab controversy, but the debates surrounding it clearly articulated political issues specific to their national contexts. This is, therefore, a case of a regional cultural commodity being localised or 'nationalised' as it is drawn into locally specific political issues. Consequently, in order to comprehend the political implications of reality television in the Arab world, studies ought to be strongly contextualised. It does not suffice to macro-analyse regionally successful television programmes, implicitly assuming that Arab countries are a monolithic sociocultural or political bloc. Rather, the most important political, sociocultural, even economic issues of each Arab country must be carefully described and analysed. In turn, that description and analysis should serve as a foundation for further study of the political implications of television in general and reality television programmes in particular.

There is a second conclusion that derives from analytical differentiation between how different Arab countries 'reproduce' reality television in variegated ways, namely that there are several registers of difference between Arab countries. Established sub-regional foci, such as 'Gulf states' or 'Mashreq' or 'Maghreb', while descriptively useful, may be analytically obfuscating. National size, geopolitical history, identity and other factors may bring countries closer across these categories. For instance, this chapter has compared the political lives, so to speak, of *Star Academy* in Kuwait and Lebanon, two Arab countries that are located in two different sub-regional areas. Although they are rarely compared in academic studies, Lebanon and Kuwait share many characteristics. They are both small in size. They have similar geopolitical circumstances, with larger, more powerful neighbours (Syria and Iraq) making historical claims on their territories. Both Lebanon and Kuwait have a history of a pluralistic press and robust public debate. In that regard, it is interesting to note that, in the now famous *Star Academy* prime-time show on 25 February 2005, the producers integrated a special tribute to Kuwait's national day, perhaps as a way of recasting the programme in a different light within the Kuwaiti public sphere, which witnessed strong opposition to *Star Academy*'s first season in 2003/2004, but also as a gesture of solidarity with another small and vulnerable nation.

The third and most important conclusion that can be drawn from this chapter is that, notable exceptions such as the 25 February show notwithstanding, the political impact of reality television is best grasped in terms of indirect articulations rather than direct causations. Because of its huge popularity, *Star Academy* pervaded Arab public discourse by being drawn into a circle of contested cultural reproduction consisting of nearly endless commentary and counter-commentary, always robust, sometimes heated. Appropriated in political demonstrations, the language and style of reality television has a powerful impact because, by saturating public space and achieving wide notoriety, it becomes the centre of intertextual references that most Arabs recognise. In other words, reality television's political potency resides in its ability to provide an idiom of contention. It gives people a new, alternative, camera-friendly and widely understood language of politics. This is of potentially enormous significance for the democratisation of Arab societies, for several reasons. First of all, the wide recognition of this language by the population enlarges the space of political participation by allowing more people into the political process even if they do not master more traditional political 'vocabularies'. Second, while *Star Academy* was popular across demographic categories, its most numerous viewers and most ardent fans were young Arabs. As it is widely acknowledged that youth involvement is crucial for meaningful political change, the entertainment–politics nexus can be a recruiting ground for more participants in political life. Having said this, the question of whether reality television ultimately has any real and sustainable political impact will depend largely on the ability of activists to transform popular energy into political institutions – an area in which Arab countries have dismal records.

- 5 -

Arab Internet Use: Popular Trends and Public Impact

Albrecht Hofheinz[1]

Important things happened in Arab cyberspace in 2005. In a year that saw several Arab elections, with some countries holding them for the first time and others appearing to allow voters more freedom than before, there was also the emergence in earnest of Arab blogging and an invigoration of websites working for greater political transparency. Some of these sites even appeared to gain a sufficient audience to begin to have an impact on the broader public. Governments, however, strongly resisted these trends. Indeed, the Internet, often extolled in the 1990s as a harbinger of democratic change, had not, by end-2005 at least, caused the collapse of autocratic Arab regimes.

As if to prove the breakthrough of blogging as a serious part of the Arab mediascape, the first arrests of bloggers took place in Libya, Iraq and Egypt.[2] Government resistance to civil society demands caused the Forum for the Future conference in Bahrain in November 2005 to end without agreement on a final agenda for regional political, social and economic reform.[3] At the World Summit on the Information Society (WSIS) in Tunis the same month, the Tunisian authorities turned a deaf ear to international criticism of their heavy-handed censorship of the online and offline activities of journalists and civil society groups.[4] In this ambiguous situation, with governments struggling to retain control in the face of citizens' resourceful Internet use, hope has alternated with frustration regarding the political impact of activities in Arab cyberspace.

CENSORSHIP'S MIXED EFFECTS

Ambiguity is evident first and foremost in censorship and its mixed effects. Although censorship is rife, not all countries exercise it to the same degree, and, even in countries with the tightest control on traffic, the Internet has opened windows and expanded horizons for those who seek to express dissent. Out of 15 states identified by Reporters sans frontières (RSF) in November 2005 as 'enemies of the Internet', four were Arab: Libya, Saudi Arabia, Syria and Tunisia.[5] The filtering and blocking of sites deemed inappropriate for moral or political reasons is also common in Yemen and the United Arab Emirates (UAE). Often, all traffic is routed through a single provider or proxy system controlled by state authorities, where the commercial, US-produced SmartFilter content software is used to restrict citizens' access to the Internet.[6] SmartFilter, also widely used in US companies and educational institutions, offers a constantly updated control list of millions of web pages in more than 60 languages, organised into over 70 categories 'for flexible policy enforcement options'. This permits the authorities not only to filter but also to monitor web use from behind proxy servers.

Saudi Arabia has been the most explicit about its access restrictions, which are directed by a special 'security committee' chaired by the Ministry of Interior and implemented by the Internet Services Unit (ISU) of the King Abdul-Aziz City for Science and Technology in Riyadh. It was not until 1999, when the Saudi authorities felt sure they had the technology to control Internet use, that they opened it to public access, several years later than most other Arab states. Stated Saudi policy is that 'all sites that contain content in violation of Islamic tradition or national regulations shall be blocked'.[7] Research by the OpenNet Initiative (ONI) shows that filtering in Saudi Arabia focuses most effectively on pornography and sexually explicit material and that this type of filtering has strengthened over the years. Sites promoting gambling, drug use or conversion to Christianity are actively targeted as well, as are tools to circumvent filtering, such as alternative web proxy servers and encryption tools. The filtering of content on alcohol, gay/lesbian issues, women's rights and political opposition is much less strict. The primacy of 'moral' issues over political concerns helps to explain the considerable popular support that filtering enjoys in the kingdom. Users can help to 'keep the net clean' by submitting requests to ban objectionable sites. But they can also ask to unblock sites mistakenly blocked by the ISU.

A similar situation obtains in the UAE, the region's most wired country, with one-third of the population online. The message UAE users receive, to tell them an Internet site has been blocked, announces that the largely state-owned Etisalat, hitherto the sole Internet service provider (ISP), aims to block sites 'inconsistent' with the country's 'political, moral, and religious values'.[8] According to reports for 2002, 60 per cent of domestic subscribers in the UAE favoured retaining filtering, mostly to protect family members from offensive material.[9] Like Saudi Arabia, the UAE employs SmartFilter extensively to block material related to pornography, gambling and religious conversion, and circumvention tools such as anonymisers or translation sites. Unlike Saudi Arabia, the UAE also blocks the entire Israeli top-level domain (.il), but not Israeli sites registered elsewhere. Attempts are also made to block gay/lesbian sites, dating sites in English (but not in Arabic) and sites critical of Islam. Political blocking – other than that of the Israeli domain – is limited, although sites specifically targeted include the Arab-American *Arab Times* (http://www.arabtimes.com).

In Tunisia, in contrast, political blocking by means of SmartFilter software has been aggressive. Besides preventing access to pornography and circumvention tools, Tunisia also works hard to block sites for political opposition and criticism of its record on human rights.[10] Analysing this pattern of online censorship, Human Rights Watch concluded that Tunisia's policy had been 'guided less by a fear of terrorism or incitement to violence [a reason often given to justify censorship] than by a fear of peaceful internal dissent'.[11] Although filtering was eased somewhat in the run-up to WSIS in Tunis in late 2005, with many sites unblocked, users were uncertain whether this would last. Political control of Internet use in Tunisia relies not only on filtering (which is carried out at the network backbone in order to encompass all ISPs) but also on heavy legal pressure. Internet cafés, required by law to monitor customer access, adopt methods known across the region, such as placing screens so that they are visible to staff and registering customers' identity card numbers. Unlike their Saudi and Emirati counterparts, Tunisian users are served only a generic failure page when trying to access blocked sites, which means that details of state censorship are not transparent. But citizens are made clearly aware that Internet use is being observed by the authorities and can be used against them in court – a practice which made Tunisia home to the first 'martyr of cyber-dissidence' in 2005.[12] Zouhair Yahyaoui, publisher of a webzine critical of the regime (www.tunezine.com), was arrested and sentenced to 28 months in prison in 2002 for 'disseminating false information' and 'stealing Internet services'. Released under international pressure in November 2003, Yahyaoui stopped publishing and, allegedly exhausted as a result of police harassment, died of a heart attack in March 2005, aged 36.[13]

In a widely publicised case, a group of young men from Zarzis in southern Tunisia received long prison sentences in 2004, having been convicted of plotting terrorist attacks based on prosecution evidence that included printouts from websites with information on jihad, weapons, explosives and fraud. Another case, involving 13 youths accused of downloading inflammatory material, occurred the same year. In 2005 human rights activist Mohamed Abbou was arrested and sentenced to three and a half years in prison after publishing an article critical of President Ben Ali on the banned news site tunisnews.com. Despite being banned, this site is widely described as the most popular source of online news in Tunisia.[14] Given Tunisia's reputation for running one of the Arab world's harshest Internet regimes, local and international commentators were highly critical of its selection as the venue for WSIS.

The Syrian authorities, like those in Tunisia, have been very wary of the Internet's potential for free communication. When Bashar al-Assad, founder of the Syrian Computer Society (SCS), succeeded his father as Syrian president in 2000, hopes were raised that political liberalisation in the country would encompass the Internet. Sure enough, Internet access was opened to the public that same year, placing Syria among the last Arab countries to do so. It soon became clear, however, that access was being affected by one of the most debilitating filtering systems in the region. This blocked opposition and political information sites, including some of the best-known international Arabic-language media, such as *Al-Hayat*, Elaph, IslamOnline and *Al-Quds al-Arabi*, as well as anonymisers and circumvention tools. But it also interfered with the very set-up of the Internet, by blocking the means to upload websites, encrypt communication or send e-mail via all but government-controlled servers. A Syrian student declared: 'It's not the Internet, it's the "Enter-not".'[15] Detentions in Syria for Internet-related charges quickly outnumbered those in other Arab states.[16] Citizens were held without charge for months or jailed for years for forwarding political jokes or news clippings to friends, or e-mailing information criticising, or even just documenting, Syrian policies to Arab and international media. A journalism student, Masoud Hamid, who used the Internet to disseminate photographs of police violence against a demonstration by Kurdish children in 2003 won the RSF-Fondation de France prize for 'cyber-dissidents' in 2005. In a move clearly timed to intimidate his fellow journalist students, Hamid was arrested a month after releasing the photographs, while he was taking university exams. He was held in solitary confinement for a year and allegedly badly tortured before being tried and sentenced to three years in prison.[17]

By early November 2005, weeks after Syria's first local private ISP (aya.sy) had started up in August, it was reported that restrictions on services such as chatting, uploading, encryption and e-mailing had been partially lifted. Although Aya had initially applied the same restrictions as the two government-affiliated providers (ste.net.sy and scs-net.org), it soon relaxed many of them, while SCS-Net also tried a limited opening.[18] Possible reasons were said to include the availability of improved technical controls for use by the security organs, although others believe that site blocking in Syria is primarily a tool of blackmail and corruption.[19] The apparent easing came as the government promised a new media law that would end the legal vacuum surrounding the Internet by introducing restrictions on Internet publishing.[20]

Elsewhere, in states such as Bahrain, Qatar and Jordan, filtering is much less restrictive, being targeted mainly at a few political opposition or pornographic sites. Since alternatives to these sites are readily accessible, such filtering efforts are largely symbolic. All the same, freedom of information is limited. In April 2005 Bahrain's authorities announced a campaign to register all Bahraini websites, but, true to their previous lack of political clarity, they failed to pursue this goal. Instead, in November 2005, they blocked around 40 sites without warning. One was Multaqa al-Bahrain (bahrainonline.org), a popular discussion forum established in 1999 that is used by the country's Shiite opposition to organise protests and evade the police. First blocked temporarily in 2002, the site had been blocked again in early 2005, after displaying a UN report criticising government discrimination against Bahrain's Shiite majority. Its founder, 27-year-old Ali Abdel-Imam, was arrested, along with two technicians. All three were released two weeks later, but without having been cleared of the charges. In contrast, the government unblocked the Voice of Bahrain (www.vob.org), mouthpiece of the London-based Islamist Shiite opposition Bahrain Freedom Movement.[21] The fact that Bahrainis inside Bahrain continue to post to sites such as bahrainonline.com demonstrates the limited effect of Bahraini filtering.

In sum, the impact of censorship across the region is mixed. The determined and the technologically adept can bypass it quite easily, as can those with the means to connect through a provider in a neighbouring state. At the same time, however, it combines with well-publicised crackdowns to induce self-censorship and deny access to banned sites for the general public. For the majority, expense remains another obstacle. Even in countries where unfiltered access has long been available, the high cost of access has long limited it to a tiny elite. This is slowly beginning to change but, even here, forms of censorship still exist. On 21 November 2005 Morocco blocked the main Polisario sites (arso.org, spsrasd.info, cahiersdusahara.com and wsahara.net) and followed this up swiftly by blocking anonymizer.com after it had been recommended as a circumvention tool.[22] Egypt partially blocked a site of the opposition Muslim Brotherhood, the regime's strongest rival in the 2005 parliamentary elections (http://www.ikhwanonline.com), as well as the online edition of the Labour Party's banned bi-weekly, *Al-Shaab* (http://www.alshaab.com). However, mirror sites such as http://www.ikhwanonline.org continued to be accessible, leading even Human Rights Watch to conclude that criticism of government policies and of individual officials can be freely expressed online in terms not permitted in print.[23]

Overall, despite persistent censorship, governments have not been able to silence dissent on the Internet or prevent activists from increasing their use of the technology to communicate and coordinate among themselves. Whereas banning access to certain sites diverts the mass of average users, it does not hinder the most determined, who can counter official control with relative ease. Fear of reprisals persists. Yet, as a human rights lawyer in Sudan told this author, 'The government knows what we think anyhow […] If they want to arrest us they do so whether or not we put our opinion out on the net, so we don't let that restrain us.' Even in Syria, Tunisia and Saudi Arabia, the boundaries of freedom of expression have been pushed back. Supporters of Zouhair Yahyaoui say he 'managed to open a breach',[24] and the Tunisian government's strongest detractors concede that the 'Internet is the major window for Tunisians in a context of total lack of freedom of press and information'.[25] Regimes themselves are split over how to manage the phenomenon. The Syrian writer Ammar Abdel-Hamid, founder of the Tharwa Project (www.tharwaproject.com, aimed at raising awareness of minority groups' living conditions in the Middle East, under the slogan 'Difference is Wealth'), has noted that, despite a generally gloomy picture for Syrian media, some reform-minded members of the regime seem willing to allow the voicing of limited dissent in state-owned outlets. He suggests that tolerance of Internet-based initiatives, which allows opposition figures to disseminate electronic bulletins even though public access to their websites may be blocked, fits the pattern of liberalisation being reflected in print first, before the broadcast media.[26] As to whether such limited openings owe more to external or internal pressure, many local activists became concerned in 2003 that the US government's so-called democracy initiatives in the region would effectively hijack their age-old call for political reform and put it under the control of a superpower known for its long-standing support of autocratic regimes. In the end, however, the view gained ground that, whatever the US agenda, civil society groups should simply intensify their own lobbying for genuine reform. The likely success of such efforts via the Internet depends on who uses the Internet in the Arab world and what they use it for.

WHO GOES WHERE?

Growth in Internet use in Arab countries has been dramatic since 2004. By that year, close to 17 million people were users, equivalent to 6 per cent of the population in Arab countries.[27] Since late 2004, with broadband connections increasing rapidly, many Arabic websites have registered a clear, exponential growth in access numbers. In 2002 it was predicted that Arab Internet users would number around 25 million, or 8 per cent of the population, by end-2005[28] – a forecast that now seems entirely realistic, with further growth to at least 11 per cent feasible by end-2006. To date, most of this growth has come from Egypt and Saudi Arabia, together home to over a third of all Arab Internet users, with Egypt reporting 4.4 million and Saudi Arabia 2.54 million by November 2005. More bandwidth and lower prices in Morocco pushed the number there to 4 million by end-2005, representing more than 13 per cent of the population.[29] The prominence of certain users and their relative purchasing power helps to shape the content that surfers of Arabic cyberspace are most likely to encounter.

In recent years Internet use has spread fastest among young people and women. The 20–30 age group are the most avid users, as indicated by statistics showing their percentage among net users in 2003 to be twice their share of the total population. The most rapid growth in Internet use has been among the under-20s. In the UAE, around half of 15–24-year-olds were connected in 2004. Women, who in 1998 allegedly constituted only 4 per cent of Arab net users, are now approaching the 50 per cent mark. But, while some data are available on the age and gender of users, the same does not apply to their income and education levels. Regular Internet use entails costs that people on lower incomes find difficult to justify. Costs, combined with a less developed infrastructure in rural areas, explain why Internet use has so far remained strongest among urban middle- and upper-class groups. Among the younger, educated elites, however, it increasingly is a fact of life.[30] Today, unlike the 1990s, when Internet communication was mainly for middle-aged professionals, it is rapidly becoming a factor in the socialisation of the younger generation.

What do all these Internet users do when they log on? Over the past six years for which statistics have been available, patterns of popularity have remained relatively stable. Table 5.1 shows the most-visited Arabic sites on the Internet in January 2006. Data from other sources give a similar picture to the one presented in the table. For example, the Saudi censorship authorities release monthly statistics of the sites most frequently accessed from Saudi Arabia, in which many of the addresses in Table 5.1 reappear. Among other sites, the most consistently popular in the kingdom

TABLE 5.1 TOP 20 ARABIC INTERNET SITES[31]

Name	Description	URL	Established	Traffic Rank 03/11	Traffic Rank 05/05	Traffic Rank 06/01
Google Saudi Arabia	The third Arabic interface page of the search engine Google (after google.ae and google.com.ly). 25% of requests are for images compared with 8% on the international Google.com, 32% on Google.ae and 15% on Google.com.ly (January 2006).	google.com.sa	August 2004	n/a	163	191
MSN Arabia	Incarnation of the worldwide Microsoft Network portal site localised for users in the Arab world, in Arabic and English. Run by Microsoft together with LINKdotNET, Egypt's largest Internet provider (over 40% market share), produced in Cairo and Dubai (Dubai Internet City). Apart from the fact that it comes pre-installed as	arabia.msn.com	September 2001	300	250	200[32]

63

Name	Description	URL	Established	Traffic Rank 03/11	Traffic Rank 05/05	Traffic Rank 06/01
	a home page on all Windows computers sold in the region, and the close intertwining of MSN with popular services such as MSN messenger, the partnership with LINKdot NET contributed much to the success of MSN Arabia, which by July 2004 had over 4.5 m. registered users.					
Maktoob	The first web-based e-mail service to allow use of Arabic as well as English. Jordanian-owned. Became the most-frequented Arabic website by 2000, perhaps earlier. Had 1 m. registered users in 2001, 3.5 m. in November 2003 and 4.3 m. in January 2006, equal to one-fifth of all users in the Arab world. Has added chatting, e-cards, news, polls, shopping, games and blogs to its offerings.	maktoob.com	October 1998	1405	134	201

Name	Description	URL	Established	Traffic Rank 03/11	Traffic Rank 05/05	Traffic Rank 06/01
Al-Jazeera	Internet edition of the Arab World's most famous satellite TV station. News in Arabic and English. Streaming video and syndicating services were made paid services after initial pilot projects.	aljazeera.net	August 1998	575	332	288[33]
Al-Saha al-Arabiya	One of the oldest (since April 1998) and best-known Arabic discussion forums, popular among all political persuasions, especially in the UAE and Saudi Arabia.	alsaha.fares.net/alsaha.com	November 1996	1519	352	303
Google.ae	Google's first Arabic version.	google.ae	December 2002	3145	473	375
Kooora	Soccer portal.	kooora.com	September 2002	>20,000	1007	391
Hawaaworld	Portal for women, conventional outlook. Based in Saudi Arabia. Discussion forum is by far its most popular service, with 181,000 members in January 2006,	hawaaworld.com	September 2000	17,874	781	453

Name	URL	Description	Established	Traffic Rank 03/11	Traffic Rank 05/05	Traffic Rank 06/01
		over 400,000 threads and over 5.4 m. postings. Ranking has to take account of additional visitors to its other address, hawaaworld.net.				
6arab.com	6arab.com	RealAudio files of popular Arabic music.	April 1999	1538	589	481
Al-Ahram	ahram.or.eg	Internet version of Egypt's oldest and best-known daily. Domain popularity is also caused by readers of the English-language *Al-Ahram Weekly* and the French *Al-Ahram Hebdo*.	?	1085	505	499
Tarab	6r.com	Music portal.	August 2002	4591	798	548
Mawqiʿ al-Ustadh Amr Khaled	amrkhaled.net	Site of Egyptian-born London-based pietistic preacher Amr Khaled, especially popular among the young. Discussion forums drew 36% of site's total traffic in January 2006, with more than 316,000 members up from 76,800 in November 2003. Percentage breakdown of visitors	January 2002	4595	389	560

Name	Description	URL	Established	Traffic Rank 03/11	Traffic Rank 05/05	Traffic Rank 06/01
	by source gives Egypt 43, Lebanon Syria, Palestine and Jordan 20, North Africa 14, the Gulf 10, North America 5 and Europe 4.[34]					
Vip600 Iqla'-Soft	Arabic-language software guide, technical forums; Internet services based in Riyadh.	vip6.com	January 2002	>20,000	1557	602
Swalif	High frequency discussion forums (2.5 m. postings by January 2006, but no membership numbers published). A search engine across 30 external forums (so far) adds to the site's attractiveness.	swalif.net	August 1999	6684	1283	610
Tadawul: Saudi Stock Exchange	Securities trading, clearing and settlements system for Saudi Arabia.	tadawul.com.sa	October 2001	7773	1003	770
Jeeran	'Arab Web Hosting Community': offers free space and a sub-domain. Hosts private homepages, communities	jeeran.com	January 2000	3131	926	786

Name	Description	URL	Established	Traffic Rank 03/11	Traffic Rank 05/05	Traffic Rank 06/01
	photo galleries, discussion forums and since late 2005, blogs.					
Tariq al-Islam/ IslamWay	Salafi 'Islamic broadcasting': audio lectures and articles on Muslim belief and practice; Quran recitations. Arabic and English; selected content in French, Dutch and other languages. Launched on initiative of the salafi Islamic Association of North America, registered in Saudi Arabia. Strong popularity growth in 2005.	islamway.com	August 1998	ca. 4040	ca. 1800	806
Gawab	Web mail service, established in Egypt.	gawab.com	March 2000	2446	597	875
Shabakat Oz	Kuwaiti portal: chat, clubs, pictures software downloads. With discussion forums (>358,000 members, >5.8 m. postings and >420,000 threads by January 2006), where entertainment,	ozq8.com	July 2001	7827	1112	881

Name	Description	URL	Established	Traffic Rank 03/11	Traffic Rank 05/05	Traffic Rank 06/01
	music, *Star Academy* ringtones and greetings are the most popular areas.					
Al-Gomhuria	Third-largest Egyptian daily. Sports pages are most popular online as in print.	algomhuria.net.eg	(2001?)	2921	1043	885

throughout 2002–2005 were: Yahoo! (with Yahoo! Groups, chat, mail); Lycos.co.uk (private forums and home pages); Bawwabat al-Arab (arabsgate.com, a secular Saudi portal with the most highly frequented discussion forums in the Arab world, plus a variety of services); Zawgaty.com (matrimonials); Geocities (private forums and home pages); Eqla3.com (an anti-Islamist Saudi site offering a satirical perspective on Arab affairs, with discussion forums on culture, society and sports); *The Times of India*; *Al-Watan* (reformist national Saudi daily); Muntadayat Jawwal al-Arab (mobile4arab.com, forums on mobile phones); Mubasher. com.sa (real-time prices from the Saudi Stock Exchange); Muntada al-Shasha (alshashah.com, a financial discussion forum that has meanwhile been replaced by a host of other stock market forums); and Elaph.com (a liberal pan-Arab electronic newspaper).[35]

The rising profile of female and young users is reflected in the growth of traffic on sites such as Kooora, Hawaaworld or Shabakat Oz, as shown in Table 5.1. Other examples of steep growth include: Arb3 (a portal and forum for women, on all aspects of married life); 'Alam al-Romansiyya ('World of Romance', made in Saudi Arabia); Startimes2 (discussion forum of a satellite TV portal); Afdal 1000 Mawqi' 'Arabi (web guide to 1000 best Arabic sites); Fosta (entertainment site, mostly for young males); Dalil MBC (web guide for young people, made in Saudi Arabia); Lakii (a conventional site for women); and Bint al-Halal (a matrimonial site from Egypt with Islamic orientation). In 2005 the biggest popularity gains among the top 20 were made by the software guide Vip600, the salafi portal IslamWay, the soccer site Kooora and the discussion forum/search engine Swalif. Meanwhile, Gawab and Maktoob appeared to be struggling against competition from new service providers, and Amr Khaled's online popularity also dipped. If we look more generally at the dynamics among the 200 most popular Arabic sites during 2005, we find that forums related to the Saudi stock market,[36] sports,[37] sex education and pictures,[38] general youth portals (especially from Egypt),[39] girls' and women's sites,[40] music downloads[41] and chat,[42] as well as Syrian[43] and Palestinian[44] sites, performed particularly well.

What these data illustrate are the needs that visitors to Arabic-language Internet sites seek to satisfy. In approximate order of priority, reflected in overall traffic, these are to: facilitate and extend social contacts through e-mail and chat; obtain news from reliable non-local sources; discuss almost everything under the sun, especially topics in the realms of religion, politics and relations between the sexes that have traditionally been taboo; enjoy entertainment, especially in the form of music downloads, sports and games; and take moral guidance from what is perceived as a contemporary Islamic perspective on modern life, including how to live as a Muslim woman in the modern world. Sites are also used to answer questions about fashion, family, food, relationships, sex life and work, and to provide match-making services and business information.

DEVELOPING TRENDS IN MOBILISATION

Given its growing reach among elites and the young, the next question to consider is how far the Internet is being used to mobilise citizens for civic action. Some commentators think the 'new trend of interactivity', with weblogs increasingly used as information channels, may force established organisations to 'become more competitive' and 'aggressively seek the truth'.[45] Journalists and non-governmental organisations (NGOs) were among the first professional Internet users in the Arab world; most Arabic newspapers have at least experimented with online content, and many of the larger NGOs have websites. In both cases the effect was to speed up communication with the outside world. Local NGOs relied on e-mail and websites to coordinate with parent bodies and attract donors, while journalists hunted the web for information, wire stories or images and to reach readers in national diasporas in the Gulf, Europe or America. Importantly, however, the Internet has long lagged far behind other means of reaching the public at home. Online editions of national newspapers are hardly accessed in their countries of origin[46] and civil society groups rely on the telephone (especially mobile phones and SMS (Short Message Service) text messages), along with faxes and face-to-face contact, when they want to mobilise local support. The reasons are obvious. Printed editions of local newspapers remain more affordable than online time, and Internet penetration is not yet broad enough to justify the cost to most local groups of creating and maintaining campaigning websites.

The same reasons may explain why Arab political parties, whether in government or opposition, still generally have only a weak presence on the Internet. Likewise, e-government services, despite improvements in Egypt, Qatar and the UAE in 2005, have remained at the pilot stage almost everywhere else. For the purposes of mobilisation, SMS has much wider reach than the Internet, in line with the penetration of mobile phones. SMS messages served in organising protests against the US-led invasion of Iraq in March 2003 (the first spontaneous mass street protests in Egypt since 1977), just as they played a major role in the Lebanese demonstrations in spring 2005. But governments have also exploited this potential. Subscribers to Sudan's state-controlled mobile phone monopoly received a text message from the authorities in March 2005, calling on them to march in protest at the UN's request to the International Criminal Court to investigate allegations of crimes against humanity committed by Sudanese officials in Darfur. The success of mobilisation via SMS contrasts sharply with most party websites' rather static appearance. Morocco had a widely publicised site for its 2002 elections, the main purpose of which seemed to be to show the country and its electoral commission in a modern light, rather than provide useful content. The Saudi Ministry of Municipalities and Rural Affairs set up a much more elaborate site (www.elections.gov.sa) to inform about, and publish, the results of the 2005 municipal elections; 53 per cent of users polled on the site said they did not think it useful.

Islamist groups have long been more successful in their Internet designs than their liberal or secular counterparts. This was the case since the earliest days of the World Wide Web in 1993, when Muslim student associations in America and Europe were quick to embrace the new medium to promote a global Islamic consciousness. Their mailing lists – early examples of news aggregators, which were widely read at the time – helped to strengthen identification with the struggles of Muslim communities in places such as Kashmir, Bosnia, Chechnya and Palestine that became focal points for ideas about defending Muslims against outside aggression. Today, with web technology more advanced and the use of Arabic no longer a problem, web-based news portals have taken over this role. The most successful of all jihad-oriented news sites is Mufakkirat al-Islam (islammemo.cc), founded when the US and UK invaded Iraq in March 2003. With the fight for Faluja in November 2004, IslamMemo became more popular than the older Moheet.com, a populist portal appealing to Islamic and Arab national sentiments that was established by the Dubai-based Al-Mutahida Group (arabia-inform.com) in 1998 and is produced in Egypt. Al-Mukhtasar li'l-Akhbar (www.almokhtsar.com), founded in November 2002 by radical Wahhabis opposed to the Saudi regime but not openly agitating against it, is the second jihad news aggregator to feature among the top 100 most popular Arabic sites. Yet conservative Islamic sites that toe the Saudi government's line continue to attract significantly more visitors than the jihad pages. This is especially the case for the audio-file site IslamWay.com, for al-Khayma al-Arabiyya (www.khayma.com), one of the first Arabic web directories, established in 1999, and for its offshoots, the portal Raddadi.com and the Wahhabi missionary site Said al-Fawa'id (www.saaid.net).

Islamist extremists use the Internet to communicate, often via Yahoo! groups and similar electronic communities that are as easily abandoned as they are created. The Global Islamic Media group attracted attention in the

West, because a strategy paper suggesting a terrorist attack in Spain to influence elections was published there three months before the Madrid attacks of 11 March 2003.[47] Since membership of groups such as these ranges between a handful and a few hundred at most, they are not mass platforms but forums for communication among insiders already converted to a cause. Militant websites, constantly migrating to escape clampdowns, can only ever reach the devoted few, who have to follow their tracks on electronic bulletin boards. One of the more persistent examples is Dalil Meshawir, among whose many different addresses meshawir.cjb.net had stayed open for quite a while at the time of this writing.[48]

Islamist groups were particularly adept at using both SMS and the Internet during elections in 2005. In the Saudi municipal elections, so-called 'Golden Lists' promoted conservative clerics and provided clear 'Islamic' orientation to voters baffled by the hundreds of candidates who were supposed to stand as individuals, since political parties are banned. It came as no surprise when almost all candidates on these lists won, since the Islamic Awakening (Al-Sahwa) is the best-networked socio-political trend in Saudi Arabia.[49] During the 2005 parliamentary election campaign in Egypt, the Muslim Brotherhood not only went house to house but also used websites, e-mail and SMS to mobilise the electorate on a scale not seen before. Even secular commentators agreed that these online efforts put campaigns by other political forces in Egypt, including the government, 'to shame'.[50] That is not to belittle secular initiatives such as Shayfeenkum (Arabic for 'We are watching you', www.shayfeen.com), a website established in June 2005 to enable voters to report irregularities in the Egyptian elections. But, whereas Shayfeenkum had lapsed by January 2006, the Muslim Brotherhood had capitalised on its strong showing to send 'mass emails' canvassing feedback on voters' expectations of their MPs and reasons for voting for or against them.[51] The web data service Alexa shows how much more traffic went to Ikhwan Online than to the site of the secular opposition movement Kefaya during and after the election period (Figure 5.1).

Arab Internet users, whether of Islamist or secular leanings, express a strong wish for political reform and greater public participation through their preference for media that are not state-controlled. In 2004 the decidedly liberal Elaph.com overtook the respected pan-Arab daily Al-Hayat in popularity among Internet readers, becoming the leading news site accessed from Saudi Arabia after aljazeera.net. Longing for reform is one thing, however, and actual political change is another, as is regularly acknowledged by participants in the thousands of online polls conducted on Arabic sites in recent years. The results of such polls are surprisingly consistent. Internet users believe their regimes cling to power not only because they are power-hungry but because of nepotism and the fear of being held accountable by democratically legitimated successors. Before the US-led invasion of Iraq, they blamed their own repressive governments much more than outside interference for the weakness of democracy in the region.[52] These long-standing attitudes help to explain why Internet users are sceptical about the possibility of an 'Arab Spring'. 'Does the uprising in Lebanon ring in a new age of popular uprisings in the Arab world?' asked aljazeera.net on 5 March 2005. The response was weak (only 3452 votes) and divided, with 55 per cent of respondents answering 'No'.[53] In September 64 per cent expressed doubt that the presidential elections in Egypt hailed the beginning of a real democratic process.[54] In January 2006 59 per cent did not believe the Moroccan reconciliation process would succeed.[55] As to whether external pressure is needed to strengthen internal reforms, Arab net-citizens are similarly uncertain. At the end of March 2005 aljazeera.net asked if the US-led invasion of Iraq had been necessary to push the Arab world towards reform and change. Of a mere 2793 votes cast in this poll, one-third agreed with the proposition. The poll was later pulled from aljazeera.net's archives.

FIGURE 5.1 COMPARATIVE POPULARITY OF IKHWAN AND KEFAYA WEBSITES

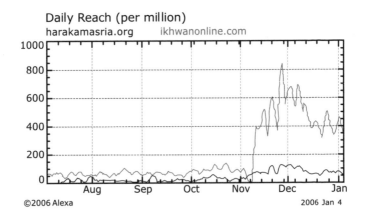

Source: Alexa, 4 January 2006.

REGIONAL SPECIFICITIES: RELIGION AND DISCUSSION

Based on the main Internet uses identified earlier in this chapter, it can be said that Arab patterns of Internet use are very similar to worldwide patterns; expanding and facilitating social networks and accessing information and entertainment are ubiquitous goals that the Internet helps to satisfy. But, drawing on the analysis above, it can also be said that Arabic cyberspace has two special characteristics. First, religion has a greater weight than almost anywhere else. Second, Arab users are particularly eager to discuss, especially politics, religion and sex. In both domains, a growing assertion of the individual as an active speaker and decision-maker, not a passive recipient of authoritative discourse, is apparent.

Of the 100 most frequently visited Arabic websites, eight have a decidedly religious and specifically Islamic character. This comparatively high ratio of religious sites is surpassed only in Kiswahili (21 per cent of only 38 sites) and Malay (11 per cent), and is not observable in any of the other official languages of the UN.[56] By far the most popular religious sites in Arabic are not the militant ones but those promoting a moral renewal of the individual, inspired by the Quranic injunction that 'Allah will never change the condition of a people until they change themselves'. Foremost among these is the site of Amr Khaled (born 1967), who, while still in his thirties, developed a huge following first in his home country and then in other Arab states, especially from among the 15–24 age group, where, as we have seen, Internet use is growing most rapidly. From mid-2004 to mid-2005 AmrKhaled.net (established in 2002) overtook the much older IslamOnline.net (established in 1997) as not only the leading Muslim site on the Internet but also the most popular religious site worldwide. IslamOnline was inspired by Yusuf al-Qaradawi, a preacher also from Egypt, whose roots lie in the Muslim Brotherhood and who became extremely influential in the 1990s through his regular programme on Al-jazeera satellite television. Amr Khaled appears on the Saudi-owned Arab Radio and Television (ART) television network, including the religious channel Iqra. One assessment of his success attributed it to the fact that young people, 'fed up with the traditional political and religious disputes', had

> been given what they have been denied for many years [:] a belief in their abilities to change and to act. [...] True change came into existence, not by restricting thought and forcing direction, but by accepting accountability and believing in one's ability. [...] Thirsty to be active and to be empowered, Arabic youth flood the Amr Khaled forums with over 4000 comments about the [TV] show and over 3000 posts about the weekly

homework. [These are] young people who believe that creating a positive change is much better than criticizing a negative reality.[57]

It is interesting to note how this assessment considers that real change has occurred, even though one might argue that no substantive change has taken place on the political level. The change referred to here is one of personal attitude and belief, which can be acted out first in the virtual sense, on Internet forums. Nevertheless the Egyptian government does not believe the phenomenon to be innocent of political implications. It was after it banned Amr Khaled from public preaching, in 2002, that he went into exile and started his website.

Internet discussion forums, such as the one provided on Amr Khaled's site, are the second distinctive feature of Arab cyberspace. No other language group debates as avidly on the Internet as Arabic-speakers. One of the oldest and still most popular forums is Al-Saha al-Arabiyya (literally 'the Arab forum', www.alsaha.com, dating from April 1998). Swalif.net (established August 1999) and Arabsgate.com (July 2000) have also been much frequented for years. There exist hundreds of dedicated discussion sites (I counted over 750 active ones in November 2003, of which about 60 were high-frequency), but forums on portal sites such as Amr Khaled, IslamOnline or Hawaaworld also play a very important role. Participants in discussion exchange tips and news on mobile phones, computer games, sports, music and film, but the hottest topics of debate are those that were traditionally taboo in Arab public discourse, namely politics, religion and relations between the sexes. All shades of political opinion are represented and, especially when the medium was novel in 2000–2002, outright 'wars' were fought on many forums between Islamists and their opponents. After the novelty had worn off and many of the original participants tired of the strident language and repetition, often without reasoned exchange of arguments, a certain disillusionment set in. But, when the old hands withdrew, they were soon replaced by new members from the under-25 age group, which is the fastest-growing on the Internet. These newcomers are clearly as interested as the pioneers in marking their presence and making their voice heard. The Internet proved an ideal medium for breaking the limitations traditionally imposed on who was allowed to speak in public, and what it was proper to say – or even think – regarding the social, moral and political order.

Disillusion with discussion forums may explain why blogs (web logs or diaries, kept mostly by individuals) made an entry into Arabic cyberspace when they did. Whereas blogging took off in the West in 2001, and quickly became an extremely important feature of Persian Internet use,[58] few blogs were published from the Arab world before 2004. Those that were, including that of Salam Pax, famous for chronicling his life in Baghdad from September 2002 to August 2004,[59] were mostly in English. By early 2005, however, frustrated with the often uncivilised tone in discussion forums and the occasional censorship exercised there, Arabs began increasingly to say 'good-bye to the forums', announcing they would henceforth concentrate on blogging.[60] One of the early bloggers, Abdallah al-Miheiri from Abu Dhabi (born 1979), who started blogging in March 2004 at serdal.com, is credited with having come up with the Arabic translation of 'blog' (al-mudawwana). Arab blog rings and aggregators were set up to network the community and the idea of an Arab 'Bloggers Union' was launched to represent the 'new cultural movement'.[61] The first annual Best Arab Blog Awards were voted for in February 2005, prompting press coverage of the phenomenon.[62] On Harvard's Global Voices Online (a hand-picked guide), Arab blogging guru Haitham Sabbah is the most active contributor.[63] Towards the end of the year grand old Jordanian portals Maktoob.com, Jeeran.com and Albawaba.com began offering blogging services. Prior to that the US charity Spirit of America, which seeks to promote 'freedom and democracy' in Iraq and Afghanistan had helped to develop a tool to allow blogging with an Arabic interface; it hosts blogs from Iraq at friendsofdemocracy.net. But most Arab bloggers are as critical of outside interference as they are of their own regimes. During presidential and parliamentary elections in Egypt, bloggers were active as (often self-appointed) election monitors, publishing reports on their sites that became important sources for traditional media.[64] The first blogs by Egyptian soldiers also emerged in 2005.[65] For promoting freedom of expression, the well-known Egyptian blog Manal and Alaa's Bit Bucket (www.manalaa.net) won the special RSF award at the November 2005 Deutsche Welle International Weblog Awards. At the beginning of the year Moroccan Tarik Essaadi's Aljinane.com had received RSF's 'Freedom Blog Award' for Africa and the Middle East.[66] Al-Hayat's well-known columnist Jihad el-Khazen, after weighing the pros and cons of blogs during 2005, strongly defended them in early 2006. He said they had further eroded censorship by creating 'a generation of "citizen journalists" who are in contact with each other, conduct impromptu dialogue, and see that their opinions reach anywhere in the world'.[67]

Meanwhile, the next Internet craze, podcasting, is beginning to appear in the Arab world, giving rise to the latest incarnation of an age-old question: 'Will podcasting bring democracy to the Arab world?'[68] Among the very first Arabic podcasts, some still in the test phase, we find everything from secular music and chat to Quranic recitations and Islamic chants. Again, the plethora of voices, although not overtly political in the conventional sense, clearly indicates an important social trend. Podcasts and blogs are ideal tools for individual expression, more suitable than discussion groups for coherently presenting an individual's point of view. This may be one of the reasons why Arabic blogs have been especially popular so far among 'secular' individuals and less so among more authority-oriented Islamists, who were quick to embrace discussion forums.[69] The 'I' that speaks out is put ever more to the fore. The attitude expressed by 'Big Pharaoh' (www.bigpharaoh.blogspot.com) – 'Hi, I am from Egypt. This is my first blog ever. I would like to use it in making my voice heard' – is one that well reflects young Arab Internet users' increasing self-confidence, self-belief and impatience with negativism. It is the same with the 'I'm a maker, not a taker!' motto on T-shirts worn by admirers of Amr Khaled. Along with this greater self-assertion, Internet users say they have become more selective about 'what I really want' and more independent of help from others.[70]

At the same time, the socialisation that Internet users experience online, through surfing and choosing as well as through participating in public debate, is one of exposure to a greater diversity of opinion than has traditionally been provided in the context of close-knit offline communities. Users discover that people have different opinions, that one's own views are not necessarily self-evident to all, that one has to find arguments to justify one's beliefs, has to rationalise them, and has to accept (if grudgingly) that one will not be able to convince everybody. As doubt competes with traditional world-views and power hierarchies, individuals become more conscious of their individuality. Although not necessarily more autonomous, they may be more distinctly aware of the role of choice in creating social communities, knowledge and values. There is, for example, increasing fragmentation of discussion forums on the basis that 'if I don't like the one I'm currently in, I emigrate and create a new one'.[71] Individuals are growing more assertive in expressing what some call 'my Islam', referring to their own personal understanding of what Islam really means, as distinct from views held by others, be they popular preachers, government-paid scholars, extremist fanatics or the 'misguided masses'.[72]

CONCLUSION

Growing individual choice, better networking, the faster spread of information, and more options to express oneself in public: these are some of the elements that contribute to an increasing sense of empowerment among Internet users, especially among the young, in whose socialisation the Net plays an ever more important role. As one commentator put it in early 2006, a new generation of users who grew up with the Net are set to become more vocal, with blogging and other forms of self-expression continuing to grow in importance.[73] Sociologist Fatema Mernissi (www.mernissi.net) celebrates what she sees as the subversive zapping power of the satellite television viewer and the civic openings created by the new 'Sindbads', as she dubs Arabs navigating the new frontier, cyberspace.[74] These new spaces of freedom are lately being recognised even by those who are extremely critical of government control and repression on the Net. Thus, Human Rights Watch wrote in November 2005: 'The Internet's role in strengthening the Egyptian human rights movement is a trend that looks likely to continue' and 'even those who know all too well the reasons to be afraid speak of the importance of Internet in Syrian society.'[75] Greater transparency and broader possibilities for participation are key issues here. These are precisely what Arab Decision (www.arabdecision.org) seeks to further by making institutional information about the Arab world easily obtainable by citizens. If enough people are informed about what executive, legislative, judicial, administrative, economic, financial, educational, media and civil society institutions exist in their countries, what their purpose is supposed to be, who is staffing them, what the background of these officials is, what the laws say, and so on, those people will be better empowered to act as citizens who know their rights and are able to claim them.

- 6 -

Satellite Television: A Breathing Space for Arab Youth?

Imad Karam

People ask a lot of satellite broadcasting in Arab countries. They look to it to solve society's most deeply ingrained problems. They expect it to promote democratisation, to give a voice to the voiceless, and even to end the occupation of Palestine and Iraq. Of course, rational thinking shows objectives such as these to be primarily the responsibility of civil and public organisations – indeed, of society as whole. Yet it is also reasonable to expect satellite broadcasting to facilitate the mission of bringing about change by acting as a catalyst, making the public better informed, opening space for free debate and, yes, giving a voice to the voiceless, especially women and youth.[1] That, in turn, raises the question of whether the voices of young Arabs have ever been heard in public arenas in Arab countries. If not, maybe it is too much to ask of satellite channels that they should push Arab societies and governments towards changing the habits of generations in inauspicious conditions.

Why satellite television and youth in particular? There is, of course, the obvious yet telling point that the young are the coming generation, so what they learn now will bear upon the future. There is also the fact that the young, especially young men, have come to the fore in terms of public action. It is they who took to the streets during the Palestinian intifada, they who suffer the consequences of military crackdowns, they who mobilise for change. How satellite television speaks to and about them is of manifest importance. However, the special significance of the relationship between Arab satellite broadcasting and Arab youth lies in two other factors. First, Arab youth spend many hours a day watching television, most of it beamed by satellite. This is because Arab youth have plenty of free time, either because they are jobless or still at school. Second, research shows that Arab youth tend to be less resistant to messages received via satellite channels than they are to messages coming from state television, from school or from the family.[2]

Young people in the Arab world[3] spend on average more time watching satellite broadcasts than they spend in school or with their families. My research with 17–26-year-olds in Egypt, Jordan, the United Arab Emirates and Palestine shows that 97 per cent of young people watch television and that many of them spend several hours a day doing so. Over half of the 200 respondents to my questionnaire said they watched television for up to three hours a day during a typical school or work day; 17 per cent said they watched four to six hours a day; 7 per cent said they watched television for more than six hours a day. Fewer than one-quarter (24 per cent) said they watched television for less than one hour a day.[4]

What Arab satellite channels are offering to young Arabs is mainly music, film and drama of a kind that does not at first sight appear effectively to address young people's concerns and aspirations, such as employment, education, marriage and issues about sexuality. This chapter therefore examines what it is that Arab satellite television offers youth in the region, and how young men and women regard the programmes on offer. In doing so, it raises questions about the representation of youth audiences on satellite channels and those audiences' responses to satellite programming. Inevitably, it asks questions about democracy and democratisation, insofar as these questions are related to problems of youth and the contribution of satellite channels. Based on focus group interviews and a questionnaire among 17–26-year-olds, both male and female, in Egypt, Jordan, Palestine and the UAE, the chapter ultimately considers whether Arab satellite broadcasting offers Arab youth a voice and a forum in which to express their opinions, or whether what it offers could more aptly be described as simply a breathing space, a place where young people can temporarily escape their realities and maybe live a virtual reality or a dream.

GAPS IN SATELLITE TELEVISION PROGRAMMING

The public sphere is necessary for democracy because it produces informed citizens, which democracies need in order to function properly.[5] Citizens, in order to access and exchange information and ideas, need to be able to engage in debates and interact through the media. Thus one of the fundamental prerequisites of democracy is free and open dialogue among people, both as citizens and as representatives of community institutions and governments. Since the general pattern of governance in the Arab world leans towards authoritarian regimes, satellite broadcasting is claimed to be playing a significant role in pushing Arab governments towards openness and democratisation by providing uncensored information and enabling Arab citizens to express their views freely. For the first time in decades they are able to debate and be critical of the policies of their respective governments. Numerous scholars have drawn a connection between satellite television and political change. For example, Annabelle Sreberny has argued that changes in the media landscape should be considered a major component of the pressure, internal as well as external, for political liberalisation and eventual democratisation being exerted on authoritarian Arab regimes.[6] Marc Lynch maintains that Arab satellite broadcasting gave rise to a new Arab public sphere by undermining state censorship and government control over the media and information. He nevertheless recognises that this public sphere does not substitute for democracy, since the new media are not accompanied by political channels through which public preferences can be translated into policy outcomes.[7]

What Sreberny, Lynch and others omit to mention is that most of this new Arab space for criticism and debate is one-dimensional. A closer look shows it to be dominated by one set of issues, while many others pertaining to the daily lives of Arab citizens are largely ignored. The public sphere that the Arab satellite channels create is largely taken up with discussion of international politics and issues relating to Arab relations with Israel, the US and other Western states. This leaves little room for domestic issues, such as national political reforms and development indicators, policies on poverty and unemployment, or a plethora of social and health problems including AIDS, drugs and the increasing divorce rate.[8] My own analysis of the subject matter covered on the three most popular weekly live talk shows on Al-Jazeera, over a period of ten weeks between April and June 2005, demonstrated how international interventions in the Arab world were given more attention than internal matters. Only three out of a total of 30 episodes of *Al-Ittijah al-Muaakis* (*The Opposite Direction*), *Akthar Min Rai* (*More than One Opinion*) and *Bila Hudud* (*Without Limits*) during these ten weeks were directly related to the principles and practice of democracy, reform or development. The remaining 27 dealt with issues such as the post-Arafat era in Palestine, Syrian withdrawal from Lebanon, Sudan, international politics, and US and foreign interventions in Arab affairs. Thus, although it is quite true to say that Al-Jazeera talk shows provide a platform for the criticism of Arab governments, it is also true to counter this, as Kai Hafez has, by saying that the shows make little contribution to a concrete democratic agenda within which people develop a vision of how to act and which political direction to take.[9] Without this, the criticism of Arab governments is in danger of making no real impact on political development in the region.

It is difficult at this point to see how Arab satellite broadcasting contributes to the creation of a public sphere that is representative, open and free. Arab satellite channels set the agenda of the public sphere they create, not just by controlling the issues covered and debated but also by controlling the information exchanged and who takes part, whether as guest, panellist or member of the audience phoning in a question live on air. Ownership considerations also mean that these channels are limited in the extent to which their programmes can include criticism of powerful interest groups in the Arab world. For example, Abu Dhabi TV or the Saudi-owned Al-Arabiya have limited scope for criticising the UAE or Saudi governments, and criticism of friendly co-members of the Gulf Co-operation Council is also off-limits. Functioning under these conditions and sensitivities makes it even harder for satellite channels to address controversial issues related to youth, such as political, economic and social participation and integration.

YOUTH PERCEPTIONS OF POLITICS AND ENTERTAINMENT

Arab youth are a very important segment of Arab society. According to the *Arab Human Development Report 2004*, children under 15 years old accounted for at least 25–29 per cent of the total population in Bahrain, Kuwait, Lebanon, Qatar, Tunisia and the UAE, rising to 37–39 per cent in Jordan, Oman, Saudi Arabia, Syria and Sudan, and 46–48 per cent in Palestine and Yemen. In Morocco, Algeria and Egypt the proportions were 31 per cent, 32 per cent and 34 per cent respectively.[10] For the 16–27 age group considered in this chapter, precise statistics are hard to come by, but it is known that rates of unemployment are highest among young people. According to a 2004 report by the Arab League's Arab Economic Unity Council, the overall unemployment rate in the Arab world reached 20 per cent in 2003, of which 60 per cent was among the youth. The report described the situation as a 'time bomb', especially since the number of unemployed in the Arab world is increasing by 3 per cent per year.[11] Not surprisingly, many reports indicate that young people experience a growing sense of alienation, while their social, economic and political chances seem to be declining.[12] They are highly marginalised and, although everybody talks about them and wants to give them advice, no one appears willing or able to give them a 'voice'.

The results of a 2002 United Nations Development Programme (UNDP) poll conducted among 15–20-year-olds in 22 Arab countries indicated clearly that job availability was the most common concern of youth.[13] The same poll showed that 51 per cent of young people expressed a desire to emigrate to other countries.[14] The *Arab Human Development Report 2003* reported that 'roughly 25 per cent of 300,000 first degree graduates from Arab universities in 1995/96 emigrated'.[15] In my questionnaire, I asked young people whether they wanted to emigrate and, if so, why. In total, 69 per cent of the respondents said they had thought of leaving their home countries. As Table 6.1 shows, when asked why they would want to leave, 27 per cent gave politics and a quest for freedom as their answer. Another 25 per cent cited jobs, 20 per cent gave educational reasons, and 10 per cent said there were social reasons behind their desire to emigrate. Clearly, Arab youth must be dissatisfied with the political and economic conditions and future prospects in their home countries to want to leave in such large numbers.

Anxiety about this state of affairs is growing among concerned specialists. Iman Bibars, who founded the Association for the Development and Enhancement of Women (ADEW) in 1987, expressed those worries in an article in Egypt's leading daily *Al-Ahram* in 2004. Having run three workshops with young Egyptian adults from all backgrounds through the ADEW, Bibars said she was concerned about the status of Egyptian youth and about their potential for political and social participation. In particular, she found that most lacked any substantial understanding of basic concepts such as human rights and did not know about civil society

TABLE 6.1 YOUNG PEOPLE'S REASONS FOR WANTING TO EMIGRATE

Reason	Percentage
Politics and freedom[a]	27.0
Economic	24.7
Educational	20.0
Exploring and experience	15.3
Social	10.6
Other	2.4
Total	100.0

[a] 3.5 per cent specified politics, while the 23.5 per cent who cited freedom included political freedom in that category.

Source: Author's survey.

institutions or their role in the society. Many did not even know about different political institutions in Egypt such as political parties, the People's Assembly and Shura Council, or have any idea of their legislative roles or the nature and purpose of the constitution. In other words, they did not know about the channels available for political and social participation. Bibars warns:

> The youth are Egypt's real wealth. The current attention paid nowadays to their development is not enough. In order not to find this 'wealth' torn between extremism and blind imitation of the West, they need to find the legitimate channels that allow them to participate in public life. And I do not mean only political participation, but also social. The youth need to know the society with all its frames, be it the different political institutions and parties or civil society institutions and the role of each in development.[16]

Bibars believes that the older generation got caught up in struggles over development and national problems and forgot to prepare the next generation for playing its part. 'We forgot to provide them with the right channels for participation,' she says, concluding:

> Our youth are lost in the midst of this life. No one wants to listen to them. They are surrounded from all directions by orders and prohibitions. They have no clear channels to express themselves and how they feel. They feel excluded from decision-making and dialogue. Information channels are also limited for them. All they understand from the term 'human rights' is their economic and social right; that is their right to work and eat.[17]

These sentiments are corroborated by comments made in the focus groups I conducted with mixed groups of young people from several Arab countries. Sarah (aged 21),[18] a Saudi Arabian studying in Egypt, complained that young people do not have a voice. She said: 'Our voice does not count. They [the older generation] simply do not take us seriously.'[19] In the focus groups young people from different countries talked of being 'pushed away' from politics. When I asked them why young people seem not to be interested in news and current affairs, I was told over and over again that the reason lies in the lack of freedom of speech. Put simply, as one of the participants explained, when young people watch news, which is largely about the killing of fellow Arabs, they feel involved. But when they try to protest, they get harassed by the authorities. Mustafa (19) said:

> We do not have the freedom of expression to freely demonstrate to support the Palestinians or to protest against the war in Iraq. For example, in this country when the [Palestinian] intifada broke out and we all went on a demonstration, the guys who were in the first rows of the demonstration

were taken in by the intelligence service. [...] We cannot even talk politics in cafés. [...] I hear about a place in Britain where you can go on Sundays and say whatever you like and criticise any president you like. This is democracy.[20]

Moreover, young people say they feel helpless and hopeless about the situation ever changing or the possibility that political leaders will do something about it. They say it is because they see existing leaders as part of the problem rather than the solution that their feelings tend towards frustration or indifference. Ibrahim (20) said:

If we feel that there is any hope, then we can watch and follow up the news and get involved, but there is no hope. So, whether we watch or not watch it is not going to make a difference. So, when hope is lost, we start looking for entertainment.[21]

Similar comments were made by others:

We are not interested in news and politics, because it means getting involved and going out to the streets to protest. When we do protest, nothing happens; what happens is only what the president says. I used to be interested in the news and I used to go out in demonstrations, but demonstrations die out soon and the president's standpoint stays on by the end of the day. That's why it is all for nothing and we had better stay out of it (Ahmed, 19).[22]

The leaders are not doing anything about the situation and there is not much that we can do about it. At least if the leaders meet and take a step towards doing something about it, then one could get involved (Amjad, 19).[23]

Participants in another focus group expressed their feelings as follows:

Can anyone in our Arab societies talk about politics? No we cannot. We have undemocratic regimes, and any one who attempts to be critical of politics will disappear from the face of the earth immediately (Hassan, 18).

Even when one is in a conversation on economics and the moment it gets close to politics, somebody will automatically remind the rest not to talk politics. So, it becomes the norm not to talk politics (Saleh, 18).

The problem is that the youth have no influence on politics in their own country and society; I mean they are not allowed to be influential or make a difference. They are only allowed to watch and observe rather than participate in politics. And since you will be seeing the same scene time and again, you get tired and fed up, so you stop watching. So, if youth had the kind of influence we are talking about, for example, if the youth can talk freely to the ruler or any other official, then everything would be different (Hassan, 18).

No one is interested in attracting youth to politics. On the contrary they push you away from it. And if you do talk politics, then you may be in trouble. But with singing, they attract you. They put for you what you like: nice and sexy girls. And if you vote in a TV programme you may win (Zakaria, 20).[24]

Young Arabs protest that they have no voice in serious television programmes, be they political, social or economic. In one of the focus groups in Egypt, Najah (19) pointed out that 'all the political and economic programmes have only old people...I've never seen a political programme that has young people commenting or discussing the issues involved.' In the same group, Nadia (20) said that 'in politics there is no voice for young people. That is a no-go area.'[25]

In another focus group,[26] Medhat (19) noted that, if TV programmes claim to be for or about youth, most of the time it is because they are offering songs and music. 'Young people are asked for their opinion only when the topic is music, songs and films,' he said. Karim (18) added: 'Yes, most youth programmes are about music, films, etc. I've never seen a political programme hosting young people or seeking the voice of young people.' Agreeing with both of them, Mona (18) reminded them that 'sports is another area where young people's voices are also sought and heard'. Medhat then gave an example from Egyptian TV, generating the following exchange.

Medhat: When they want to advertise a serious programme that will discuss Egyptian politics and economics, for example, they bring someone who is very dull instead of bringing in someone with expertise in advertising who would attract many people to watch the programme. However, if the programme is on music, they bring in the most charming and articulate person so that they attract many people and thus make profits. They do this because they think that youth are interested only in music and dancing...
Karim: Which is the truth...
Heba (18, objecting): No, not at all...
Maher (19): What they should do is swap the two presenters.[27]

Karim insisted that the problem could be in the youth themselves rather than the media. He said: 'Our problem is that we are no longer interested in good stuff. Most of the youth would for example rather watch *Star Academy* [a reality gameshow song contest on LBCI] rather than a programme on Al-Jazeera, which would of course be...'. Shady (20), interrupting him, suggested: 'It is because we sometimes feel suffocated. We escape from and try to avoid news programmes as they make us feel suffocated.'[28] Karim, continuing, asked other group members: 'We do not watch Al-Jazeera everyday, do we?' They all replied 'No'. He went on: 'Even though it [Al-Jazeera] has terrific programmes and is even better than the BBC and CNN. However, Mazzika and Melody [music channels] are on all the time. It is because that is what we are interested in and that is who we are.'[29]

The young people taking part in these exchanges made clear their conclusion that they have no voice in any so-called public sphere created by Arab media. In their eyes there was no difference between Arab satellite channels and terrestrial state television when it comes to giving a voice to the young. On the other hand, Arab satellite channels seemed to be winning the loyalty of youth audiences on account of the variety of entertainment they provide. Even so, the acceptance of entertainment on Arab satellite television was far from universal among participants in the focus groups. Opinions differed in all the groups when the interviewees were asked whether they thought entertainment – especially music video clips and singing competitions such as *Super Star* (the Arabic version of *Pop Idol*) – were helpful for youth. There was a divide between those who approved of such programmes and those who did not. However, what was striking was the consensus that such programmes attracted them. Those who said these programmes were not healthy for the young or the wider society confirmed that they still watched and enjoyed them.

Pressed on this point, the participants indicated that they resort to entertainment on television as a means of getting away from the burdens and problems of life, whether political, social or economic. They told me that they have enough seriousness in their lives already without trying to get more of it from television. Entertainment, they said, gave them the chance to forget about their problems. Nada (18), from a middle-class family in Cairo, said that television helped her to 'escape from her problems'.[30] She explained: 'Had it not been for TV, my problems would stay in my face all the time. TV gives me the chance to break away from my problems.' Amjad (19) said that he goes to the television, especially music video clips and movies, when he feels bothered. 'For me, when I feel bothered or bored, without knowing what's wrong with me, I go and watch music video clips. I think that most young people do the same.'[31] Mohammed (20) agreed. 'I do the same,' he said. 'If there is something on my mind or something that I would like to forget, problems that I try to ignore, I watch music on television … Just like some people go to sleep if they feel concerned or bothered.'[32] On another occasion, Atef (19) echoed the same sentiment. He put it as follows: 'Most people, when they feel suffocated and would like to breathe, they say: "Let's watch television, listen to music, watch comedy programmes on TV." […] They have a laugh, feel better, and they have the right to do so and feel that way.'[33]

With a growing feeling of malaise as a result of the conditions in their countries, Arab youth seem to find in entertainment on Arab television a means of distancing themselves, albeit temporarily, from their problems. In this connection, Atef's analogy of a 'breathing space' in relation to entertainment programming is revealing. The idea of a breathing space seemed to take precedence over any sense of satellite channels offering a voice for young people or representing their social and political needs.

DIDACTICISM, MONOLOGUES AND NEWS ABOUT KILLING

The Arab satellite television landscape is fluid and fast-changing. The explosion in the number of satellite channels is causing Arab audiences to fragment. To attract, retain and maximise viewership, satellite channels have adopted a policy of segmentation through the launching of specialised channels targeted at specific audience groups. In 2003 Saudi-owned MBC launched Al-Arabiya, a 24-hour news channel, to compete with the Qatar-based Al-Jazeera. It also turned MBC2 into a free-to-air movie channel with Arabic subtitles.[34] By end-2005 Al-Jazeera had launched Al-Jazeera Sports, Al-Jazeera Live and Al-Jazeera Children's Channel and was preparing to launch Aljazeera International (in English) and Al-Jazeera Documentary Channel. Rotana, which started out as a 24-hour music channel, expanded into three music channels and one movie channel. The same goes for two other music channels, Melody and Mazzika.[35] All these developments were clearly aimed at young audiences as an important consumer group.

Yet, despite these innovations, the most widely watched Arab television programmes remained relatively homogeneous. A review of media output included in the *Arab Human Development Report 2003* found that light entertainment was the most common offering, and described it as predominantly 'superficial, repetitive in content, and promot[ing] values that encourage consumerism and a reduction of work'.[36] Among the proliferation of satellite channels are those specialising in culture (such as Nile Culture and Tanweer from Egypt), religion (notably the Saudi-funded Iqra and Al-Majd), education and so on.[37] Yet these channels are not popular among Arab audiences in general, and least of all with youth. My research among people in the 16–27 age group showed they strongly preferred movie channels such as MBC2 and Rotana Cinema, music channels such as Rotana, Mazzika, Al-Nojoom and Melody, entertainment-oriented channels such as LBCI and Future TV, and 24-hour news channels such as Al-Jazeera and Al-Arabiya. During my focus group interviews with young Egyptians, I asked participants if they watched specialised Egyptian channels such as Nile Culture and others; they all replied in the negative. Karim (17) described these channels as 'a complete failure'. 'They have failed and it is because of finances,' said Maher (19), adding: 'These channels are state-owned and it is just like the case of state schools as opposed to private schools, where the standard of the staff, teaching and the curriculum are much higher [in the private sector].'[38]

Like youth elsewhere, Arab youth need information and opportunities to talk about their feelings and problems. This, it would seem, is not being provided by the media, and especially not by television – at least, not in an effective way. There remains a need for programmes that address the issues still considered largely taboo in Arab society, such as relationships between boys and girls. This does not mean that these 'sensitive' issues get no airing at all. What it does mean is that the airings provided take the form of monologues, not dialogues. In their study, published in 2000, Barbara Ibrahim and Hind Wassef commented: 'Whenever dialogue is opened with young people on such issues, the occasion is seized upon by adults as a didactic opportunity to convey messages about right and wrong.'[39] Amina Khairy, Cairo correspondent for *Al-Hayat*, has made a similar point. Writing in 2003 she said Arab youth want to be addressed as adults, not as teenagers or kids. They prefer programmes to be live and not recorded and many would like programmes to host parents and teachers to enable them to listen directly to young people's opinions, needs and complaints.[40] Participants in my research felt the same way. Hana (19) complained that youth programmes speak about youth, but never to them. 'There are no programmes that address the concerns of young people,' she said. 'There should be programmes that dialogue with the youth. We need such programmes that talk to the real youth. The programmes that we may see on TV would have a set-up audience of youth who do not represent the real youth.'[41]

In a focus group in Jordan, Farah (20) pointed out that there are plenty of what she called 'corrupting' programmes for young people on television – programmes which are very popular among the youth – but, she argued, there is 'not even one' good, non-corrupting programme that attracts young people. 'There are programmes on youth issues, but they discuss youth issues from the viewpoint of older people rather than the young. They are very dull and very upsetting. I feel as if it is my grandfather who is talking to me.'[42] Maher (19), who has an interest in business and economics, complained that most of the time when he turns the TV on and flips through the channels all he finds is music, dancing and films. 'It hardly happens that I find serious programmes and when I do, the presenter would be a very old man, someone who is about to die. We need to see and hear young people. We would love to hear ideas and problem solving from young people.' He continued:

> During the period of the floating of the Egyptian currency, there was a business programme on Egyptian TV and they invited a man with 30 years of experience to offer his ideas and solutions. What I really would like to see is people like me… I want to see what they think of the situation. […] I want to know if there is a group of people thinking like me or is it just stupid me.[43]

This does not necessarily mean that the programme was unsatisfactory in its own terms. But it does give a clear indication of how young people are put off just by seeing older people on television giving opinions and advice.

Thus doubts are expressed as to whether the rise of new channels has created new and lasting opportunities for dialogue among and with young people on television. Zen TV, launched in 2001 as the first Arab channel specifically for a youth audience, did indeed bring up issues long avoided by other channels. It tackled taboo subjects such as sex, the growing generation gap and emotional conflicts, by means of a large number of talk shows, game shows and dubbed movies.[44] The channel, which stopped its regular programming in 2003 and turned into a 24-hour music and video clip channel instead, seemed overtly Western in the eyes of many Arab youth. Although 65.5 per cent of the respondents to my questionnaire said they knew about the existence of Zen TV, only 30 per cent said that they had ever watched it. A year after its switch to 24-hour music, a young observer noted online: 'It turned out that the problems and concerns of Arab youth are – from Zen's perspective – mainly to do with hairstyles, fashion, cellphone ringtones and artists' websites.'[45] Another agreed, saying that, according to Zen, the interests of Arab youth are limited to dancing, music and fashion.[46]

This is despite the fact that, as my research showed, movie and music channels are most popular among Arab youth, who watch television largely for entertainment rather than education or knowledge. As Table 6.2 indicates, the bulk of the time my informants spent watching television was dedicated to watching movies or video clips on music channels. About 33.3 per cent of the respondents to my questionnaire said that movies were their most-watched programmes on television, followed by 17.5 per cent for singing, music and video clips.

Most of the young people interviewed in the focus groups said that the 24-hour music channels are on all the time while they are at home, whether in the foreground or the background, as they are doing other things. These channels – Rotana, Melody, Al-Nojoom and Mazzika – feature non-traditional dancing by assertive female singers in the latest Arab music

TABLE 6.2 MOST-WATCHED TV PROGRAMME GENRES AMONG 16–27-YEAR-OLDS

Type of programming	Percentage[a]
Movies	33.3
Singing and music	17.5
News and current affairs	15.1
Religious programmes	10.6
Talk shows	6.5
Soaps	6.5
Sports	6.5
Documentaries	1.6
Interviews with celebrities	1.6
Other	0.8
Total	100.0

[a] Of respondents putting the genre at the top of their list.

Source: Author's survey.

video clips. News and current affairs came lower down the list as a reason for watching television, with about 15 per cent of the respondents to my questionnaire saying that news and current affairs were their most-watched programmes on television. When asked about news and current affairs, most people in the focus groups said they found the news dull and repetitive, as well as depressing. Mustafa (19) said: 'I watch mostly entertainment. News and politics is so boring. It is not as important as it used to be and now it is very much the same. Nothing is really new and that is boring. It is also depressing as it is all about death, death and death.'[47] Saleh (18) pointed out that the news is more or less the same. In contrast, he said, 'There is always something new when it comes to songs. Even if one does not approve of the song, one still likes to see something new.'[48]

Young people watch the news mainly when big events happen and follow up only for a short period. This was predominantly the view of young people across the focus group discussions. Mohammed (20) pointed out that there was much interest in the news when the second Palestinian intifada (uprising) broke out in 2000, but this interest did not last for long. Ansar (20) added: 'In the beginning of the intifada one could easily get affected by seeing the images of the killings in the news. One could even become depressed, but then it becomes usual and even normal.'[49] The Palestinian intifada, the attacks of 11 September 2001 in the US, the subsequent wars in Afghanistan and Iraq, and the 2005 assassination of Lebanon's prime minister, Rafiq al-Hariri, were mentioned as the biggest events that made young people watch the news. But my respondents also said it added to their depression. Sharif (19), from Egypt, said that watching the news makes young people more depressed. 'The news are depressing and we are already depressed about everything that is going on in our country. It's crowded and the economic situation is bad, so we do not need to get more depressed by watching the news. We have enough of what's going inside our country.' Sarah (21) said that she finds the news mostly boring, 'except for the critical parts like the assassination of Hariri … events that change things'. Saber (19) complained that young people lack opportunities to comment on news and current affairs. 'The way they present the news – it's always the same. I'm not saying they should change it, but at least they should add some features that concern young people. Like just to give a chance for young people to appear on TV as well, and discuss their opinions about political ideas.'[50]

As young people find news and politics unfair, depressing and dull, entertainment seems to be the way out. Entertainment appears to be the most common way to distance young people from the problems of their lives and from politics. Yahya (19) said: 'We watch entertainment channels to escape from the depressing atmosphere of politics. Politics is dull and depressing and that's why people stay away from it and go towards entertainment.' In the same focus group, Ibrahim (19) echoed Yahya, adding that entertainment attracts young people because they get enough of politics on all the different channels. 'All you get in the news is "seven Palestinians were killed during the day and 17 were killed during the night"; it becomes routine. There is nothing pleasant about news.'[51] In a different focus group, Assem (19) argued that young people stay away from politics because it is depressing. 'Nothing is new,' he said. 'It's all about killing.' Saleh (18) added that political programmes do not offer any solutions and that he finds them even insulting to youth intelligence.[52] Over half the respondents to my questionnaire said they like to watch entertainment exclusively. Table 6.3 shows that only 9.6 per cent ticked both boxes, for entertainment and information. Another 10.4 per cent said they watched television to pass the time, while 4.8 per cent said they watched to escape from the problems of their lives.

Esmat (17) from Egypt stated outright that she did not like watching serious programmes. 'I only watch light programmes for entertainment. […] I love television and it is on all the time. For example, I have books to read, I have access to the Internet, but I find it easier to just lie down and watch television. I'm not saying it's a good thing, because it makes me lazy as I exert no effort.' Lamia (17) agreed, adding: 'TV makes me very lazy. I could have 100 different things to do, but I prefer to sit and watch TV.'[53]

TABLE 6.3 REASONS FOR WATCHING TELEVISION AMONG 16–27-YEAR-OLDS

Reason	Percentage
Entertainment	52.8
Information and knowledge	20.8
Both entertainment and information	9.6
Passing time	10.4
Escaping reality	4.8
Other	1.6
Total	100.0

Source: Author's survey.

CONCLUSION

Traditionally, Arab youth have had no voice at home, at school or out in the wider world. In both private and public they have been expected to listen to the advice of older people and act on it. This does not appear to have changed with the advent of Arab satellite broadcasting. More than a decade and a half after the emergence of this phenomenon, programmes that allow young people to represent themselves to each other and to decision-makers are still lacking. Arab satellite channels have attracted young people with films and music, but not with quality factual programming that entertains while it educates and informs. My research suggested that existing attempts at informative programmes for Arab youth have been not only ineffective but counter-productive. It is ineffective to have a middle-aged presenter hosting a group of middle-aged men and women to discuss youth problems in front of a staged youth audience. My respondents, who know their own problems, said they wanted to be given the chance to talk about their problems and debate possible solutions. The didactic tone, with direct guidance and advice, that Arab media adopt when dealing with youth programming has put young people off. They want to feel involved in shows that address issues from their perspective and not that of an older generation. They want younger presenters and talk show hosts.

To date, Arab satellite broadcasting has largely ignored youth problems, especially those directly related to government, politics and social issues such as unemployment and the under-representation of youth in politics and public affairs. Meanwhile, Arab youth have failed to find a voice in the

Arab media. What they have found instead is a breathing space, a space in which entertainment offers a brief chance to escape reality, to imagine themselves in roles and situations unattainable in their real lives. As it stands, this space does not seem to be structured or planned. However, more research is needed to discover whether the expansion of entertainment on satellite channels is purely commercial or whether it serves a political agenda. Critics contend that Arab governments encourage entertainment provision to 'hypnotize the already snoozing Arab mind and drive it away from issues that really count and problems that actually matter'.[54] In the meantime, whatever the motive, one of its ironic consequences has been to lay the foundations of something that has come to be viewed as 'Arab youth culture'. Given the extent to which my respondents expressed feelings of being unrepresented and unfulfilled, any notion of 'Arab youth culture' should be treated with care.

- 7 -

Democracy and the Media in Palestine: A Comparison of Election Coverage by Local and Pan-Arab Media

Giovanna Maiola and David Ward

This chapter assesses the extent to which pan-Arab satellite channels offer a counterbalance or substitute for failings in the structures and output of nationally based media in the Arab world. The Palestinian presidential election in 2005 offers an entry point to assess the roles of both the local media and pan-Arab satellite broadcasters in providing the electorate with a range of news and viewpoints.[1] One of the central questions it addresses is whether pan-Arab satellite channels offer a real alternative to the national state broadcasters that are prevalent throughout the Arab world. More specifically, the chapter reports on the findings of a content analysis conducted on a sample of television channels during the election campaign period. Through those findings, and through insights gained from interviews with members of the Palestinian media community, it examines the features shaping the public portrayal of candidates, the electoral process and the issues of the campaign. It also assesses the relationship between the media and the political system, and ways in which this relationship can shape the range of information available to viewers during an election campaign.

Our basic assumption is that the media's capacity to operate freely depends on the kinds of relationship that the media develop with political powers. The key issue is how far the media are able to impose or suggest cultural and political ideas and thus how far the public are able to access critical information.[2] For citizens to be actively involved in the public sphere – and it is perhaps very premature to talk about such a participatory sphere throughout the Arab world – they must have access to a range of information and debate. Elections offer the ideal litmus test of participation in political dialogue through the media, as they are one of the

96

events in the political calendar during which questions about representation and diversity are perceived to be crucial. However, even in those Arab countries where elections take place, a free media environment has been rare.[3] For this reason, and given the extreme conditions in the West Bank and Gaza at the time of the January 2005 presidential election, it is a unique case study. The research therefore attempts to isolate the characteristics of the coverage of the presidential election while also analysing similarities and differences among channels and seeking to explain the editorial policies of specific local and pan-Arab television channels.

The chapter argues that, if the pan-Arab media are affecting the standards and content of local media, this should be reflected in local Palestinian broadcasters' election coverage. If the pan-Arab channels are 'encouraging a plural political culture', as suggested by Marc Lynch,[4] then the changing relationship between the audience and political elites should be reflected in local television. It concludes that, although satellite broadcasters contribute overall to the plurality of television in Palestine, there are fundamental characteristics in the nature of current affairs and news coverage that remain country-specific and these are reflected in the different hierarchies of the news agenda, which for the local broadcasters is still governed by critical political and social pressures.

THE PALESTINIAN MEDIA LANDSCAPE

The Palestinian media sector remains plagued with problems and, at times, expansion in the number of television channels seems at odds with the climate under which they operate. Unlike many other parts of the Arab world, the West Bank and Gaza Strip have a diverse and burgeoning broadcasting sector, which, despite extreme political and economic pressures caused by decades of Israeli occupation, provides a total of 40 television channels. At first sight, exponential growth in the number of broadcasters in recent years appears to reflect growing pluralism. Yet the proliferation of media outlets is very far from indicating political or economic development in the sector overall. On the contrary, occupation and the conflict this has caused have affected all areas of social, political and economic life, including the media. In the early 2000s the World Bank estimated Palestinian unemployment at over 50 per cent, with 60 per cent of the population living below the poverty line, on an income of less than $2 per day.[5] Palestinians who depended on jobs in Israel were seriously hit by restrictions introduced after the second intifada broke out in September 2000, and a 2003 UN report suggested the country resembled a war-torn economy. Revenues for the burgeoning commercial media reflect this decline and are relatively tiny. Saeda Hamad estimates that the average price of an advertisement in a national newspaper is approximately $50, while an advertising slot on a national television channel can be bought for a meagre $12–15.[6]

Despite the collapse of the economy, the television sector has shown growth in the total number of broadcasters as regional channels have sprung up throughout the territories (Table 7.1). However, pan-Arab channels are an extremely dominant force in Palestinian television, as their popularity with the audience dwarfs that of local broadcasters.

According to a survey conducted by the Jerusalem Media and Communications Centre in 2003 (Table 7.2), Palestinians tend to watch

TABLE 7.1 MAIN PALESTINIAN TELEVISION CHANNELS

Name	Coverage	Ownership	Name	Coverage	Ownership
PBC[a]–Palestine TV	Ramallah, Gaza[a]	National	Peace	Nablus	Private
Al-Mahd	Bethlehem[b]	Private	Baladna	Qalqilia	Private
Bethlehem	Bethlehem	Private	Qalqilia	Qalqilia	Private
Shepherd	Bethlehem	Private	Al-Nasser	Ramallah	Private
Al-Amal	Hebron	Private	Amwaj	Ramallah[b]	Private
Al-Majd	Hebron	Private	Al-Quds Educational	Ramallah[b]	Al-Quds University
Al-Nawras	Hebron	Private	Sharq	Ramallah	Private
Al-Farah	Jenin	Private	Watan TV	Ramallah[b]	Private
Jenin al-Markazi	Jenin	Private	Al-Bilad	Tulkarem	Private
Jenin Star	Jenin	Private	Al-Fajer	Tulkarem	Private
Al-Nour	Jericho	Private	Al-Salam	Tulkarem	Private
Afaq	Nablus	Private	Tulkarem	Tulkarem	Private
Gama	Nablus	Private	Tulkarem al-Markazi	Tulkarem	Private
Nablus	Nablus	Private			

[a] Palestinian Broadcasting Corporation also operates a satellite television service.
[b] Also covers neighbouring area.

satellite television in preference to local and national alternatives, with Al-Jazeera identified as the key channel by viewers in the West Bank and Gaza. In response to the question 'Which television station have you recently watched the most?', Al-Jazeera emerged as by far the most popular, being named by 51.7 per cent of respondents as the channel they had recently watched more than any of the others. It was followed by other satellite channels, while PBC TV received only 3.7 per cent of the positive responses. The survey showed the extent to which the Palestinian television sector is dominated by pan-Arab satellite channels. The attraction, according to interviewees in the survey who watch pan-Arab television, is the quality and range of programming and the lack of similar programming on national and local media. Such popularity has led to some rather grand claims as to the impact of the pan-Arab media on the political and social structures of the Arab world. Hence, for example, Lynch has written:

> New Arab media has [sic] eroded state monopoly over information, embedding in its audience an expectation of choice and contention that undercuts authoritarian political culture. Satellite television stations are encouraging a pluralist political culture, one in which individual voices

TABLE 7.2 MOST-WATCHED CHANNEL AS REPORTED BY PALESTINIAN RESPONDENTS, 2003

Channel	Percentage of respondents		
	Total	West Bank	Gaza
Al-Jazeera	51.7	51.2	52.5
Abu Dhabi	14.2	12.4	17.3
Al-Manar	7.8	7.4	8.6
Al-Arabiya	5.3	4.3	7.0
PBC TV	3.7	1.2	8.0
MBC	1.7	2.0	1.1
Iraq	1.6	2.4	0.2
Al-Amal	1.2	1.7	0.2
Jordan	1.0	1.6	0.0
Others	10.3	13.9	4.1
Don't watch	1.1	1.3	0.7
No answer	0.4	0.6	0.3
Total	100.0	100.0	100.0

Source: Jerusalem Media and Communications Centre, April 2003.

can be heard, disagreements openly aired, and nearly every aspect of politics and society held open to public scrutiny.[7]

Despite the growth of pan-Arab satellite channels, Palestinian media, like local media in other parts of the developing world, suffer serious weaknesses that work to distort their ability to produce and distribute quality news and information. Members of the media community, interviewed for our research, highlighted a number of influences.[8] In order of priority, these were: restrictions imposed by Israel and the Israeli occupation; lack of an adequate legal framework; the omnipotent role of Fatah in Palestinian political life and the life of the Palestinian Authority (PA); self-regulation by journalists; a lack of professionalism; and the lack of a sound economic base for the development of the mass media in general. Although journalists working for the satellite channels are protected from some of these features, they are not isolated from the pressures of working in an environment in which restrictions and pressures on journalists are almost part of daily life. The question is how these pressures are reflected in broadcast content and whether, given that satellite broadcasters enjoy better conditions than their local counterparts, their content is markedly different from local coverage. In an election campaign any difference would be apparent in the themes and range of information communicated to the public, testing whether the satellite channels offer a real alternative to the national media in serving the needs of local democracy.

COVERAGE OF THE 2005 PRESIDENTIAL ELECTION

Our content analysis of the media coverage of the presidential election was conducted according to a quantitative approach, based on content analysis as interview. This technique surveys textual data by means of a standardised or semi-standardised form to record properties of a given whole of units of analysis, such as television programmes or newspaper articles.[9] The research analysed a sample of television channels in the West Bank and Gaza over the two-week campaign period, from 25 December 2004 to 8 January 2005. We particularly examined the coverage provided by PBC TV and Al-Jazeera. The rationale for this choice was in the role these two channels played in informing the public as well as in contributing to defining voters' perceptions of the political alternatives. If there is erosion of state monopolies over information as suggested by Lynch,[10] this would presumably be evident in the public service broadcaster PBC TV, especially as it is also under certain legal obligations to provide balance and pluralism in programming. It is important, therefore, to reflect on differences and similarities revealed between these two channels over the election period, with a particular emphasis on the models of election coverage proposed by the pan-Arab satellite channel on the one hand and those adopted by the publicly owned national broadcaster on the other.

Politically pluralistic media coverage is the product of a number of editorial choices, of which the allocation of airtime and space for political contestants is only one indicator. The amount of coverage alone cannot be considered a reliable indicator of fairness and balance; the way candidates and political parties are portrayed is also a key factor in assessing how the media contribute to informing the electorate about political alternatives. The agenda-setting function of the media within the electoral process also represents a crucial sphere of investigation. The main assumption of this theory is that 'the mass media set the agenda for each political campaign, influencing the salience of attitudes towards the political issues'.[11] As a result, the issues and the events with which candidates and parties are associated when covered by the mass media represent both an opportunity and a challenge. This is because they help to define public attitudes and perceptions towards candidates in terms not only of policies proposed to the electorate but also of their credibility and authoritativeness. Issues are therefore a political resource within an election campaign, and they represent tools to create images. Through these political resources candidates attempt to establish the issues that voters will consider when they make their choice about whom to vote for.[12]

The first level of our analysis relates to the amount of electoral and political communication, conceived as the airtime devoted to coverage of candidates and other political actors. As Table 7.3 illustrates, PBC TV allocated the most time to reporting on the activities of the parties and candidates, followed by the privately owned local broadcaster Watan TV. Coverage of the election on the two transnational channels was considerably smaller. Whereas the presidential election, the campaign activities of candidates and the dynamics between political parties constituted the main issues of the news agenda for Palestinian television stations, for the two pan-Arab channels such issues were only one dimension, albeit a highly relevant one, of a wider agenda that encompassed news from around the Arab region.

For pan-Arab channels, the election in Palestine represented an important event that had to compete with other items on the news agenda. For national television channels the election was one of the key issues around which they could focus their coverage, representing the core of their output. Moreover, the legal framework regulating election campaigns in the media imposed a certain level of obligation on PBC TV involving free

TABLE 7.3 TOTAL AIRTIME ALLOCATED TO POLITICAL ACTORS[a]

Channel	Time (minutes)	Percentage of total for these four channels
PBC TV	1811	52.32
Watan TV	1363	39.38
Al-Jazeera	197	5.70
Al-Arabiya	90	2.60

[a] Candidates and non-candidates.

Source: Authors' survey.

additional airtime for candidates' party political broadcasts. These two factors – newsworthiness and legal provisions – can explain, to some extent, the different levels of attention paid to election-related news by the national media and pan-Arab broadcasters. The difference clearly reflects their different markets and vocations, different target audiences, editorial

TABLE 7.4 TIME ALLOCATED TO ELECTION AND POLITICAL COVERAGE[a] BY PROGRAMME TYPE

Programme type	Percentage of total				
	Al-Arabiya	Al-Jazeera	PBC	Watan	Total
Free airtime	0.0	0.0	72.4	0.0	37.9
Current affairs/ election programmes	0.0	59.7	15.2	62.7	36.1
Paid airtime	28.1	0.0	0.0	36.6	15.1
News	49.2	40.3	12.4	0.7	10.3
General talk shows	20.8	0.0	0.0	0.0	0.5
Other	1.9	0.0	0.0	0.0	0.0
Entertainment	0.0	0.0	0.1	0.0	0.0
Total (percentage)	100.0	100.0	100.0	100.0	100.0
Absolute values (minutes)	90	197	1811	1363	3,462

[a] Candidates and non-candidates. Rounding of subtotals means overall totals may not add exactly in this or subsequent tables.

Source: Authors' survey.

standards and news priorities. However, other differences emerge from a comparison of the range of formats employed by broadcasters. In this case the editorial choices adopted differed not only between national and transnational broadcasters but also from one local broadcaster to another (Table 7.4).

PBC TV's election coverage was concentrated in a programme entitled *Palestine Votes*, which provided candidates with free airtime, as required by law. It was aired after prime-time news, and repeated later in the evening. Each of the seven presidential candidates had the chance to present their manifesto and discuss it with a panel of journalists, according to a standard format and structure that was the same for all contestants. The editorial line followed by PBC TV clearly tended to concentrate election coverage within this specific format and to focus on other issues in regular news and current affairs programmes. This meant that airtime amounted to 22 hours, including both *Palestine Votes* and unpaid campaign advertising spots. The total airtime dedicated to the candidates within PBC TV news and current affairs coverage was considerably less; only one hour was dedicated to coverage of candidates out of nine hours devoted to political and electoral information in these genres. Meanwhile, Watan TV displayed a different editorial strategy. Its information on the election and politics was generally limited to current events programmes, while paid spots represented a considerable part of its election coverage. The channel did not have its own news production facilities and sporadically re-broadcast Al-Jazeera's main news bulletin. Watan TV also re-broadcast some episodes of *Palestine Votes*, particularly those devoted to Mustafa Barghouti, as well as some of Al-Jazeera's programmes devoted to the candidates and elections.

Al-Jazeera's coverage of Palestine during the elections was carried in news bulletins and current affairs programmes as well as a specially tailored programme, *After Arafat*, which allowed candidates to discuss their political manifestos. All seven candidates were interviewed in the week prior to election day and, even though they did not receive equal airtime, the programme provided a significant opportunity for the candidates to reach both the national public and wider Arab public opinion. Furthermore, Al-Jazeera covered Palestinian political issues and the presidential election in several of its regular weekly political debates, such as *The Opposite Direction* and *More than One Opinion*, displaying a constant interest in facts and events. As for Al-Arabiya's election coverage, this followed a different approach, being more concentrated in formats such as general-interest talk shows and news bulletins. The channel also sold airtime to candidates, and this was exploited by Mustafa Barghouti throughout the campaign period.

Along with the formats adopted for reporting, the distinction between the amount of coverage assigned to presidential candidates and that allotted to other non-competing political actors represents a further indicator of the significance assumed by the election within the more general political agenda of news media. Here there was a marked difference between national and pan-Arab channels (Table 7.5) For Palestinian broadcasters, the presidential candidates represented the heart of their coverage. Both PBC TV and Watan devoted more than two-thirds of their coverage of political issues to covering candidates and campaign activities. On Al-Jazeera the candidates received more limited attention, although quantitatively it was still signficant. Al-Jazeera actually devoted more airtime to covering actors who were not competing in the presidential race, thus confirming the idea that the elections were just a piece of news, albeit a significant one, in a competing hierarchical news agenda.

Analysis of the way PBC TV and Al-Jazeera shared out time among political forces facilitates a clearer understanding of their different editorial lines (Table 7.6). PBC TV devoted the largest part of its political programming to coverage of the elections. It gave small amounts to other political actors. Within this limited coverage, Fatah dominated news and current affairs, due to frequent reports of the activities of its most prominent representatives. Coverage of the ruling party was denoted by clear institutional framing, and most content relating to Fatah members focused on representatives of the Palestinian Authority carrying out official duties or as members of the

TABLE 7.5 DISTRIBUTION OF POLITICAL COVERAGE BETWEEN CANDIDATES AND NON-CANDIDATES

Channel	Percentage distribution		Total
	Non-candidates	Candidates	
PBC TV	24.1	75.9	100.0
Watan	10.8	89.2	100.0
Al-Jazeera	58.9	41.1	100.0
Total[a]	20.7	79.3	100.0
Absolute values (minutes)	700	2672	3372

[a] Data are unavailable for Al-Arabiya.

Source: Authors' survey.

Palestine Liberation Organisation (PLO). Other political forces received very limited attention, suggesting a relationship of close proximity between PBC TV and the political sphere, particularly the ruling party. The lack of coverage for Hamas members was even more illuminating.

Although Hamas decided to boycott the presidential election, it was one of the main parties running for the first round of local elections, in which it won a number of constituencies. Also, despite its decision to boycott the presidential race, Hamas represented a crucial interlocutor for all actors involved in the election and one of the main referents within the political debate concerning the future Palestinian president. It was therefore significant that PBC TV followed a policy of silence towards this key political actor, whose members were largely covered by Al-Jazeera's programming. Hamas was far more prominent on Al-Jazeera, where it received the same amount of coverage as Fatah. This allocation of time gave a more accurate reflection of the spectrum of political forces active in the Palestinian context and their respective weight in terms of popular support and political influence.

TABLE 7.6 ALL PROGRAMME AIRTIME ALLOCATED TO POLITICAL FORCES (NON-CANDIDATES)

Political force	Percentage of total		
	Al-Jazeera	PBC TV	Total
Fatah	35.2	87.5	76.8
Hamas	37.3	1.0	8.4
Islamic Jihad	2.3	5.8	5.1
Independent	3.4	4.9	4.6
Popular Front for the Liberation of Palestine	14.7	0.0	3.0
Palestinian National Initiative	2.7	0.5	1.0
Palestine Democratic Union	3.4	0.0	0.7
Palestinian Authority	0.0	0.3	0.2
Palestinian People's Party	0.7	0.0	0.1
Arab Liberation Front	0.3	0.0	0.1
Democratic Front for the Liberation of Palestine	0.0	0.0	0.0
Total (percentage)	100.0	100.0	100.0
Absolute values (minutes)	116	436	552

Source: Authors' survey.

In respect to the shares of airtime among the presidential candidates (Table 7.7), the editorial line followed by the four channels was noticeably different. With the exception of Watan TV, Mahmoud Abbas was the candidate who received the most coverage. However, it is important to point out that the distribution of airtime among candidates also varied considerably, based on the different media appeal of individual candidates. The satellite channels, Al-Jazeera and Al-Arabiya, focused their coverage on two candidates, Mahmoud Abbas and Mustafa Barghouti. Nevertheless, a significant difference emerged between the channels. Al-Jazeera, while devoting the largest amount of election coverage to the head of the PLO, also covered the other candidates and provided fairly balanced coverage, particularly during the last week of the campaign. In contrast, Al-Arabiya's election reporting focused almost completely on the two main candidates, with its coverage tending to favour Mahmoud Abbas. Watan TV provided Mustafa Barghouti with extensive coverage compared to the other candidates, particularly in genres such as current affairs and election programmes and in paid spots.

PBC TV's coverage demonstrated an attempt to balance the tight control exerted on the channel by the Palestinian Authority and the perceived need to afford equal opportunities, formally at least, to all the candidates to present their political manifestos. During the two-week official campaign period, PBC TV strategically reduced election-related reporting

TABLE 7.7 TIME ALLOCATED TO CANDIDATES ACROSS ALL PROGRAMMING

| Candidate | Percentage of total | | | | |
	Al-Arabiya	Al-Jazeera	PBC TV	Watan	Total
Mustafa Barghouti	36.0	17.1	11.8	41.4	25.8
Mahmoud Abbas	62.8	38.4	19.0	10.0	17.1
Bassam Salhi	0.9	7.6	14.1	14.7	13.8
Abdel-Halim Ashqar	0.0	9.1	16.1	11.0	13.1
Taysir Khaled	0.2	8.2	13.1	14.1	13.0
Shaikh Sayed Baraka	0.0	7.0	14.9	3.9	9.4
Abdel-Karim Shubair	0.0	12.5	11.0	4.8	8.0
Total	100.0	100.0	100.0	100.0	100.0
Absolute values (minutes)	90	81	1,376	1,216	2,763

Source: Authors' survey.

in its news bulletins and concentrated its coverage of the candidates in the specially tailored programme *Palestine Votes*. This strategy represented a highly meaningful shift from the pre-election period, when the news was dominated by coverage of Mahmoud Abbas and Fatah.[13]

At the start of the official campaign period, PBC TV clearly modified its style and approach when covering the electoral process. Election reporting was reduced in the news from a daily average of 22 minutes before the official campaign started to an average of 15 minutes per day afterwards. Only a very limited amount of this time was devoted to coverage of candidates. During the campaign period, the amount of information concerning candidates was less than one hour, most of which was dominated by Mahmoud Abbas, who was mainly covered in the context of his institutional duties (see Table 7.8). This change of communicative strategy seems to be confirmed by an analysis of data related to the coverage of candidates in the different programmes' genres. The distribution of free airtime for party political broadcasts and campaign advertising responded to a logic of equal treatment, not only in terms of time allocation but also in terms of formats adopted for the presentation of candidates.

TABLE 7.8 CANDIDATES' SHARES OF PBC TV ELECTION COVERAGE DURING OFFICIAL CAMPAIGN PERIOD

Percentage of total

Candidate	Free airtime	News	Current affairs/ election programmes	Total
Mahmoud Abbas	15.3	93.8	100.0	19.0
Abdel-Halim Ashqar	16.9	0.3	0.0	16.1
Shaikh Sayed Baraka	15.6	0.3	0.0	14.9
Bassam Salhi	14.7	1.8	0.0	14.1
Taysir Khaled	13.7	0.3	0.0	13.1
Mustafa Barghouti	12.2	3.0	0.0	11.8
Abdel-Karim al-Shubair	11.5	0.3	0.0	11.0
Total	100.0	100.0	100.0	100.0
Absolute values (minutes)	1,312	57	7	1,376[a]

[a] Includes one minute of entertainment programming featuring Mahmoud Abbas.

Source: Authors' survey.

Al-Jazeera was not obliged to abide by any laws regulating Palestinian election broadcasting. It therefore enjoyed a large degree of autonomy in its editorial choices related to the coverage and access of presidential candidates. In its news programmes it allotted a total of 23 minutes of coverage to the candidates, which was a relatively limited amount compared with the time allocated by local broadcasters (Table 7.9). It also tended to cover the candidates only when they were involved in newsworthy events, such as the Israeli arrest of Mustafa Barghouti in East Jerusalem and again in Hebron, or the restrictions imposed on the election process by the Israeli army. Coverage of Mahmoud Abbas was largely related to his institutional position; this often put him in the news, with his status offering him considerably higher visibility than the other candidates. However, the channel offered all candidates the possibility of access, by providing them with a series of five-to ten-minute slots called *After Arafat*, in which they were interviewed and presented their manifestos. This decision represented an acknowledgement of the need to respect some sort of pluralism in covering the Palestinian elections in order to offer a balanced picture of the alternatives for voters. Al-Jazeera therefore granted all candidates the ability to present themselves and their political projects not only to the Palestinian electorate but to wider Arab public opinion. This approach, based on mediation between

TABLE 7.9 CANDIDATES' SHARES OF AL-JAZEERA ELECTION COVERAGE
DURING OFFICIAL CAMPAIGN PERIOD

	Percentage of total		
Candidate	Current affairs/ election programmes	News	Total
Mahmoud Abbas	24.9	72.1	38.4
Mustafa Barghouti	14.7	23.1	17.1
Abdel-Karim al-Shubair	17.5	0.0	12.5
Abdel-Halim Ashqar	12.8	0.0	9.1
Taysir Khaled	10.9	1.6	8.2
Bassam Salhi	9.4	3.2	7.6
Shaikh Sayed Baraka	9.8	0.0	7.0
Total	100.0	100.0	100.0
Absolute values (minutes)	58	23	81

Source: Authors' survey.

journalistic priorities and the acknowledgement of social responsibility towards the public, was fully consistent with the 'Code of Ethics' that Al-Jazeera had adopted in July 2004. Under the code the channel commits itself to 'adhere to the journalistic values of honesty, courage, fairness, balance, independence, credibility and diversity, giving no priority to commercial or political considerations over professional ones'.[14]

For the purpose of the analysis, the tone of each broadcaster's coverage of candidates was also measured (Table 7.10), by taking into account two complementary concepts: the journalist's explicit judgement (evaluation) about the political actor, and the framing (value) of coverage. In this respect, the coverage of all broadcasters in the sample was characterised by the absence of negative reporting of the candidates, and this was especially pronounced on the Palestinian channels.[15] The two satellite broadcasters' coverage had slightly more critical journalistic styles, particularly in their coverage of Mahmoud Abbas. This tendency was mainly a result of the topics covered in the news. The negative tone of some of their coverage can be attributed to the fact that Mahmoud Abbas acted as the head of the PLO, and, even though he was regularly accredited as the most likely winner of the election, coverage of his activities was often associated with problematic aspects of Palestinian affairs and challenges likely to be faced by the new president after the election.

A major difference between the television channels lay in the different modalities employed, based on positive and neutral coverage adopted when reporting on contestants. While PBC TV and Al-Jazeera tended to have neutral coverage, positive tones were dominant in Al-Arabiya and in Watan TV. In this respect, the coverage of Al-Jazeera and PBC TV demonstrated an attempt to adhere to a model of public broadcasting by tending to refrain from any kind of explicit commentary by journalists. That is to say: despite being characterised by favourable reporting of Mahmoud Abbas and his party in terms of the amount of airtime they received, PBC TV attempted to provide non-evaluative coverage of the candidates. Even so, a number of episodes of indirect campaigning in favour of Mahmoud Abbas were observed on the public channel during the election campaign. For instance, during a PBC TV interview with the Palestinian foreign minister, Nabil Shaath, the interviewer kept shifting from the main topic, Yasser Arafat, to ask about Abbas's religious affiliation. Thus Abbas was mentioned on several occasions by both the interviewer and Shaath, who kept praising the PLO chairman. PBC TV also broadcast a six-second still image showing Arafat and Abbas with the PA logo in the middle. Similar images were shown at regular intervals, clearly implying that Abbas embodied the continuation of Arafat's legacy.

TABLE 7.10 TONE OF COVERAGE RECEIVED BY PRESIDENTIAL CANDIDATES[a]

Channel	Candidate	Percentage of total		
		Negative	Neutral	Positive
Al-Arabiya	Mahmoud Abbas	11.5	12.0	76.5
	Mustafa Barghouti	0.0	23.7	76.3
	Bassam Salhi	0.0	70.0	30.0
	Taysir Khaled	0.0	100.0	0.0
	Abdel-Karim al-Shubair	0.0	100.0	0.0
	Abdel-Halim al-Ashqar	0.0	100.0	0.0
	Sayed Baraka	0.0	100.0	0.0
Al-Arabiya total		9.9	14.5	75.6
Al-Jazeera	Mahmoud Abbas	4.3	93.2	2.5
	Mustafa Barghouti	0.0	100.0	0.0
	Abdel-Karim al-Shubair	0.0	100.0	0.0
	Abdel-Halim al-Ashqar	0.0	100.0	0.0
	Taysir Khaled	0.0	100.0	0.0
	Bassam Salhi	0.0	100.0	0.0
	Sayed Baraka	0.0	100.0	0.0
Al-Jazeera total		1.7	97.4	0.9
PBC TV	Mahmoud Abbas	0.0	95.2	4.8
	Mustafa Barghouti	0.0	100.0	0.0
	Bassam Salhi	0.0	100.0	0.0
	Taysir Khaled	0.0	100.0	0.0
	Abdel-Karim al-Shubair	0.0	100.0	0.0
	Abdel-Halim al-Ashqar	0.0	100.0	0.0
	Sayed Baraka	0.0	100.0	0.0
PBC TV total		0.0	95.4	4.6
Watan	Mustafa Barghouti	0.0	60.9	39.1
	Bassam Salhi	0.0	64.4	35.6

Channel	Candidate	Percentage of total		
		Negative	Neutral	Positive
	Taysir Khaled	0.0	54.2	45.8
	Abdel-Karim al-Shubair	0.0	19.6	80.4
	Abdel-Halim al-Ashqar	0.0	2.2	97.8
	Sayed Baraka	0.0	3.0	97.0
	Mahmoud Abbas	0.0	76.8	23.2
Watan total		0.0	49.5	50.5
Overall total		0.8	54.5	44.7

[a] All programmes, excluding party political broadcasts and political airtime.

Source: Authors' survey.

A final area of analysis involves the linking of topics with candidates and political actors (Table 7.11), since it is possible by examining the news agenda for each channel to assess whether the agenda was favourable to candidates or damaging in terms of their credibility and reliability. The agendas of PBC TV and Al-Jazeera were very different, reflecting the specific vocations of the two channels – one having its main focus on Palestinian affairs, and the other projected more into the broader Arab world.

The two broadcasters therefore handled the issues based on different models of news values, which in turn reflected different levels of autonomy for each of the two media systems from the political sphere. PBC TV adhered to a model whereby the media construction of reality was deeply influenced by institutions and parties, thus revealing the dominance of political logic over media logic.[16] Al-Jazeera seemed closer to a model in which media logic prevailed and professional practices were the guiding principle in the selection, treatment and packaging of facts and issues. The editorial agenda defined by PBC TV was a reflection of its official nature. Many of the issues it covered were linked to the sphere of institutions and most of the actors associated with these issues were representatives either of the PA or PLO. Second, the information environment created by PBC TV's overall editorial agenda produced a favourable frame for Mahmoud Abbas by emphasising the topics shaping his official campaign. His link with Yasser Arafat, international credibility and capacity to restart the peace process all enjoyed positions of prominence in PBC TV's coverage.

TABLE 7.11 TOPICS LINKED TO CANDIDATES[a]

Topic	Percentage of total Al-Jazeera	PBC TV	Total
Electoral process	1.0	25.5	18.6
Arafat's legacy	0.0	18.1	13.0
Local elections	11.0	12.0	11.7
Election campaign	31.1	2.1	10.3
Demilitarisation of intifada	30.2	0.0	8.5
International relations	0.1	9.1	6.6
Fatah celebrations	0.3	8.7	6.4
Peace process	1.2	6.6	5.1
Palestinian resistance	8.1	1.7	3.5
Religion	0.0	4.6	3.3
Israeli attacks	4.9	2.0	2.8
Release of prisoners	0.3	3.0	2.3
Attacks against candidates	3.6	0.7	1.5
Israeli restrictions on presidential election	2.3	1.1	1.4
Public administration	0.0	1.8	1.3
Inter-party relations	4.0	0.0	1.1
Institutional activities	0.4	1.2	1.0
Economy/finance	0.0	0.7	0.5
Institutional reform	1.0	0.0	0.3
Boycott of elections	0.3	0.0	0.1
Party activities	0.3	0.1	0.1
Total, including other	100.0	100.0	100.0
Absolute values (minutes)	197.5	500.7	698.1

[a] All programmes, excluding party political broadcasts and paid airtime.

Source: Authors' survey.

The main area of discussion and reporting was related to the electoral process. Facts and comments on the technical aspects of voting – such as voter registration, voting procedures and the activities of the election administration – amounted to more than 25 per cent of the overall time devoted to politics by PBC TV. The second most relevant issue was the one defined as 'the Arafat legacy'. This thematic area was particularly favourable to the candidacy of Mahmoud Abbas, who was frequently linked to this topic and implicitly identified as Arafat's most credible and reliable successor. Similarly, all the topics related to the PA's international relations, constantly presented in news and current events programmes, represented an opportunity for Mahmoud Abbas to increase his media exposure as a candidate enjoying strong links with the international community and accredited at international level. In spite of its success in local elections, Hamas received very limited coverage on PBC TV, and the main actors associated with the theme of local elections were representatives of the PA. News and debates about Fatah's anniversary celebrations constituted another core issue of PBC TV programming, thus confirming its celebratory stance towards institutions and the leading political forces.

Al-Jazeera's coverage reflected its professional vocation and journalistic values. Coverage focused on a range of topics that were not potentially beneficial to any of the candidates and covered a broader spectrum of problems and issues. The election campaign itself was a main theme within this channel's agenda, while a second theme dominating programmes was related to disarmament of the second intifada. This issue was particularly problematic for Mahmoud Abbas, as it referred to wider discussions on the future of Palestinian resistance and the relationship between institutional and social forces. Being potentially problematic, this area of debate was generally ignored by PBC TV. Al-Jazeera, in contrast, made space for alternative voices, such as that of Hamas, and thereby it represented a forum of debate and discussion for this political group. Al-Jazeera consistently covered issues that were often neglected by Palestinian broadcasters. During the campaign period these included: discussion on the idea and strategies of Palestinian resistance; Israeli attacks against Palestinians; relations among Palestinian political parties; and the need for reform. The result was a very diverse agenda which gave the public access to a wider range of issues and debate.

THE FINDINGS IN CONTEXT

It is assumed that transnational channels, most notably Al-Jazeera, have introduced profound changes in the media culture of the Arab world. The question is whether this change can be imported to other media structures so as to produce more pluralistic, more independent and better-quality journalism and information. The findings of our research have to be placed in the Palestinian context, especially the context of the role of local Palestinian media. The struggle against Israeli occupation has deep implications for the relationship between these media and the political sphere, as well as the conditions in which journalists operate in the West Bank and Gaza. According to interviews conducted during the research, the main obstacles affecting journalists' ability to report freely were basically related to the situation of constant conflict.[17] A journalist summed this situation up as follows:

> Pressures on journalists are intertwined with security and the lack of a desire to be critical of ourselves. There are travel restrictions that have affected media coverage of the elections. Movement is OK for the bigger media outlets as we have journalists stationed around the region so we do not have to get around when things are closed down. The big Arab satellite broadcasters have better conditions and are treated differently, but local media are treated as second-class.[18]

Tight control exerted by Israeli and Palestinian authorities on information; lack of freedom of movement in the region; physical assaults and harassment; 'red lines' which journalists are not supposed to cross in their coverage; limited economic and human resources: these are the key factors that dictate what the Palestinian media are able to cover. In these circumstances, possibilities for covering the election and the candidates as well as openly representing views and opinions were dictated by factors beyond the control of the media. This does not mean that journalists working for the satellite broadcasters were immune to such pressures, merely that they were less exposed to them. Moreover, news production is linked with the very nature of the Palestinian broadcasting system. The development of such a system, based on the Oslo Agreements, represented a cornerstone for the development of a Palestinian media sphere, autonomously managed by Palestinians representing

> [a] conversation … [which was] not simply about crisis, and not only one engaged in moral legitimisation and political persuasion, as the pre-Oslo public discourse of Palestinians so often was, but one whose main currency could be ordinary civic, social life.[19]

Working in parallel with this, the development of broadcasting structures implied another level of commitment in the nation-building process and recognition of the PA as a fully legitimised institution. In this respect, national television in Palestine reveals its multi-purpose nature: it is a channel for the creation of Palestinian identity and a means to strengthen and endorse the authority of the PA. Coverage of the presidential election was dominated by this latter trait even while the broadcaster tried to combine competing priorities. On the one hand, PBC TV attempted to offer the electorate the possibility of receiving information on the candidates and their manifestos, in order to fulfil its legal obligations. On the other hand, its role as an institutional channel placed it under the guardianship of the PA, and consequently Fatah. There is little doubt that PBC TV is intrinsically linked to Fatah, as is nearly every sphere of Palestinian social, political and cultural life; this stems from the fact that, in the context of Israeli occupation and lack of sovereignty, Fatah perceives itself *as* the Palestinian state. In the presidential election, this symbiotic relationship imposed a style of reporting as well as an editorial strategy aimed at consolidating the political status quo, emphasising continuity of leadership. It imposed a journalistic mindset that portrayed Mahmoud Abbas as the natural and most credible heir to Yasser Arafat. Meanwhile, coverage by the private channel Watan TV was characterised by greater independence from the ruling party and might be assumed to have been shaped by a different set of values. However, Watan's editorial line unequivocally endorsed the candidacy of Mustafa Barghouti, thus representing another model of militant broadcasting that, although not favouring the ruling party, was directly involved in the political struggle. In both cases the channels assumed the role of political actors, linked to particular factions of the overall political arena.

In contrast, the satellite channels were outside the jurisdiction of Palestinian law and theoretically immune from the influence and control of the Palestinian political sphere. Both channels devoted relatively limited coverage to the presidential election and its candidates and focused their coverage on Mahmoud Abbas. In a journalistic context exempt from externally imposed obligations and, ideally, guided purely by professional considerations, the weight afforded the incumbent candidate was a result of newsworthiness criteria and reporting priorities. However, the nature of the coverage on the two channels diverged considerably, with Al-Arabiya opting for a commercially oriented approach by offering candidates the chance to buy airtime for their campaign broadcasts. This strategy was not an effective means for ensuring access for all candidates, as many of them could not afford the fees. Mustafa Barghouti was the only candidate to purchase airtime on the channel. Al-Jazeera adopted an approach closer to the model of public service in broadcasting, by guaranteeing airtime for all candidates. Although limited in extent, this approach gave candidates an opportunity to communicate with voters and put forward their programmes and manifestos. To a degree, therefore, Al-Jazeera acknowledged its moral responsibility to provide its viewers with complete and accurate coverage of the candidates. Airing the candidates' interviews during prime time on the eve of election day also represented a significant counterbalance to the overwhelming coverage of Mahmoud Abbas in news programmes.

CONCLUSION

There is little doubt that Al-Jazeera and Al-Arabiya played a part in the Palestinian presidential election. Despite their different editorial policies, they contributed to creating a healthier range of information and news about the event. They were able to build on their relationship with the Palestinian public, which perceived them as enjoying a greater degree of independence. PBC TV and some other private local broadcasters have yet to establish this kind of symbolic and cultural relationship with the Palestinian public.

The model of journalism adopted by the pan-Arab channels might represent a paradigm for strengthening a local broadcasting system to make it capable of delivering a service that engages with the public and acts to build trust and credibility. However, transnational channels do not constitute an alternative to a 'national' television system. For organisational and production reasons, they cannot be entirely focused on the agenda of a single country because they select news according to a logic of competition between facts and events. The specific issue of an election, however relevant to a wider public, cannot be expected to become a core of their news agenda. At the same time, there are other, purely symbolic considerations suggesting that the function of local broadcasters cannot be replaced. These are related to the role of such media in providing viewers with local news, as well as in representing the social and political diversity of Palestinian culture. More importantly, their role in building national identity in the absence of sovereign independent statehood is crucial in understanding PBC TV's role in the politics of state-building. According to the dimensions isolated in this chapter, the Palestinian media sphere can be interpreted according to a model of collateralism between media and the political system: broadcasters act following a logic of proximity, if not symbiosis, with the political sphere. They do not represent a fourth estate but, rather, they assume the same positions and stances as parties and political forces, thus creating an information environment in which political logic prevails over media logic. On the other hand, the two transnational Arab channels covered here, while not exempt from pressures and contradictions, served in the specific context of the Palestinian presidential election to provide information that was consistent with a model of competition. In the case of these channels, particularly Al-Jazeera, media actors became autonomous public players competing with the political sphere to set priorities, represent groups, mirror and lead public opinion and, in many cases, to mobilise the public on a number of issues. This is a model in which media actors are able to impose their agenda in terms of topics and personalities to fully exploit their power of framing problems and issues.[20]

On a final note, the two models of broadcasting, transnational and national–local, suggest that, to date, two parallel television systems have developed with different production and editorial boundaries. There is little evidence that the generally superior quality of the satellite broadcasters' coverage is trickling down to national broadcasters. Nor is there much evidence that the overall coverage of a satellite broadcaster, whose audience is by definition pan-Arab, can meet the needs of local viewers at election times when those viewers require more intense and regular election coverage. However, it is interesting that Al-Jazeera's coverage focused on a wider range of issues than that of its local counterparts. Perhaps this is no coincidence, as Palestine has become a focal point for pan-Arab politics of resistance to the Israeli occupation, whereas the specifics of the Palestinian election lacked wider audience appeal outside Palestine.

- 8 -

Palestinians, News and the
Diasporic Condition

Dina Matar

News stories about events affecting Palestinians are an almost permanent feature of the international media landscape. From the outbreak of the second Palestinian intifada in September 2000, to Yasser Arafat's death in November 2004, to legislative elections for the Palestinian Legislative Council in January 2006, critical events repeatedly grab headlines. Journalists and politicians vie to interpret and explain their ramifications for the intractable conflict between Israel and the Palestinians. Each time they do so, as with the 9/11 suicide attacks in the US, the 'war on terror' and the invasion of Iraq, the combination of news coverage and uncertainty surrounding the events themselves serves to bring Palestinians living in other countries into the public gaze. Equally, it raises fresh questions in the Palestinians' private (intimate) sphere about 'Palestinian-ness', what it means to be Palestinian.

Amid heightened tension about the repercussions of terrorism and the relationship between the Middle East, Islam and the West, questions in the public domain are often concerned with whether the pluralisation of 'publics' into public 'sphericules',[1] embodying the particular interests of different social and cultural groups, may challenge the overall collective interests of the nation state. Such questions, which relate to the Habermasian normative ideal of the public sphere, have been central to contemporary debates about the globalisation of the media and about the real and perceived challenges this poses to the old, taken-for-granted ways in which people thought of and experienced cultural and political space.

This chapter, based on a qualitative audience study of the uses of news among Palestinian individuals, households and groups in London and Manchester between November 2001 and June 2003, does not concern itself with whether Palestinians in these contexts constitute a 'sphericule' or a 'counterpublic'.[2] Rather, drawing on a larger, original empirical study of the social and political consequences of news to the Palestinians in Britain, it examines how the participants[3] in that study think about themselves, their identity and the community through their engagement and talk about news. It addresses the contexts according to which they use news to mark boundaries. These are the common frames that people use to negotiate positionings between the familiar and unfamiliar, the national and transnational, the local and the global. Such positionings may enhance their transnational connectivity, which may in turn affect their participation in, or withdrawal from, public life.

The context of the larger empirical enquiry on which this chapter draws was the continuing conflict between Israel and the Palestinians and other related, unplanned media events[4] mediated by a diverse array of news media, including Western, local, global and/or transnational broadcasting channels. The period of investigation, November 2001 to June 2003, witnessed the most serious escalation in hostilities between Israel and the Palestinians since the beginning of the second Palestinian intifada in September 2000. It was also a period that can be described as involving intense grassroots political communication between Palestinians in Britain and similar others in other diasporic spaces and in the homeland. Palestinians' awareness of their transnational connectivity had by this time been enhanced by the proliferation of, and easy access to, diverse news media, including transnational satellite television in Arabic. But the intensification of conflicts in the Middle East and beyond, and the uncertainty they create, must also be understood as having exacerbated a deep collective identity crisis among those involved in the broader research – a crisis centred on what it means to be Palestinian (Palestinian-ness) and what it means to feel Palestinian (Palestinian-ism). The Palestinians' condition is arguably unique in terms of the Israeli–Palestinian conflict's centrality to Middle Eastern developments and international affairs. In an age of 24-hour news, framed according to diverse cultural and ideological perspectives, the participants in this study cannot simply be understood as a news audience normatively understood as a reasoning and detached public. They must also be understood as addressees, summoned to coalesce around particular news dramas as an engaged collective.

In the interviews carried out for the broader research, hardly a conversation was started without informants referring in some way to their attachment to the imagined collective. However, their talk suggested that they were involved in a continuous negotiation of positionings between what it means to be Palestinian and what it means to be cosmopolitan in the diasporic space. In other words, while their conversations claimed distinctiveness and imagined the collective in particularistic terms, they also appealed to universalistic principles of human and citizen rights. This suggests that, even while retreating into essentialising positions about themselves, their community and the other, informants were reaching out to participate in a diverse set of public spheres (outside their own intimate one), including a British public sphere. Put differently, in taking up particular positions, the informants were asserting their distinctiveness and using this as a means to mobilise for action, demand recognition and negotiate parameters of cultural and political citizenship.

IDENTITY CONSTRUCTION BY MEMBERS OF A DIASPORA

As numerous studies and theoretical paradigms over the past few decades have demonstrated, analysis of the media must involve deconstructing politicised debates around the relationship between media and identity. Questions about the formation and transformation of self and collective identities are not exclusive to postmodern enquiry. They have been a major concern in approaches to communication structured around notions of globalisation, development or dependency. Since the 1980s much of the interdisciplinary literature on the relationship between globalisation processes and national or collective identities has drawn on two diametrically opposite theoretical perspectives on the fate of the nation and nationalism. One, the 'hegemony approach', sees globalisation as predominant and homogenising in its effect. The second, the 'heterogeneity approach', maintains that national dimensions remain paramount and that nations remain central to media cultures and policies. However, in an age of flows that are increasingly transnational, we need to integrate these two paradigms and address them as overlapping. Such an understanding is particularly relevant when discussing diasporic groups, for whom the global reach of news media and the immediacy of 24-hour news broadcasts mean that they remain largely, although not solely, focused on nation-centric news dramas.

The term 'diaspora' has gained currency in recent years, with the realisation that it could serve as a theoretical tool for understanding migration processes and experiences. There has also been a recognition that links between diasporas and their countries of origin, on the one hand, and their host societies, on the other, are more complex and ambivalent than was assumed in the ideal-type model of diaspora popularised in the old migration and colonialism literature. That said, there remains a tendency in the field of media studies and the new sub-area of research focusing on diasporic media to prioritise the relationship with the homeland. This tendency, which arises from general assumptions that migrants remain loyal to their origins, directs attention away from the creative possibilities opened up by the activities of diasporas in local and transnational contexts, and away from the fluidity of identity transformation through relocation, cross-cultural exchange and interaction.

Drawing on Annabelle Srebreny's suggestion that a focus on diaspora seems to invite a looking around, not only in and back, but also a 'scoping all-round gaze',[5] this chapter argues that it is this ability to 'look around' that makes the term 'diaspora' meaningful for academic study. It allows for an exploration of how members of a diaspora may mobilise around their awareness and imagining of themselves as a diaspora and also as members of a particular collective – doing so through dialogue, debate and negotiation around who their members are and what it means to be who they are. This understanding allows us to address the contexts that propel members of a diaspora to mobilise and coalesce as a particular collective within the complex set of linkages made possible by contemporary transnational dynamics. Such contexts include alternative spaces of communication, in which the meaning and boundaries of diasporic identity are continually constructed, debated and re-imagined. To understand diaspora in this way is not to subscribe to binary analysis of globalisation processes as either global or local, national or transnational. Binary thinking obscures the actual interdependence and interweaving of these processes. Instead, this approach foregrounds the need for any analysis of how diasporic members make use of their connectivity through media or other potential vehicles of globalisation to take into account the interweaving between the national and the transnational. Interweaving is about continuity and overlapping movements between the particular and the cosmopolitan,[6] rather than about competition over a meeting place between the two.

Importantly, this understanding allows for an exploration of how identity is constructed through continuous dialogue, or a discursive process of identification that acknowledges tensions between the self and the other, between the self and the collective, and between the national and the cosmopolitan. Put differently, this approach allows us to problematise identity and identity politics in the transnational context. It allows us to address the different contexts through which transnational social actors, diasporic groups and marginalised people can be understood.

These notions provide the framework in the current study for analysing the informants' talk about news. They emphasise that social terms we use and take for granted – 'identity' and 'community' – are the products of ongoing debates or political struggles. What this means is that people's thinking and talking about their identity can oscillate between essentialising versions and versions that are more open to possibilities. In other words, categorical identities can be invoked and given public definition by individuals or groups even when they are not embodied in concrete networks of interpersonal relationships. Therefore, rather than assuming a simple opposition or dichotomy between essentialism and social constructionism, it is important to acknowledge that people can think about and construct their identities in multiple ways. The point here is that, under certain circumstances, self-critical claims to strong, basic and collective (national) identities are important to acknowledge. Where a particular category of identity has been repressed, de-legitimated or devalued in dominant or public discourse, it is possible that it may be invoked in an essentialist way.

The sequence of unplanned media events related to the Palestinian–Israeli conflict has served to bring into the open a deep collective identity crisis over what it means to be Palestinian (Palestinian-ness). This in turn has been central to Palestinian national consciousness (Palestinian-ism) ever since *al-nakba* (the catastrophe) of 1948 and the ensuing exodus, which has become a significant and emotional site for individual and collective memories and mythologies of the Palestinian people. The history of Palestinian migration predates that event. It began in the late eighteenth century, when mainly Christian families, motivated by socio-economic or personal interests and family considerations, began migrating to the West. Politically motivated flight was triggered before 1948. A peak period was the Great Revolt of 1936–1939, a popular uprising against the Jewish institutions that were beginning to take a foothold in Palestine. But this was on an altogether smaller scale than the estimated departure, forced or otherwise, of some 750,000 Palestinians from their homes after the 1948 Arab–Israeli War.

Statistics on Palestinians in Britain are limited, with the result that details about their composition and whereabouts continue to elude researchers, including myself. Part of the reason is a general trend, followed by the British and other European governments, to place Palestinians in a generic 'Middle Eastern' category. This renders them invisible within the prevailing ethnic profiling methods used in the UK. For example, the 2001 general census[7] clustered Palestinians in a generalised 'other' category comprising a variety of ethnic groups. Furthermore, since census figures are based on place of birth, Palestinian children born in Britain are recorded as British, not Palestinian. Palestinians are, anyway, not easily identifiable as a separate ethnic group since they share language, customs, traditions and religion with other Arabs. That said, estimates suggest there are around

20,000.[8] This number is small compared to an estimated 80,000 in Germany, and small in relation to the number of Palestinians worldwide. Palestinian Authority estimates put this at 8.7 million, of whom 3.7 million were in the West Bank and Gaza Strip in 2003.

In the larger project, I spent a great deal of effort trying to track down the emerging institutional infrastructure of the Palestinian diaspora in Britain, such as community associations and schools. This work revealed, first, that the Palestinians in Britain are not clustered in specific geographic areas and, second, that there was a degree of flux in the community, with some activities ending and others starting up during the course of the research. The wide dispersion of the Palestinians, even in the London area, also meant that their experiences were different from the experiences of other minorities and ethnic groups in the UK.

The media environment available to the Palestinians in Britain is one of the richest in the Palestinian diaspora, comprising a variety of print and broadcast channels with different orientations and claims on their audiences. The Arabic print media, for example, include a number of daily newspapers, printed in Arabic in London, all of which carry a great deal of news and commentary about events from Palestine and the Arab world. *Al-Quds al-Arabi*, in particular, addresses the dispersed Palestinian diaspora as members of a larger Palestinian people (*al-shaab al-falastini*). Transnational satellite television in Arabic, developed inside and outside the Arab world since the early 1990s, means that the Palestinian diasporic space is constructed through a great variety of cultural activities and media channels. It is therefore necessary to examine the role the media play in the complex set of psychological, sociological and cultural dynamics that comprise diasporic reality.

DISCOURSES OF IDENTITY, NEWS AND PUBLIC LIFE

I now turn to consider how members of the Palestinian diasporic community in Britain talk about news. In doing so I address the relationship between news and discourses of identity, and how this pertains to the question of what makes people participate in or withdraw from public life. The approach to identity adopted here draws on Stuart Hall's theoretical framework of 'identification as discourse', which sees identities as social discursive constructs that are created, maintained and called upon in various cultures and in different contexts.[9] Though my approach is informed by social constructionism, which broadly assumes that knowledge is constructed and deconstructed through ideological discourse, I propose to use the terms 'consolidation' or 'recreation' when referring to identity. These terms assume that the basic material for knowledge already exists, but that this can be manipulated, shaped and polished by various actors in different contexts. My perspective acknowledges individual reflexivity and creativity, but rejects a simple binary opposition between social constructionism and essentialism. This is because, under certain circumstances, self-critical claims to strong, basic and primordial identities, including religious and national identities, are important to acknowledge. What is vital to explore are the contexts within which some identities are more readily summoned than others and the ways in which people shape or consolidate different versions of these identities.

Interviews with Palestinian participants in my research indicated that what it means to be Palestinian (Palestinian-ness) and what it means to feel Palestinian (Palestinian-ism) were, for them, key concerns. Most of those interviewed for the larger project identified themselves as Palestinian. Some said they were becoming 'more Palestinian'. Others suggested that being Palestinian meant being different and/or unique, that being Palestinian meant being the underdog or the victim, but also resisting and struggling. In this, they reiterated official and nationalistic discourses about Palestinian-ness. Some suggested that what it means to be Palestinian is different from what it means to be Arab or Muslim.

> I was born a Palestinian and I have memories. In Palestine, you are with your family so what can I tell you? I do not depend on the community or the idea of the community. When I see a Palestinian, I feel very happy. To be honest with you, there is a problem with the Arabs and the Gulf people. We have our own culture and our own dialect even. Even though we were born outside Palestine and live outside it, we still feel Palestinian. Our thoughts are Palestinian. Everything: our customs, our traditions, and even our food and the way we bring up our children – we tell them we (and they) are Palestinian (Wael, 25).

Similar particularistic (exclusionary) dimensions of what it means to be Palestinian weave through many of the informants' accounts of 'belonging'. However this is also interspersed with reflexivity about longing and belonging, suggesting that where people feel they belong (the cultural or ethnic home) may not match objective ascriptions of membership (to the political or civic home), because 'belonging' separates into 'being' in one place, and 'longing' for another. For instance, Mona, a 32-year-old Palestinian woman from west London, says that she feels integrated in British society and that is reflected in her 'social' interactions. But still she makes the crucial distinction that her 'feelings' are Palestinian: 'Psychologically, I cannot but be Palestinian.' Omar, a 35-year-old middle-class businessman, is more reflexive in his assessment of belonging and the tensions involved:

> London is an extremely cosmopolitan city and it is difficult to define exactly who is a traditional British person here. The standard definition of what it means to be British is blurred. This country is my home now and I feel integrated inasmuch as I am capable of doing anything in this country that anybody purely British can do. At the same time, however, I have my political identifications and attachments to Palestine... I guess it is because I also feel comfortable when I go back.

In talking about and around news, many respondents voiced concerns about themselves and their families and the collective, meaning the Palestinian nation. Their concerns seemed to underline the continuous tensions between the personal and the political (national) and between individual and collective memory that come into play during such moments. This comes across clearly in the following exchange in a group interview in Manchester (emphasis added):

> Mahmoud: [W]e [the Palestinian nation] are at the centre of the mess now, not isolated. The impact on *us* and on politics has been huge. *We see this at our own level because we are Palestinians.* The reason that we speak a lot about politics is that what we watch on television has an impact on us. It is a direct impact really. We have families in the Occupied Territories and when we travel, we also suffer. We feel it in our everyday lives.
> Maha: Yes, this mess has made others become anti-Palestinian, anti-Arab and anti-Muslim. *The whole world now does not see our side of the story.* Sharon has done all his deeds and there is not a single word of protestation against it. Before, it was different. Now everybody is silent.

Similar perceptions of an 'imagined community in crisis' weave through most of the informants' accounts about news, even though they may not be personally directly involved in the news events they talk about: relentless violence since the start of the second intifada, the 11 September attacks in the US, the US-led 'war on terror' and the invasion of Iraq. Indeed, the interview material shows that these events triggered notions of instability and insecurity among a majority of respondents, irrespective of their age or gender. This is how Nadwa, a 55-year-old Palestinian in London, put it:

> Look at the situation we are in. We do not feel secure any more. Look at what the UK government is doing, can you trust them as every minute they come up with something new, some new law? I cannot explain to you how I feel, because what you see is totally impossible. This is beyond our imagination.

Discourses of crisis were articulated across the board. Women respondents were generally more emotional and agitated in discussing these concerns; they tended to focus on the human and social aspects of the meaning of news and on how they themselves, their children, their family and friends might have been affected by these news accounts. Male informants, in general, were more circumspect in their reflections on the sense of crisis. They concerned themselves with attributing blame or offering analyses of the evolving situation. More interesting was that the informants shifted from voicing concerns about themselves and their immediate families and friends to voicing concerns about the collective, meaning the Palestinian nation as whole, serving to underline the continuous interweaving of the personal and the political.

There is little doubt that the notion of crisis relates to the specific timing of the larger research. While taking the timing into consideration, it is important to acknowledge that, in making sense of the news, informants were forced to deal with the narrative as addressees as well as a news audience. This meant that they had to negotiate its meanings as an attached and engaged collective rather than as a detached audience. Some respondents said they had become obsessed with news. Some said they were eager to find out what was happening next in order to make sense of the unfolding drama. Others said they were constantly switching channels to assess the different mediations and representations in the news. Mona, for example, said:

> I switch channels. I change from Arabic channels to English ones to see what they are covering and what they are saying. In the end, though, I turn to the one news programme that meets my needs and moves me, or leaves an impact.

Almost all the respondents said they engaged with diverse news media, including mainstream Western news media, such as the BBC, as well as Arabic-language media, particularly Arabic satellite broadcasting channels. Their talk about their news viewing routines reflected how access to diverse news media is something they demand and expect to have in their everyday lives.

Some of the younger informants said that the continuous news story of the ongoing conflict between Israel and the Palestinians was the catalyst that propelled them to install satellite dishes. They wanted pan-Arab satellite channels as these provided them with alternative narratives that they saw as countering the dominant discourses of mainstream (Western) news media, such as the BBC and CNN. Dominant discourse is not a manifestation of a monolithic or static set of ideological concerns but of a broader process of communication, which serves as a matrix for the discussion of various issues by members of a society. In this sense, dominant discourses reflect the ever-changing structures of power, shaped by continually evolving and often contradictory combinations of assumptions and world-views of socio-economic and intellectual elites.[10]

The research period coincided with a proliferation of alternative news sources and there is little doubt that the availability of transnational news media provided the respondents in this research with compelling accounts of events. The simultaneous availability of diverse sources, from English broadsheets and the BBC to Arabic-language sources, together with diverse ways of telling news stories, created a contested context for engagement with news. That is to say: tense, contradictory and polarised dynamics surrounded these informants' experiences of news, drawing attention to a deliberate process of interaction and interweaving between the local and the transnational.

> I am not only satisfied with just hearing the news as it is. This is not enough. It is important to hear the news from different viewpoints and then you decide. There is a big difference. When it comes to the Palestinian story, Arabic channels, particularly Al-Jazeera, show us exactly what happens, even showing us pictures of dead Israelis (from suicide bombs). But Al-Manar is the best really because it is the only Arab station focusing on the Palestinians (Hussein, 45).

At the same time, however, many of the informants suggested that their consumption practices were also dictated by *what* was being said, pointing to how their making sense of news has to be seen as linked to perceptions of power and to struggles for recognition and membership in a national public sphere.

> The media are basically indifferent. I would not go as far as to say they are positively biased towards Israel. What I would say is that they probably leave on purpose large sections of the story. They would tend to say five Palestinians were killed today on the West Bank, whereas, if they wanted to, they could show graphic pictures of those five people, etc. Very, very powerful images that would be very damaging to Israel and they don't do so. They obviously have access to those images, but they show the Israeli images definitely (Omar, 32).

Comments referring to cultural exclusion were articulated across the board. However, they were particularly notable in the way respondents contrasted between diverse news narrations and in their comments on the narration of events in the Palestinian–Israeli conflict by dominant news media. Many said that the latter reflected cognitive scripts and models of behaviour shaped by the experience and narration of previous events. Put differently, they saw the narrations as fitting traditional journalistic 'frames' deployed to make sense of violence, terrorism and Islam. The use of frames is a common journalist practice and is often manifested in the predominance of 'crude binaries' in news reporting, particularly during times of trauma, as journalists strive to make sense of events and attempt to lend authority to their narrations. Such frames, particularly noticeable in news reports related to 11 September, have attracted much scholarly attention, and there is little need to expand on them here. Instead, the relevant point here is that the process of framing serves to focus attention on discourses of 'us' and 'them' in the national (British) public sphere. Discourses that tend to establish essentialist and polarised news accounts based on dichotomies between 'us' and 'them', or the 'West' and the 'rest', belie complex realities and create conflicts of identification for Palestinians in Britain. Significantly, it was in relation to these polarised contexts that many informants, irrespective of gender and age, tended to question the mainstream media's representation of events. Many said they felt bracketed within such categories as 'Islamic fundamentalists', and 'supporters of terrorism'. The bracketing served to catalyse dogmatic modes of thinking, bringing to the fore discourses emphasising political and religious identifications.

> The news affects us in many ways. I do not think there is a lot of discussion about the background. For instance, if we talk of the intifada, they [the Western media] rarely give any explanations. The only one thing that is said is that we are Islamic and terrorists and that we are brainwashed... The mainstream media does not want to say anything else. It makes me feel different (Leila, 28).

Informants' dissatisfaction with news media bias and their criticism of it reflected how they were taking on the role of engaged and concerned citizens. By engaging in criticism they were challenging hegemonic discourses, at least in relation to media portrayals of the Palestinian–Israeli conflict. Their criticism of Western news media contrasted with their often favourable comments on alternative news narratives, particularly those of Arabic satellite channels, such as Al-Jazeera. It suggested that the news media can act as a symbolic forum for thinking and arguing. 'We find in Al-Jazeera a way to vent our feelings and emotions. It is the most objective and balanced of all the channels' was one recurrent answer. 'As Palestinians, we feel there are people who care for you' was another.

> I like to watch Al-Jazeera and Al-Manar. The news is very interesting and [...] you feel that they say what is in my heart and express what is in my mind. Most of their news and images... even when they have intervals

or adverts, they put pictures of the intifada and music and Arabic songs about Palestine. Al-Manar, for instance, does not report from south Lebanon as much as it does on Palestine (Nuha, 45).

What emerges from these comments and others is the sense that the informants in this research do not turn to news only for information but because it confirms their ideological consciousness of what it means to be Palestinian. Some informants said they were fed up with news because nothing is going to change. Others, however, suggested that the advent of Arabic satellite television provided them not only with a choice of viewing but also with the incentive to be able to negotiate and publicly criticise news narratives. This seemed to confirm that the news media can mediate between public institutions and private or collective interests. Indeed, some of the women interviewed for the larger research, particularly those with grown-up children, said their access to diverse news sources since the second Palestinian intifada had spurred them to take part in protests criticising Israeli and US policies or in fund-raising events for Palestinians in the Occupied Territories. Their response contrasts sharply with Palestinians who arrived in Britain in the 1960s and 1970s and shied away from any involvement in political action. Many older-generation Palestinians tended to live on their memories, not wishing to visit their former homeland, even though they had British passports. It was as though, for them, the place that was now Israel had been frozen in 1948, like a photograph – an Arab country with Jews in it, not the other way round. Unlike that generation, respondents in my research not only talked of involvement in sit-ins, protests and fund-raising campaigns but said that it was because of diverse news narratives that they had become more active in organising events. This comment by Mona captures this clearly:

> [Engaging with diverse Arabic news] allows me to have the strength to discuss things with people out there [in the British public sphere]. Watching the news and the different coverage of events has given me the strength to open a debate with the British and the others … it has given me permission for entry [into societal dialogue] and to show them the double standards of coverage.

It becomes apparent that the availability of diverse news media can enable more active and public participation in private and public debates. Indeed, some of the informants said that access to diverse news enabled them to experience what it means to be Palestinian in intimate space and what it means to be a citizen in the British public (national) space. Some young adults and those born in Britain said this active participation was linked to the increased and continuous news coverage of critical events, such as the second intifada, which coincided with the proliferation of pan-Arab satellite news media. This phenomenon confirms the importance of addressing the contexts according to which collective identities are summoned. Though these actions are clearly driven by the interests of the informants as members of a particular collective, the public expression of private interests serves to address some of the normative concerns underlying the Habermasian model of the public sphere.

Conversely, many informants were not convinced about the degree of news media diversity and expressed strong suspicions about covert political and economic interests of media channels. These informants were particularly critical of pan-Arab television channels' alleged political agenda. Their criticisms suggested that, although the narratives produce a shared 'ideological' agenda for conversation – a social and political forum for discussing shared agendas and concerns – there was no sense that these representations created a convergence of ideologies. Nadwa, a 55-year-old Palestinian widow, said: 'Al-Jazeera, I am afraid of. There is something inside me which tells me there is something behind it. At first, I watched it, but then I started to feel the programmes are made as a cover for something else.'

However, the informants' critical interpretation of Western (mainstream) news narratives contrasted with their preferred readings of the mediated representations of pan-Arab satellite broadcasting news channels. It was as though their preferences were dictated to a certain extent by conflicts between the different cultural discourses of news and their own experiences, real and imagined, resulting in active 'identity work' through dialogue or through their talk about news. Evidence of this active identity work was apparent throughout the interviews, but came into especially stark relief when informants contrasted between narratives of the same event by Western news media and pan-Arab transnational television. It was in these contexts that questions relating to what these respondents perceived as their distinctiveness as members of a particular political and national group came into central focus. The role played by news in the coming together of audience members as a distinctive collective came across in assertions of a 'communal and political identification', a hardening of divides, and the construction of frames of 'us' and 'them'. This emerged in the following comment by Maha, a 32-year-old Palestinian in London:

> Now they are saying we [the Palestinians] are terrorists. What we see on television [the Arabic channels] actually opens the question of where terrorism is, with us or with them [sic]. They are our enemies or, as they claim, we are their enemies, but they are harming us in a way that we are not harming them. If we talk exclusively about Palestine... What has made the world feel with Israel or show sympathy to it. It's because they

always show that image. We don't have that image. They [Western media] show that Arabs are always the problem. This is our problem. Our media is not the same as theirs. Our media has ignored certain things. The Europeans, the Americans and the Jews, the media there is stronger than ours. This is because they are with Israel. They always tell us the roots of the Arabs and also show things that may not apply to us or be within us. For instance, now they are saying that we are terrorists. What we see on television raises the questions of where terrorism is, with us or with them.

It was also within such contexts that comments such as 'Now, I am Palestinian' or 'I am becoming more Palestinian' were voiced by various informants, irrespective of age, gender, socio-economic or socio-religious situations. Comments such as these suggest that the informants' active identity work can be understood as defensive and emotional cognitive reactions to perceptions of exclusion and non-visibility in the British public sphere – perceptions that come to the fore in their appropriation of news framed according to different cultural and/or political perspectives. And it was in this polarised context that most informants, irrespective of gender and age, tended to question the mainstream media's representation of events which many said bracketed them within such categories as 'Islamic fundamentalists' and 'supporters of terrorism', a double-categorisation[11] that served to catalyse dogmatic modes of thinking about the continuous crises, bringing to the fore discourses emphasising the informants' political and religious identifications.

> The news affects us in many ways. I do not think there is a lot of discussion about the background. For instance, if we talk of the intifada, they [the Western media] rarely give any explanations. The only one thing that is said is that we are Islamic and terrorists and that we are brainwashed … The mainstream media does not want to say anything else. It makes me feel different (Nada, 32).

Conversely, many of the informants said they were comfortable being in Britain and that their experience of living in Britain was positive in many ways. Their accounts reflected a sense of belonging to the cosmopolitan, or an identification with the cosmopolitan aspect of living in Britain. Such notions were particularly evident among respondents who lived in London. Such is the case of Mansour, who has been living in London since the mid-1960s:

> I feel I am integrated with the cosmopolitan aspect of Britain, of London. We are all foreigners here, I feel. Living in London reminds me of the Palestinian *hara* [neighbourhood]. I have no problems in Britain. Whenever I come back to London [after a trip], I feel it is home.

In his examination of the various discourses among South Asians in London, Gerd Baumann juxtaposed the notion of dominant discourses, which refers to essentialist discourses reifying culture and identity, against demotic discourses, which challenge existing reifications.[12] He argued that the dominant emphasises the conservation of existing communities while the demotic allows Southallians to re-conceive community boundaries and contest the meaning of culture. According to Baumann, the demotic discourse thus allows Southallians to create new communities as well as to subdivide or fuse existing ones, and is used to undermine the dominant one 'whenever Southallians ... judge it useful in any one context'.[13] In contrast to an instrumental reification, I suggest, based on the evidence presented here, that open and closed discourses (like the demotic and dominant discourses Baumann refers to) coexist in tension. They are not simply discursive reifications of the distinctiveness of the community[14] but also articulations of desired realities that may materialise in the future.

Indeed, the informants' talk points to the emergence of a Palestine-centred identification, a *discursive imagination* with an entity called 'Palestine' that may materialise in the future, but which has a double meaning. In some contexts it excludes others; in other contexts it demands recognition and visibility in the national public sphere. While these two strands of imagination are not irreconcilable, there is a sense that what is foregrounded here is not only collective harmony or a political identification with an increasingly metaphoric Palestinian nation but, rather, a longed-for sense of self-respect and individual possibility.

In talking about news, the respondents' imaginations of what it means to be Palestinian alternate and/or coexist with imaginations of what it means to be a cosmopolitan or what it means to be a British citizen. Interestingly, the respondents' affective and subjective articulations of what it means to be Palestinian were in stark contrast with the more rational and measured discourses about belonging to the cosmopolitan or the host society. It seemed the informants imagined the cosmopolitan as a 'terrain of opportunity' for taking part in social action and interaction. What this means is that we need to pay attention to the affective sensibilities of modern audiences and the ways in which their structures of feeling contribute towards their mental maps. These are important issues to take into account. They can help us understand the contexts in which diasporic and migrant groups feel excluded, politically and culturally, and the contexts in which they essentialise their identities and exclude others. That in turn can help address the ongoing debate about the nature and benefit of multiculturalism and the ongoing struggles between dominant and alternative cultures.

CONCLUSION

The central logic of this chapter is that the availability of diverse news media, particularly transnational news media such as Arab satellite channels, has radically challenged the political dynamics and social experiences of members of the Palestinian diasporic community in Britain. While exacerbating a deep collective identity crisis centred on what it means to be Palestinian and what it means to feel Palestinian, access to diverse news sources also provided the impetus for thinking about participation in public life in the host culture. In analysing the responses and attitudes of interviewees towards diverse news narrations, I found that, even among British-born Palestinians with no personal experience of exile, there was a growing awareness of their transnational connectivity and their Palestinian-ness, as well as a growing consciousness of a Palestine-centred identification. At the same time, however, many of the respondents had become more conscious of their cultural and political positioning in Britain and of demands to negotiate the parameters of citizenship and belonging in the host country space.

The findings of the broader research resonate with recent work on migrant and diasporic groups, which has identified the emergence of new 'transnational imagined communities' made up of a growing number of people who live dual lives and who maintain regular transnational connections across national borders.[15] However, this chapter has also shown that, in many ways, it is the signifier 'Palestinian' that binds the Palestinians in different spaces as a collective. That said, the informants' growing consciousness of identification with an imagined Palestinian entity did not mean a retreat into defensive and closed identities or creating hybrid ones. Rather, as shown above, it meant a continuous movement between essentialising and more open positions. That movement challenges assumptions about the emergence of particularistic identities that are increasingly common in popular media and mainstream political discourses.

I started the chapter by drawing attention to the fact that the availability of transnational news media, such as Al-Jazeera, means that the informants cannot be seen only as a news audience. Different representational accounts summon them as addressees to coalesce around particular news dramas as an engaged collective. The material presented here showed how the informants, as an audience, could choose between different representational spaces and accounts of their national conflicts. As addressees, however, their choices were influenced by the different modes of address, by scepticism about the reliability and credibility of news sources and by the demand for more and varied information. The influencing of these choices becomes significant in specific political and cultural contexts within which different versions of identity are negotiated, polished and worked on. These contexts, as suggested above, relate to the timing of the research. But they also relate to the informants' experienced realities of everyday life, grounded in the struggles of connection and community, in the conflict around identity and identification.

That said, the power of transnational news media, such as Al-Jazeera, cannot be understood only in terms of their ability to summon particular ethnic, linguistic and/or religious groups that live within broader and diverse multicultural societies. It should also be understood in terms of the audience's ability to recognise these media as oppositional public spheres that may provoke different ways of thinking about themselves and their community. As reported above, it was in their contrasting of different mediated news accounts of the same event that the informants were able to recognise that they could seek a more 'participatory' role in the host country's public sphere.

- 9 -

Crafting the Arab Media for Peace-building: Donors, Dialogue and Disasters

Bruce Stanley

From small beginnings in the 1960s, Western governments and international non-governmental organisations (INGOs) are today spending huge sums on media intervention in Arab countries, to the point where such intervention has become an industry. Among the plethora of media projects aimed at moulding Arab public affairs are a subset intentionally framed in terms of a discourse of conflict resolution, conflict handling and peace-building. Since 1998 external donors have financed such projects bilaterally and multilaterally, with the explicit aim of replacing violence and threats among regional antagonists with mutual understanding, diversity, dialogue and exchange. When it comes to measuring their impact and effectiveness, however, the results have generally failed to meet expectations, and there have been some spectacular disasters. Despite this, the number of such projects in the region is on the increase, with an ever wider range of donors becoming involved. This chapter reviews the development of these interventions for peace. It proposes a typology for understanding their objectives, evaluates their general success and failure and concludes with some considerations about requirements for success.

WHAT CHANGED IN THE 1990s

Intentional intervention in the Arab media for the specific objective of peace-building generally emerged only as part of the donor push for regional democratisation and good governance that characterised the 1990s. Before that, however, there were precursors to the post-1990 approach.

These fell into two broad types. On the one hand were activities that sought to enhance the general professionalism of the Arab media, with the vague objective of increasing democratisation or empowerment. On the other were off-the-record dialogues for peace-building. The first approach, which might be termed 'traditional training', tended to take individual Arab journalists and editors from the print or broadcast media out of their local environment and sought to give them Western professional skills, either through technical training (in the case of the Thomson Foundation[1]) or academic training (as with the Fulbright Program, which dates back to the early 1950s; the more recent Humphrey Fellows programme in the US;[2] or AMIDEAST's training programmes for Palestinians during the 1980s and early 1990s[3]). Such projects lacked any clear causal tie to peace-building. They tended to be framed either within a fuzzy Cold War terminology of 'enhancing democracy' or by a commitment to professionalising regional reporting. The assumption was there, if unexpressed, that such exposure would lead to better, more open societies and, by implication, to greater regional stability. Arab media were viewed as indirect agents for change, and this type of intervention involved no intentional peace-building component.

In contrast, off-the-record dialogues were often instigated by non-mainstream academic, peace or faith-based organisations working on conflict resolution in the region. Groups such as the Quakers, for example, as part of their long-running activities in the Middle East, held quiet, simple meetings among influential Israelis, Palestinians and other Arabs, with journalists and editors included because of their access and insight. The media were not specifically targeted and nor were they explicitly identified as direct agents of peace-building. During the late 1980s, however, the Quakers were among the first to host Israeli–Palestinian sessions targeting journalists, and the discourse was more explicit about the media being agents of change.[4] In the same category was the work of Herbert Kelman, the Harvard social psychologist, in his interactive problem-solving approach to conflict. From the 1970s onwards he involved Palestinians and Israelis in workshops, with journalists and editors among the participants.[5]

Several factors constrained these pre-1990 efforts. The conception of 'media' was quite narrow, being mostly restricted to print journalism, as were the mechanisms and objectives of engagement. Overall there was little explicit conceptualisation of the media as a direct agent for the transformation of conflict. I have been unable to uncover any focused work by peace or faith-based groups with the Lebanese media during the whole history of the Lebanese Civil War. Nevertheless, as with the Israeli–Palestinian case, it is almost certain that some individual editors and journalists took part in behind-the-scenes dialogues seeking to rebuild the fabric of Lebanese life.[6]

The first amply funded interventions specifically aimed at empowering civil society in the Arab world followed the Middle East peace conference in Madrid in 1991 and the Israeli–Palestinian Oslo Accords in 1993. The words 'good governance' and 'civil society' started to appear in donor – and therefore also in local – discourse after 1991. The Democratic Institutions Support Project of USAID was one of the first large-scale schemes of its kind, followed by the European Union's Med Media project. By 1994 the regional map of donors and activities and their scope had changed. A veritable democracy 'industry' began to emerge, which dramatically increased the nature and amount of funding available throughout the region.[7] All this gave prominence to concerns with shaping public space in the Arab world, including the media. It also conflated democratisation with the US-led 'peace process', as the discourse for one often found its way into the framing of the other. Donors focused on civil society as a check to authoritarian governments, assuming that, along the way, the transformation of Arab governments would produce peace in the region. Sometimes the reverse assumption prevailed, suggesting that peace would create conditions for civil society to function, thus leading to democracy. The EU's People-to-People Programme of 1998 aimed to build a civil society context for the Oslo process, which, having been top-down, needed bottom-up support. The media, as one part of civil society, were to be empowered in the search for peace.

Concurrently with these developments, the sub-field of conflict resolution in international relations was coming of age. By 1990 institutions, journals, frameworks, theory, departments and conferences had all evolved to such an extent that a package justifying interventions in conflict situations via civil society actors was readily available.[8] This alternative to the traditional paradigms of conflict, security, the centrality of the state, and bounded interstate war offered new techniques, alternative frameworks and deeper understandings of dynamics.[9] As a result, in the wake of the Madrid conference and Oslo Accords, funding for conflict resolution projects in the Middle East, if framed in the language and concepts of the new peace industry, was suddenly available, dramatically increasing almost overnight the number of conflict resolution projects and the local centres or institutes for conflict resolution ready to conduct them. Although emerging partially from a regional trend towards *dakakeen* (shops: i.e. civil society institutions lacking any real substance) and projects for projects' sake, in the Palestinian case there actually was a small cadre of activists, practitioners and students on which to build.[10]

Nevertheless, it still took other factors to encourage the appearance of specific media interventions for peace-building in the Middle East. The first was the 1994 genocide in Rwanda, and the local media's implication in it. After that, northern donors, INGOs and conflict resolution institutions really began to invest time and money in media intervention projects, initially focused in Africa. By 1998 the first tranche of projects (Africa, Eastern Europe) were evaluated, and by 2002 there was a wealth of evaluations, 'best practice' reports, frameworks of analysis[11] and new findings about the power of the media for peace-building.[12] It is interesting to note that few Middle East examples are cited in these reviews. For example, a 2001 report by Media Action International, *Lifeline Media: Reaching Populations in Crisis*, made scattered references to projects in Afghanistan and Somalia, but referred only once to an early attempt to shift Israeli perceptions of Palestinians.[13] The first mainstream media intervention projects for peace-building to receive significant funding appeared in the Middle East only after 1998.

TACTICAL OR STRATEGIC INTERVENTION?

Since that time there have been hundreds of such projects, sometimes actually competing for participants,[14] while advertisements for specialists in the field indicate that the trend will continue, not least because of new funding from sources such as the US Middle East Partnership Initiative. Some donors are explicit about their objectives. But, no matter how clear they are about what they think they want, donors face unavoidable choices that will determine the nature and outcomes of their projects. One key choice is whether to commit to the substance of peace-building, as distinct from the fashionable terminology. The vast majority of media interventions today cloak their objectives in the discourse of democratisation and civil society empowerment. While the legacy of pioneers such as the Thomson Foundation continues in many training programmes, the difference today is that such programmes are wrapped in talk of democracy initiatives, the public sphere and civil society empowerment. Many of these projects take place in conflict situations such as Iraq or the West Bank and Gaza, but the majority fail to mention concepts of conflict resolution, conflict transformation or peace-building.[15] A recent Danish initiative, offering media assistance to transform the Arab public sphere, was typical in not addressing the proposed intervention's peace and conflict implications.[16] This is despite the fact that, with a wealth of conflict resolution literature now available about the impact of outside intervention in conflict situations, development strategists have started to become aware that a peace and conflict impact assessment (PCIA) is needed for all development projects, in just the same

FIGURE 9.1 DEGREE OF APPLICATION OF PEACE-BUILDING CONCEPTS

Traditional training plus

Transformational interventions

Low degree

High degree

way that assessments of gender and environmental impacts are already required. Given these choices and potential shortcomings, it is possible to place projects on a spectrum (Figure 9.1), ranging from those that employ some of the terminology, but are not informed or crafted on the basis of peace-building (low), to those that take full account of the transformational aspects of a new, powerful paradigm for conflict transformation (high). John Burton termed the latter paradigm 'provention'.[17]

The type of project we might call 'traditional training plus' carries on the professional training that has been offered since the 1970s, uses the language of democratisation and civil society empowerment and adds in 'peace' terminology, in a way not found in the democracy/public sphere work.[18] The EU funded projects such as Jemstone and Med Media explicitly because it was said they would support the Israeli–Palestinian peace process and increase mutual understanding and dialogue by bringing journalists together for training.[19] In 2000, for example, the EU reported that it funded Israeli–Palestinian–Jordanian media cooperation to the tune of Euros 2.5 million, to support the peace process. Yet conceptualisation of the media as agent of change in such projects was not fundamentally different from before, since the focus was on change percolating indirectly via empowered media. At the other extreme lie media projects that take to heart Burton's argument that conflict transformation is about developing a whole new approach to societal relations and of being 'proventive' about conflict. Such transformational intervention can be radical, using the media to craft an assault on deep societal structures and conflict behaviours. But few peace-building projects, and even fewer media peace-building projects, have adopted this objective. Those that do, such as some of the work done by Search for Common Ground (SfCG) in the region, have distinctive characteristics. They are informed by a longer-term time horizon for intervention and a clearer calculation of the media's direct agency for structural, behavioural or attitudinal change in conflict. Crucially, they conduct PCIAs.[20]

The challenge for donors is that projects fall into these different types. Some projects talk peace without being informed by conceptual thinking about what peace entails. That may be convenient if commitment to long-term structural change in minority rights in a society has implications for a donor's foreign policy, in that it jeopardises the future of elite groups who happen to be the donor's allies. Commitments to democratisation require forethought about the likely societal conflict that will result from attempts to change structures of power. Such questions have dogged most projects. Indeed, the simplistic and manipulative nature of some interventions can be blamed for the anti-normalisation movement in Jordan and the anti-dialogue stance of many Palestinian NGOs. Moreover, many media intervention projects are really about conflict management (negative peace) rather than conflict transformation (positive peace).[21] The distinction is important, since it shapes the fundamental goals of the intervention. If the EU supports a project to monitor Israeli and Palestinian media for incitement, how will the findings be used? How likely is it that the EU would pressure the Israeli government to caution newspaper editors if researchers were to demonstrate a shift towards demonisation of the Palestinian leadership in their editorials? It might be argued that US funding for a radio station in Baghdad is intended to manage the attitudes of the Baghdad population towards the US-supported interim government. That is different from trying to create a pluralistic society of tolerance and respect for others in order to transform the fundamentals that produce conflict in divided societies. A concern with negative peace is very different from one driven by a commitment to positive peace: the policies proposed, the goals articulated, the resources committed differ dramatically.

Part of this relates back to conflict transformation as an alternative paradigm for society and how it should operate. Some media projects are only tactical in that they back a particular political option (such as the Oslo process or the Road Map), aim at decreasing levels of violence (for example, through programming that sets out to counteract hate radio) or 'managing' behaviour (such as stopping suicide bombers). The alternative is for projects to be strategic and transformational, driven by an underlying sense of the longer term and the hard work required over the next hundred years to produce an alternative society.[22] Work to stop suicide bombings is merely an attempt to manage conflict behaviour. This is inadequate, according to Johan Galtung, because it overlooks the need to change not only behaviour but conflict attitudes and the fundamental structural disparities that have fed a conflict from its beginning.[23]

Projects also fall into different categories according to the media forms they target or employ. Traditional interventions, involving journalists from the print media or radio, employed a narrow definition, relevant to the technology of the time. In the 1970s global training expanded to include television staff, although examples in Arab countries were rare. Today's focus is somewhat broader and includes Internet publishing. In general, however, most media interventions still do not adopt a definition of media that is broad enough to encompass not only television, radio, newspapers and websites but also videos, video games, theatre, soap operas, cartoons, graffiti, infotainment, storytelling and blogs.[24] While most current media interventions in the Arab world focus on traditional media, donors have to decide whether this is an adequate approach. A few have ventured into theatre and video. The EU Partnership for Peace (PfP) Programme supported the production and performance of plays for schoolchildren on the subject of pluralism, and brought Israeli and Arab theatre staff together to produce and perform plays from Beirut to Cairo. It also funded *Sesame Stories* videos, using ideas from the US children's series *Sesame Street* to teach about pluralism and diversity. In one year, 2002, the National Endowment for Democracy funded two Iraqi theatrical productions on the theme of human rights, a website for Iraqi journalists advocating pluralistic media, a periodical for Sudanese writing, a stage play on non-violence targeting Palestinian youth, and a series of Yemeni radio debates on voter education.[25]

Besides the issues of vision and scope, there is a third question for donors about the timing of projects. Historically, third-party interventions in conflict have tended to occur when tension is at its highest, just before violence erupts. Alternatively, they have sought to manage a conflict that has become violent, or struggled to bring a violent conflict to a ceasefire. Today, in contrast, third-party civil society actors are intervening across all phases of conflict, from earliest manifestations to the post-conflict phase. In the view of John Marks, founder of SfCG, different strategies or types of intervention may be called for in each phase.[26] An intervention conducted in the midst of conflict may require armed guards, as HornAfrik, an independent broadcaster in Mogadishu, discovered when it upset warlords by using talk shows to give marginalised groups a voice. Marks suggests a framework based on the three phases of pre-conflict, hot conflict and post-conflict, although more sophisticated typologies exist.[27] In general, however, mainstream donors in the Middle East have paid little attention to projects targeting the full range of phases, being more concerned to use the media to help manage conflicts just before, during and just after violence.[28] As for types of intervention, Marks has also offered a comprehensive typology based around the media-related objectives of any given intervention. He identified five categories.

I. *Rudimentary journalism training*. Here the objective is to end unskilled, inaccurate, highly partisan reporting. Historically, interventions of this type aimed at teaching the importance of fact-checking and objectivity. As a form of media intervention for peace-building, Marks sees this type as raising awareness and creating a culture of best practice.

II. *Building an open media culture.* This type of intervention seeks to create an advanced culture of journalistic accountability, in which journalists rethink their attitudes to their profession. Through work on the legal and regulatory framework, or management training, it also seeks to create a context in which the media can do their job.

III. *Building a culture of peace journalism.* Here the aim is to transform the media into a proactive tool for peace-building. Through peace and conflict assessment sensitisation, re-education and introducing an alternative paradigm, the media develop a new awareness of their own role and contribution, presenting society to itself in a different way.

IV. *Targeting specific problems.* Projects of this type use the media proactively to counter hate speech, educate for elections, warn of landmines, inform about the International Criminal Court and so on, making the media a strong champion for positive change.

V. *Long-term focus on a culture of peace.* In this category, projects aim at the development of sustainable communities, using the media to modify perceptions and teach about diversity and tolerance from an early age. Such projects focus on general, deep issues of empowerment and voice versus invisibility, stereotyping and distorted development.

Types I and II in Marks's typology accord with what Pernille Jørgensen might call 'media assistance' projects[29] and what I, in this chapter, have termed 'traditional training plus'. Types III, IV and V, on the other hand, fit more closely with the notion of 'media intervention', since they are more proactive, and advocate the media as the agency for direct societal transformation.

Although the distinction between assistance and intervention is useful, I would rather distinguish between projects that actually seek some transformation of conflict and those that stick to management and handling. Having done that, it then becomes possible to unpack the degree to which media are seen as agents for transformation, since the mainstream democracy initiatives are unconcerned with this question. Currently there is little blue water between 'traditional training plus' interventions and the new types of training being supported in the Arab world by USAID, for example. All intermingle concepts of democracy, peace and media, often with little clarity as to what the relationships and connections actually are. My alternative approach distinguishes between tactical and strategic initiatives and yields three types of transformational media intervention that can be crafted from peace-building concepts and objectives (Figure 9.2).

• *Type I* applies to projects that seek to empower the media to become an active force for handling and transforming conflict through reflection on the way media function and their role in society. When this reflection takes place, peace journalism emerges.[30] Alvin Toffler contrasted between traditional 'war' approaches and this type of approach, which he termed 'anti-war'.[31] Galtung contrasted between peace journalism and traditional war journalism.[32] Here the media themselves are the target, transformed via intervention into a stronger, more thoughtful, cognisant agent for societal change. This objective requires a very different project from the majority of those currently receiving funding in the Middle East.

• *Type II* interventions make *tactical* use of the media to: handle/mitigate/reverse/transform specific conflict situations, problems or events by providing information where it does not exist, reaching an alternative audience that could otherwise veto change; counteract hate speech or support truth and reconciliation processes in post-conflict situations.

• *Type III* projects see the media as a transforming agent for the fundamentals of conflict (behaviour, attitudes and structure) and seek the *strategic* transformation of society over the long term. Here the goals may be to defuse the isolation felt by minority communities within a society before it breaks out into organised conflict; strengthen local early warning systems; or enhance traditional resolution practices.

WHAT HAS BEEN DONE?

A full range of INGOs, countries and multilateral donors have supported media intervention projects in the Middle East since 1998. The EU, for example, committed over Euros 35 million via the People-to-People Programme (1998–2000) and its successor, the PfP Programme (2002–present), in an attempt to support Middle East peace through civil society activities. Of this total, around Euros 7 million was devoted to funding approximately 18 media projects, covering everything from print journalism, theatre, film and video. The range of objectives included: providing alternative information to the public; encouraging the discussion of

FIGURE 9.2 EVOLVING TYPES OF MEDIA INTERVENTION

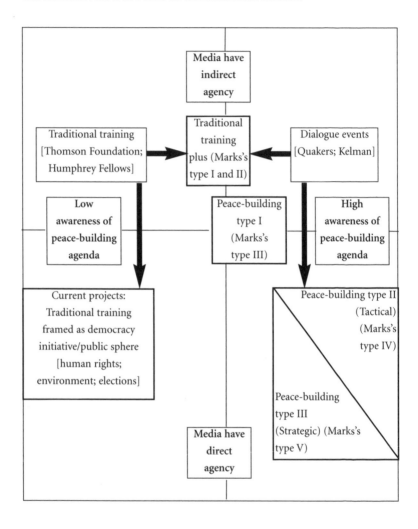

alternative policies; building networks of journalists across regional boundaries; breaking down the isolation and self-justifications of veto groups within conflicting societies; starting new types of media; monitoring hate and distortion so that it can be exposed; supporting creative programming for long-term shifts in attitudes; crafting political support for current political projects for peace; and building a constituency for peace programmes among journalists and managers.

Many EU-funded projects fall into the 'traditional training plus' category. Jemstone, a substantial recipient of funds, combined traditional training with the aim of networking across regional conflict boundaries. A smaller number were serious attempts to empower the media for peace journalism and societal transformation. The bimonthly youth newspaper *Crossing Borders*, attempting to reach young Palestinians, Jordanians and Israelis, had some success in reaching a cadre of engaged youth leaders via reporting and training for journalism as the overt rationale.[33] The EU oeuvre also contained tactical as well as strategic projects. Some were funded because tactically they sought to unblock stalled Israeli–Palestinian negotiations, to help further the consideration of alternatives or to raise the level of public support for the Road Map. Others were strategic, targeting young people who feared 'the other' and found it difficult to put a human face to the enemy.

Other donors have taken up similar issues. SfCG, for example, has crafted projects that were informed by a conflict resolution logic. Some were directed at specific needs where media might make a contribution. Among these was a television series, aired by Abu Dhabi TV as well as Israeli and Palestinian stations, in which Israelis and Palestinians talked about fears, concerns and possible alternatives for final-status issues.[34] Other projects have been concerned with the long-term shifting of values and attitudes that feed conflict in societies.[35] There are several examples of media being targeted in this way. They include projects supported by the UK's Department for International Development (DfID) since 1999;[36] the Panos Institute's work on pluralism in the Middle East since 2002, explicitly linked to conflict prevention and peace-building;[37] or National Public Radio's 'Next Generation Radio' one-day workshop with Algerian women journalists on the role of media in conflict resolution.[38] The list also includes a project by the Noor al-Hussein Foundation in Jordan with a group called Images and Education to employ actors, writers, graphic designers, musicians and puppeteers to create a 'Culture of Peace' programme for Jordanian children.[39] The Ford Foundation has both its 'Public Artist' and 'New Voices, New Visions' projects to support change in the public sphere via the role of artists.[40]

Given the range of initiatives, another avenue into comparing and assessing them would be to adopt a conflict transformation lens in place of the media lens chosen by the typologies discussed above. Adopting this approach means probing whether media interventions are truly aimed at peace-building and what key tasks they need to accomplish if conflict is to be transformed. My review of projects based on these criteria is set out below. It suggests that, of seven possible types of work,[41] all of which are required for the long-term transformation of conflict, some have received more attention than others (Figure 9.3).

TABLE 9.1 A TYPOLOGY OF MEDIA INTERVENTIONS BASED ON CONFLICT TRANSFORMATION OBJECTIVES

Project type	Objectives	Examples
Mutual understanding and dialogue, channelling communication between parties	Create cross-boundary understandings of shared humanity, shared interest in peace, willingness for reconciliation, possibilities of dialogue. Know 'the other' better through dialogue; counteract misperceptions.	*Gesher* newspaper (1986); SfCG workshops for journalists on mutual understanding; EU 'Du-Et' (2005) supplement by Jewish and Palestinian journalists; EU-supported seminar on 'Media and the Conflict' involving Israeli and Palestinian journalists (2005); *Crossing Borders* regional youth newspaper; Seeds of Peace youth magazine *The Olive Branch.*
Peace education	Spread concepts and skills for dealing with conflict and promoting peace widely within communities; embed a 'culture of peace' within key groups (youth, leaders, future leaders, media); train grassroots in peace-building.	Internews project 'Reporting for Humanity' to train young reporters in 'conflict-reducing reporting'; training in diversity reporting by International Federation of Journalists (IFJ) in Maghreb and Palestine (2002–2004); Raoul Wallenberg Institute training for Moroccan journalists on human rights (2003); Seeds of Peace media conference for youth (2003); Democracy Education for journalists from Israel, Jordan and Palestine in Cyprus (2003).
Enhancing societal capacity for doing conflict resolution	Widen the range of mechanisms available in society for handling disputes; empower traditional mechanisms for handling conflict;	SfCG Awards for Journalism; Dubai Press Club journalism awards; USIP professional training in negotiation skills (included some Israeli and Palestinian journalists); USIP

Project type	Objectives	Examples
	embed techniques especially among influential people and decision-makers; increase capabilities to handle and resist conflict at the grassroots; incubate local institutions to fill gaps for sustainable conflict handling; build sustainability in local institutions for peace-building.	professional training in negotiations and conflict resolution for Iraqi women (included some journalists 2004); EU support to put Voice of Power back on air in Israel/Palestine; UNESCO supported conflict resolution training for Lebanese journalists, 2004; National Democratic Institute/SfCG conflict resolution training for Moroccan Press Union.
Empowering marginalised communities (encouraging a balance of power)	Enhance political participation and influence of minority and marginalised groups by empowering their institutions, strengthening their organisational capacity and supporting their cultural identity. Groups under threat need to feel more secure and knowledgeable about themselves so they can participate in peace-building and take risks for peace. Empowering voice, expression of identity, representation of self to 'the other'	Thomson Foundation training in Beirut for regional journalists on reporting social issues (2004); EuroMed training for journalists on gender equality; US AID support for 3rd Arab Women's Media Centre conference (2004); EU support for Qattan Foundations Palestinian cinema project (2004); Ford Foundation projects for artistic production in Palestine and Egypt and audiovisual production in Lebanon; EU supported training on democracy and pluralism for Russian-speaking journalists in Israel; Tamer Institute in Palestine backing a youth-run newspaper and youth radio show.

Project type	Objectives	Examples
	contributes to symmetrical interaction.	
Shifting threat and intimidation	Reduce the threat and intimidation level in order to open up space for equitable win-win engagement. It is not enough to reduce verbal representations of intimidation; there must be a shift to positive alternatives for engagement away from antagonist tactics and strategies of confrontation.	Euro-Med training for media on battling xenophobia (2005); EU support of joint Keshev-Miftah project for monitoring media coverage, incitement and professionalism.
Crafting political space	Enlarge political space for discussion and representation of ideas; encourage consideration of alternatives drawn from local, national and intervention levels; challenge conventional wisdom and top-down-imposed solutions; listen and give voice; help build trust in consultation; craft an area where alternatives are discussed and seen to have a chance of adoption.	IFG MFD-MED for Democracy networks; Article 19 studies on press laws and dialogue with local governments; Friedrich Ebert Foundation training for Algerian journalists on democracy; Center for Media Freedom-MENA 2003 seminar in Casablanca on Revitalizing Media Freedom; SfCG News Service on Conflicts in the region; DfID's Political Participation Fund to improve Iraqi media coverage of elections; USAID community action programme for independent media in Iraq; Reporters Sans Frontières reports on the state of the media.

Project type	Objectives	Examples
Political options work (solution building)	Get decision-makers to consider innovative, outside-the-box alternatives to key political issues that are blocking negotiations; build the data with which to argue for alternatives; provide knowledge and alternative ideas; keep track of changes that threaten the current process; build societal support for difficult choices and decisions; sell the agreement afterwards.	EU supported SfCG five-part TV series on final status issues in Israel and Palestine; EU support for *Bitter Lemons* and *Palestine–Israel Journal*.

Although examples are given here for each of the seven possible types of work, the review as a whole shows that the vast majority of projects funded since 1998 have been directed at dialogue and mutual understanding, peace education, crafting political space and political options work. Many fewer projects sought to empower marginalised communities or to enhance the societal capacity for achieving conflict resolution.[42]

DEPOLITICISED DIALOGUE AND THE 'FEEL GOOD' FACTOR

The bias exposed by this review needs an explanation. Certainly, the attention to dialogue and mutual understanding is understandable: the objective of humanising 'the enemy' and recognising that there is a partner for peace who shares similar interests and fears has long been the core of most traditional conflict resolution activity. Often called people-to-people projects or dialogue, the vast majority of peace activities around the world involve creating cross-boundary understandings of shared humanity; in the discourse of peace, dialogue and 'getting to know you' hold centre stage. Conventional wisdom suggests that this is where progress will first be achieved. But it also offers a less threatening challenge to existing attitudes and behaviour. Such feel-good activities are depoliticised, and may, superficially, appear to be both necessary and sufficient for peace-building.[43] Many of the media interventions in the region have this as their primary objective, which fits well with particular assumptions about the deep source of conflict. If conflict is assumed to be primarily psychological and based on misunderstanding, then dialogue and getting-to-know-you contacts will be seen as key to the management of conflict. Third parties, via media interventions, feel they can then assist by increasing the 'real information' available about the other, bringing antagonists together so they can see into the eyes of the enemy, creating fora in which the humanity of the other can emerge, and then fear and distrust will dissipate. Media projects which provide information, showing the other as grieving or hopeful, attract donors because they fit this view.

A bias towards dialogue sidesteps the deeper, more divisive structural foundations of conflict. In the Israeli–Palestinian case, for example, it allows Israelis to insist that Palestinians accept them long before they themselves address the hard political realities of occupation. Decontextualised mutual understanding activities, delinked from other factors of the conflict, quickly reveal their limited effect. This is one reason why so many Arab and Palestinian groups turned so strongly against normalisation with Israeli in the late 1990s. The kind of dialogue proposed, disconnected from changes in the structural or behavioural causes of conflict, was devalued and hollowed out. Too many donors supported too many media interventions concerned primarily with mutual understanding, often one-offs of feel-good acceptance of diversity that lost any meaning because they took place within a context of despair, violence and political stalemate.

Many early media intervention projects attracted donor funding because they promised to produce mutual understanding by bringing antagonists together across the divide. Questions about how exactly the process was to occur or be sustained were often avoided. The project, mentioned above, to make and broadcast *Sesame Stories*, aimed at encouraging mutual understanding among young children. It was initially developed after the 1993 Oslo Accords but had to be heavily revised and narrowed in scope when the regional climate deteriorated sharply after 1999. Later projects tried to be more sophisticated, with stronger impact assessment calculations and clustered around peace journalism and monitoring incitement. But donor concern with documenting incitement shares a similarly narrow understanding and a focus on outcomes rather than sources of conflict. The EU and USAID have been particularly supportive of such monitoring activities,[44] even though, as demonstrated by the Middle East Media Research Institute, which distributes selective translations from the Arab press, they can be used as a political tool.

In contrast, interventions such as the EU support for *Bitter Lemons* on the Internet, or the 'Du-Et' insert in newspapers, or financing for the *Palestine–Israel Journal*, were concerned not only with providing alternative information, so as to break through the barriers of ignorance, but also with consideration of alternative political options.

The biases discussed here share much with those of the democracy projects in the region. Attention is placed on outputs and forms of interaction by citizens with the government or people to people rather than on the process of reciprocity and power distribution in society. The difficult task of actually mapping and assessing conflict is squeezed out by a preoccupation with the mutual understanding of individuals and talk about democratic ideals. Donors have shown only limited concern with the more problematic and complex aspects of peace-building, such as the specific inclusion of excluded minorities (beyond gender), the building of sustainable conflict resolution institutions and processes within communities, or that of long-term development.[45]

RESULTS OF IRRESPONSIBILITY

In the evaluations of global media interventions for conflict resolution that emerged after 2000, a number of key themes and recommendations repeatedly appeared. These advised planning on the basis of peace and conflict impact assessments; incorporating local expertise; committing to long-term support; linking media interventions into broader sets of transformational projects; avoiding consultants who 'parachute' in; and thinking in terms of transforming conflict situations, not just managing them. Such recommendations appear to have played little role in the planning, logistics and evaluation of recent media interventions in the Arab world. Donor staff remain unfamiliar with the extensive literature available from either civil society conflict resolution or best practice for media intervention. There are few codes of conduct or frameworks for intervention developed by donors to guide projects. Project portfolios have been accumulated in an unorganised and ad hoc manner, without evaluating the strategic vision of media interventions that framed the activities. Traditional delivery techniques of one-off workshops continue to dominate training approaches, disconnected from related activities where multiplier effects could be gained. The scramble to offer media training in the region has produced competition for monies, duplication of effort, a dependency culture and distraction for media staff. Evaluation procedures remain focused on technical requirements and measurement of outputs instead of being informed by PCIA perspectives.

Although measuring impact in such circumstances remains problematic, there are few clear signs that the enormous effort expended has had anywhere near the projected effect.[46] Certainly, individual participants at workshops have crossed borders and mutual understanding has resulted; struggling local institutions concerned with peace-building have acquired a skill set that will facilitate sustainability; and local media staff have been exposed to new approaches, with some actually able to undertake peace journalism. Data have been collected on incitement; new instruments for understanding the 'other' have appeared; local elites are now more cognisant of peace-building activities within civil society; and there are cross-border networks of young journalists that did not previously exist. Such projects have expanded peace-building activity in the Arab world, challenged conventional wisdom and focused attention on the new Arab media and what it could or should do in Arab society. Ultimately, however, it is the gap between promise and reality that is most disappointing. Realistically speaking, media interventions for peace-building do have the potential to produce a wide range of significant effects and impact, both in the short and long term. Yet failure of vision, distorted objectives and unquestioned assumptions have delivered meagre results. A donor preference for dialogue over structural transformation and an idealised vision of the media and its capabilities are partly to blame. The political agenda found in the Middle East Partnership Initiative and the related military goal of stabilisation produce a concern with conflict management rather than long-term conflict transformation.[47] Bias towards managing the Israeli–Palestinian conflict rather than transforming it colours work across the whole region. Since cultural imperialism has been sufficiently identified as a key risk of such interventions, it is irresponsible for donors to enter situations of open conflict without proper guidelines, clear strategic objectives framed by conflict transformation, transparency and local involvement.[48]

One fundamental problem is that the media are viewed more from the perspective of challenging the state, as a corrective to the 'fierce' states of the Arab world, or a prophylactic against state power than as an instrument for change. Donors tend to adopt the state/civil society dichotomy, with the media seen as key players in that tension. This state-centric, neo-liberal agenda colours project approval and development, and points media interventions, whether of the democracy initiative type or those framed by peace terminology, towards some tasks of peace-building but not others. In this view, strong internal processes and civil society institutions are deemed capable of handling conflict, the source of which is said to be the fierce state that is not constrained. It is a view that ignores additional factors that lead to conflict, such as regional and international forces, structural asymmetry, repression and denial of identity. Ultimately, donors have yet to make the shift from such 'theories of power' as the foundation for their policies (prevention) to a process-oriented transformational understanding in which problem-solving (provention) becomes the modus operandi for a holistic attack on societal conflict. Without such a shift, media interventions for peace are liable to become part of the problem, not part of the solution.[49]

CONCLUSION

The Arab media do have a major contribution to make to the transformation of protracted social conflict. And third-party interventions could play a role in this process, although we can anticipate that, over the medium term, they will remain significantly moulded by interest group objectives, ad hoc logistics, mistakes and circumstance.[50] But media interventions can also be shaped by appropriate strategic visions, so that the positive power of the media is unleashed rather than constrained in narrow parochial paths and left to disappear into the sand. Hegemonic control over the Arab public sphere is not an appropriate strategic vision; donors and other outsiders need another understanding of their role and objectives. Democracy, peace, conflict management, a strong civil society, media development, counteracting incitement: these are not ends to be achieved but, rather, the outcomes of processes of reciprocity and problem-solving to be nurtured within societies. A culture of peace does not spring, *deus ex machina*, from dialogue, but from informed, sustained, creative attention to the structural, attitudinal and behavioural components of conflict. The role of third parties is to support local processes and actors crafting for themselves procedures and institutions to handle and transform the inevitable conflicts, whether within or across boundaries, that will arise. Within an evolving Middle East, the media then become a facilitator for the articulation of problem-solving options within a region desperately in need.

- 10 -

In Search of the Arab Present
Cultural Tense

Tarik Sabry

If one is to ask an Arabic speaking intellectual to-day: What are the motivations and ends of Arab contemporary culture, he would feel perplexed as to the motivations, but would immediately answer for the ends by saying: they are to revive our religious Arab history, they are to cement the foundations of Arab nationalism and Arab unity.[1]

I count myself fortunate to have attended the seminar series from which the chapters in this book are drawn. The series, on the changing media landscape in the Arab region, took place in London over a period of two years.[2] I listened with great interest to more than 30 papers by scholars from all parts of the world, all of which, in my view, contributed something new and interesting. The series explored the relevance of Jürgen Habermas's normative concept of the public sphere to Arab media and the media's role in the reshaping of contemporary culture and society in the Arab world. The papers sparked challenging and critical questions, often leading to heated debate.

Throughout the series I was very much interested in the spatial and temporal situatedness – the 'where' and 'when' – of what was being said about Arab media and society and by whom. The question 'by whom?' is one that deals with narration in the sense of who narrates, in what way and from what position. Despite its importance, the question of narration is one I am prepared to suppress here so that I can turn my attention to what I believe to be far more important and pressing issues. By the 'when and where' deixis, I refer to the spatiality and temporality of the scholarly work presented in the series. In dealing with the 'where and when' of what was said, I hope to engage in a meta-series discussion, with the aim of providing a platform for continuity and further debate on the topic of

Arab media, culture and society. As I reflected on the series and its content, I became more and more preoccupied with questions of an epistemological nature, the most persistent being: how does the cultural material that was presented in the series relate to and inform 'contemporary' articulations (both sociological and philosophical) on Arab culture and society? Other ways to ask this question are: what are our points of reference for what was said, and to what epistemic space 'paradigm' did the series contribute? What do we call it? How do we connect it to the existing body of intellectual work on Arab culture(s) and society? Here I am not concerned with the question 'for whom are we writing?', as this was famously – or, perhaps, infamously – dealt with in Ahmad Aijaz's critique of postcolonial theory and its main intellectuals.[3] Instead, the questions I pose seem to lie at the heart of a crisis that is deeply seated not only in Arab 'culture' but also in prevalent modes of Arab reasoning.

A meaningful articulation of the media's role in the construction of a democratic Arab public sphere cannot take shape outside a 'thick' understanding of contemporary Arab culture and society. Such an articulation requires us to build epistemological bridges to problematics inherent to contemporary Arab thought. Habermas's 'public sphere' did not come from nowhere, and its articulation as a normative concept was no accident but a long and continuous philosophical argument that can be easily traced to Jean-Jacques Rousseau, or even Plato. Habermas's work is part of a continuous search for a rational society. The search continues. To make connections between what can be said today about Arab media, culture and society, and contemporary Arab thought, I turn to what is perhaps the most important and influential Arab and Islamic philosophical treatise of the twentieth century, namely *A Critique of Arab Reason* by the Arab philosopher Mohammed Abed Jabri. Drawing on Jabri's work, I explore in this chapter three epistemological deficits in Arab reason[4] today, which stand in the way of developing a contemporary and relevant cultural repertoire that is able to document, examine and communicate the 'cultural' as it is lived, experienced and thought in the present tense of Arab cultures. These, the chapter will argue, are inherent to: the problematic structure of what Jabri calls 'Arab reason'; the problem of the unconscious in Arab cultural temporality; and Arab intellectuals' ceaseless undermining of the 'popular' in Arab cultures. The chapter also investigates what might be learnt from the ongoing project of internationalising the field of cultural studies as a way to support the search for the Arab present cultural tense.

THE 'STRUCTURE OF "ARAB REASON"'

Making use of work by André Lalande,[5] Jabri distinguishes between two kinds of reason. One is 'la raison constituante' (Arabic: *al-aql al-mukawin*), which refers to the mental activity that creates knowledge, constructs meanings and decides on rules and principles. The second is 'la raison constituée' (Arabic: *al-aql al-mukawan*), referring to reason that is already constituted and which encompasses a whole repertoire, including the arts and sciences.[6] Lalande defines the latter as 'the reason that exists, as it is, in a given moment ... what it is in our civilization and epoch ... we should also say in our profession'.[7] This, he adds, 'presents us with two characteristics of great importance'. 'On the one hand it assures the cohesion of a group, more or less large, that claims its ownership; ... on the other hand, it can also be posed as an absolute by all those who have not yet acquired' what Lalande calls 'l'esprit critique nécessaire'.[8] It is the dialectical relationship between these two categories of reason, argues Jabri, that determines cultural repertoires and ways of reasoning. Jabri attributes Arab reason's regression over the last 600 years to its preoccupation with reproducing the old ('raison constituée') rather than creating the new. Jabri argues that the death of philosophy (critical reason) as a project precipitated stagnation in Arab thought. This imbalance in the structure of Arab reason has in turn led to confusion in Arab cultural temporality, or what Jabri describes as 'unconscious cultural temporality'.[9]

ARAB CULTURAL TEMPORALITY

How does Jabri articulate the problematic of 'unconscious time' in Arab culture? Using Jean Piaget's concept of 'l'inconscient cognitif', he calls for a structural reorganisation of the parts or phases of Arab cultural temporality, so that it can function in a linear fashion.[10] He shows how the structure of reason shares the same temporality with the culture to which it belongs. As such, he argues that Arab reason's temporality is also the temporality of Arab culture. In the case of Arab culture, and unlike European cultural temporality, argues Jabri, the old and the contemporary coexist on the same stage. Hence the confusion in Arab cultural temporality.[11]

> The temporal in recent Arab cultural history is stagnant ... for it does not provide us with a development of Arab thought and its movement from one state to another; instead, it presents us with an exhibition or a market of past cultural products, which co-exist in the same temporality as the new, where the old and new become contemporaries. The outcome

is an overlapping between different cultural temporalities in our conception of our own cultural history... This way, our present becomes an exhibition of our past, and we live our past in our present, without change and without history.[12]

The relationship between the old and the new, argues Jabri, is unconscious, as what we forget of culture does not simply vanish, but stays in the unconscious. In this case, reason as an epistemological tool produces and is constructed in 'an unconscious way'.[13] To illuminate this, Jabri presents the contemporary Arab intellectual as a migrant through cultural time, who is able to change positions swiftly from Right to Left, from socialism to democracy, and from Islamism to secularism.[14] Besides this overlapping in Arab cultural temporality, Jabri adds that the spatial and the temporal also overlap. Arab cultural history, he argues, 'is more connected to the spatial than it is to the temporal: our cultural history is the history of Kufa, Basra, Damascus, Baghdad, Cairo, Granada, Fez... which makes it a history of cultural islands'.[15]

To link these epistemological issues to the topic of Arab media, culture and society, let me give some examples from two relatively recent pieces of work. One is an article by Muhammad Ayish entitled 'Beyond Western-oriented communication theories: A normative Arab-Islamic perspective', published in 2003. The other, by Basyouni Hamada, entitled 'Islamic culture theory', appeared in 2001. Both articles strive to re-articulate or rethink Arab and Islamic media and communication, making use of a theoretical framework that draws on cultural particularities that can be said to be distinctively and inherently Arab and Islamic. In doing so, the articles play an important role in de-westernising media and communication theory. On the one hand, Ayish provides us with an interesting and insightful analysis that theorises Arab-Muslim communications and their audiences, while tracing and making use of characteristics inherent to Arab heritage that date back to the *jahiliya* (the period pre-dating Islam). Hamada, on the other hand, adduces what he considers to be a coherent set of Islamic cultural principles, which he recommends as a normative framework for the governance of the media in a 'just' and democratic Islamic society.[16] Hamada's point of reference is Islam, and particularly the Quran, a text that satisfies (and in fact preaches) all the prerequisite elements recommended by the author to guarantee a democratic Islamic 'public sphere'. These are: the right to know; the right to choose belief and behaviour; the right to read; the right to write; the right to power; the right to choose one's government; freedom to express opinion; and the right to criticise an unjust ruler.[17] The implication is that, with such empowering cultural foundations (were they only practised), the work of Habermas and a whole repertoire of Western thought on the relationship between media and society becomes superfluous. Both authors' attempts to de-westernise media and communication theory – and, in Hamada's case, to formulate an Islamic *Shura*-based public sphere – are useful. However, at the root of their analyses lies an implied definition of 'Islamic culture' that needs unearthing. What does the term 'culture' refer to in the context of 'Islamic culture theory'? Notwithstanding the importance of the Quran and the inspiration it provides for theorising a humane, just and democratic culture, it is important to acknowledge that, for such a theory to function, it is necessary that the category 'culture' is taken out of its discourse. It has to be re-articulated so that it is informed not only by the timeless and the sacred but also by an ontologically time-based world, and a 'culture' that is driven not only by the sacred but also by that which is profane, everyday: the ontological. A reworking of the idea of Arab and Islamic culture is fundamental and should precede all attempts at theorising media, culture and society in the Arab and Islamic worlds.

The following extract from Raymond Williams's analysis of George Orwell's work encapsulates what I mean when referring to the broadening of the notion of 'culture'. Williams writes of Orwell: 'He went to books, and found in them the detail of virtue and truth. He went to experience, and found in it the practice of loyalty, tolerance and sympathy. But in the end,' Williams continues, quoting directly from Orwell's novel, *Nineteen Eighty-Four*,

> it was a bright cold day in April, and the clocks were striking thirteen. Winston Smith, his chin nuzzled into his breast in an effort to escape the vile wind, slipped quickly through the glass doors of Victory Mansions, though not quickly enough to prevent a swirl of gritty dust from entering along with him.[18]

Williams writes of the dust that

> it is part of the case: the caustic dust carried by the vile wind. Democracy, truth, art, equality, culture: all these we carry in our heads, but, in the street, the wind is everywhere. The great and humane tradition is a kind of wry joke; in the books it served, but put them down and look around you. It is not so much a disillusion, it is more like our actual world.[19]

It is this grittiness in culture, the ordinary, the everyday, the profane, that must be articulated, and not only what Matthew Arnold once described as 'the *best* knowledge and thought of the time'.[20] What is required, in our pursuit of the present cultural tense in the Arab world, is a re-articulation of culture, where the concept denotes not only a fixed set of values but also a system of relations, which takes into account the gritty nature of lived experience (the social) as well as the best that has been written and said. Re-articulating the concept of culture so that it draws from the present tense of Arab cultures is a way of dealing with and changing what the present of Arab cultures holds. Change in cultural temporality, however, does not happen with time, for it is not time that brings change but what we put in it. As Immanuel Kant said, 'It is not temporality itself that changes, but something that is in it.'[21] This observation leads to the third epistemological deficit: that of Arab intellectuals' ceaseless undermining of the 'popular' in Arab cultures.

ELITIST INTERPRETATIONS OF CULTURE

Arab intellectuals' interpretations of culture are largely elitist. With few exceptions and without exaggeration, their 'take' on culture can be compared to those of the Spanish philosopher José Ortega y Gasset,[22] Matthew Arnold[23] and other modernists who could not hide their abomination for the masses and their ordinary cultures.[24] Arab intellectuals are, in general, more aristocratic than the aristocracy. Arab popular culture, for example, is still considered by many prominent and influential Arab intellectuals to be profane, unconscious, irrelevant and consequently unworthy of study. This view is symptomatic of the vast majority of Arab intellectuals, who constantly downgrade colloquial Arabic and for whom, to use Orwell's analogy, what goes on in the vile and gritty wind – the *souq* (marketplace), *makha* (café), the television pop music contest – is classified as profane. Therefore, all that is *shaabi* (of the people), be it music, television programmes or just ordinary everyday experience, remains largely under-examined. The phrase the 'Arab street', commonly used by Arab media and Arab intellectuals, reflects this elitist stance and its distance from the majority of the population. Why should there be an Arab street where there is no talk of a European, American or Indian street? The constant massification and homogenisation of Arab audiences into this redundant term – 'the street' – is proof of a major lack of understanding about how complex and stratified audiences are. 'There are in fact,' as Williams put it, 'no masses; there are only ways of seeing people as masses.'[25] There is today no substantial research using empirical methods to examine how Arab audiences interact with the media or to investigate the relationship between Western media consumption and the dynamics of imperialism. Audience research in the Arab world is fragmentary and largely underdeveloped.[26] This chapter does not permit lengthy exploration of the reasons for this.

Suffice it to say, that unlike their counterparts in Western countries, especially the UK, Arab academics have not yet grasped the need for a coherent field of cultural studies, let alone begun to develop such a field. There are no cultural studies in the Arab world as such, only fragmented works in the area, which remain largely unconscious parts of an incoherent whole. This inadequacy has wider implications for the poverty of audience research in the Arab world, most of which is quantitative, commercially driven and tells us hardly anything about who Arab audiences are or how they interact with and read media texts. It is important to add, as Jon Alterman has noted, that even the quantitative data emerging from surveys on Arab audiences 'tend to be developed for marketing studies, and thus concentrate on wealthier populations and remain proprietary'.[27] What is required is qualitative research with the potential for investigating the social world of Arab audiences and their interpretations of it.

In dealing with the threat of cultural imperialism, Arab scholars too often take audiences for granted. Jabri argues for the importance of understanding 'the phenomenon of cultural "infiltration", not only as an outside action, moved by a desire for hegemony, but also through the negative implications it has for our present cultural reality'.[28] 'Cultural infiltration,' he adds 'is in principle an infiltration of identity.'[29] Rather than unpacking how this infiltration actually takes place, Jabri moves directly to remedy.

> The answer to the question what can be done? [...] is to work inside our culture by renewing it from within. The beginning is to understand this 'inside' by reorganizing its parts so it is re-connected to us and we are reconnected with it in a modern and contemporary way.[30]

The reason we need to start work from within 'our culture', Jabri argues, is because, 'were it not for its weakness, the action [cultural infiltration] coming from without could not have carried out its effects in a way which makes it a danger'.[31] Jabri's proposition, albeit genuine and stirring, tells us absolutely nothing about where and how cultural infiltration occurs. Nor does it deal with the kind of channels that facilitate it. Arab scholars[32] have generally dealt with 'cultural imperialism' as a taken-for-granted phenomenon, its conclusiveness never brought into question, so that we are never told empirically how this 'effect' or 'action' takes place. This uniform approach gives rise to serious concern, for it seems to render superfluous any empirical enquiry into the implications of imperialism for Arab culture and structures of feeling. The danger in this line of thinking is that it risks, unwittingly, masking the very dynamics of imperialism it purports to understand.

INTERNATIONALISING CULTURAL STUDIES AND THE PROBLEM
OF TRANSLATION

The working out of the idea of culture in the Arab world has to be seen as a process, an ongoing intellectual project that is ready to accept and deal with the three problematics described above. However, this reworking of the idea of culture also requires a space where the study of contemporary culture can become a legitimised scientific practice, a space where 'culture' as a category is re-articulated and unpicked as the product of a system of relations, and as a 'process, not a conclusion'.[33] Such space must also allow for 'an articulated expression ... of new forms of aesthetics in Arab cultures'.[34] As for the urgent and pertinent questions of how such an intellectual project might be possible, and under what epistemological umbrella it would operate, Jabri's answer to the problems of Arab 'reason' is a return to rationality through the vehicle of philosophy. He has taken up the immense task of retracing where the Arab philosophical project was abandoned, by revisiting and reworking the contribution of Ibn Rushd (known in the West as Averroes). In this manner, Jabri hopes not only to resuscitate the project of rationality in the Arab and Islamic worlds but also to reconcile the past with the present.

While a return to the philosophical project is clearly indispensable in dealing with the deficits that Jabri identifies, other intellectual disciplines must also be allowed to work towards the same purpose. Philosophy alone is not enough. The question is really one of hermeneutics: upon what basis do we reinterpret Arab cultures and societies today? I propose that we base our reinterpretation on the social and the cultural, and, since the existential precedes both the social and the cultural, perhaps the existential should also be added as a third category. These three categories or determinants would form the basis upon which we can rely in our search for the present tense of Arab cultures. The articulation of these categories would take place under a new field of research that, unlike sociology, has yet to be fully introduced to the Arab world. This is the field of cultural studies. The latter is better equipped than philosophy or sociology to deal with questions concerning contemporary Arab cultures and the temporalities within which they operate. It would be naïve to think that such a field will have the effect of a magic ring, which has only to be touched for all the problems of Arab thought to vanish. But what cultural studies will guarantee, if added to Arab university curricula, is space for a whole new body of intellectual work on contemporary Arab cultures and societies.

The field of cultural studies is, above all, an epistemic space that situates the category of culture at the centre of its enquiry. It is not a 'fixed body of thought that can be transported from one place to another, and which operates in similar ways in diverse national or regional contexts'.[35] Cultural studies can be moulded and reshaped to adapt to different historical and cultural situations. As Ien Ang and David Morley have argued, the place and relevance of cultural studies 'varies from context to context, and has to be related to the specific character of local forms of political and intellectual discourse on culture'.[36] There are literally hundreds of studies, textbooks and articles on cultural studies as a paradigm and field of study, many of which revisit its beginnings in Britain after the Second World War, emphasising the role of the Centre for Contemporary Cultural Studies at Birmingham University and its intellectuals, of whom Stuart Hall was a leading figure, in shaping this distinct and relatively new project. So much has been written, in fact, that I see no need to retell the story. Here, instead, I am more interested in shedding light on the internationalisation of cultural studies, including the problem of translation and whether cultural studies, as an episteme, can be of use in our pursuit of the present cultural tense in Arab cultures.

Cultural studies have been defined as a radical project, a movement, a fashion, and sometimes, because of its interdisciplinary nature and boundless intellectual geography, simply as 'nobody-knows-anymore'. Since the 1980s it has managed to migrate to other parts of the world. Yet the term usually evokes the British, Australian, American or European incarnations of cultural studies, restricting the field's geography mainly to the West.[37] Regardless of its claim to internationalisation, Ang and Morley observed at the end of the 1980s that it remained 'largely restricted to the developed world, reflecting the fact that it is in the West that the cultural dimension of politics has been foregrounded, as a result of transformations in the social formation brought about by post-industrial and post-Fordist capitalism'.[38] One of the distinctive characteristics of cultural studies is 'its desire to transgress established disciplinary boundaries and to create new forms of knowledge and understanding not bound by such boundaries'.[39] It is the 'open-ended and experimental nature of cultural studies that guarantees its distinctiveness...as a particular discursive formation and intellectual practice'.[40] Interviewed by Kuan-Hsing Chen, Stuart Hall emphasises the need to increase the overlap rather than police the boundaries of cultural studies.[41] But Jon Stratton and Ien Ang argue that these qualities hide an implied 'unproblematic liberal pluralism'; they point out that cultural studies are 'not exempt from power relations'.[42] Ackbar Abbas and John Nguyet Erni express similar concerns in the introduction to their anthology on internationalising cultural studies, stating that a certain parochialism continues to operate in cultural studies as a whole, whose objects of and language for analysis have had the effect of closing off real contact with scholarship conducted outside its (western) radar screen. In the current moment of what we call 'the postcolonial predicament' of cultural studies, in which a broad hegemony of western modernity is increasingly being questioned among cultural studies scholars from around the world, we must consider any form of internationalisation as an effort – and a critical context – for facilitating the visibility, transportability, and translation of works produced outside North America, Europe and Australia.[43]

Their attempt to de-westernise cultural studies is, in their own words, 'a political and intellectual intervention into a state of unevenness in the flow and impact of knowledge' within the field.[44] In this context, the internationalisation of cultural studies is not regarded as the propagation of another universal body of knowledge such as sociology, for example, that is legitimised through Western discourse,[45] but as a resistance to universalism and intellectual imperialism.

What an Arab cultural studies project might look like, or how it may develop, is difficult to predict. What is clear is that, with the body of intellectual work on Arab culture and society already at hand, Arab cultural studies will quickly establish unique characteristics and particularities. However, national or cultural differentiations and distinctiveness must not be the basis upon which a whole intellectual project is defined. It is not the 'Britishness' or 'Englishness' of cultural studies that defines the field, but its radical re-thinking of the relationship between culture and society. Similarly, it is not the 'Arabness' of cultural studies that should define its intellectual agenda, but the opposite. When asked to elaborate on the internationalisation of cultural studies and the problem of translation, Hall replied:

I use 'translation' in quotation marks…translation as a continuous process of re-articulation and re-contextualisation, without any notion of a primary origin…[W]henever it [cultural studies] enters a new cultural space, the terms change; and, exactly as you find in any re-articulation and disarticulation some elements remain the same, because there clearly are certain points, certain terms and concepts in common, but then there are also new elements which change the configuration.[46]

The appropriation of 'British' cultural studies in different locales has largely been influenced by local cultural particularities. Ang and Morley observed in 1989 that, in the Netherlands, for example, cultural studies had been most influential in departments of education, where Paul Willis's 1977 study of anti-school culture had found more resonance than Dick Hebdige's 1979 study of subculture, which offered a 'less institutionally-focused emphasis on the politics of style'.[47] The explanation, Ang and Morley suggested, lay in the fact that, 'from a generalised social democratic perspective, interest in forms of cultural resistance is cast in the desire to (better) *teach* "the people", not to learn from popular experiences'.[48] Notwithstanding the importance of re-articulation and translation as necessary intellectual processes, some elements must remain the same. In Hall's words, cultural studies are '*always* about the articulation – in different contexts … between culture and power'.[49] It is, if anything, this relationship that needs to be maintained for Arab cultural studies to be credible. Indeed, maintaining such credibility depends on the ability to articulate and assess not only the dynamics of power, as they emerge in the cultural text, but also the economic structures that govern and influence cultural production in the Arab world. What I am trying to emphasise here is the importance of political economy, which should not necessarily be seen as an oppositional paradigm, as is the case in the West, but as a complementary one that enhances our understanding of cultural production in the Arab region.

An Arab cultural studies project may be critiqued or rejected on a number of premises. Here, I content myself with addressing just two. One is that, since Arab societies have not undergone the same historical conditions that influenced and shaped the cultural studies project in the West, cultural studies' applicability as a paradigm is questionable. The second is that the dominant paradigm in cultural studies interprets the world as a social and cultural phenomenon and alienates the existential aspect, which would make it problematic to translate in a world-structure where experience is determined first and foremost through the existential. While it is a truism that the historical conditions that shaped cultural studies in the West have no parallels in the Arab world, or, indeed, the rest of the world, it can be argued that, under the auspices of globalisation and its ceaselessly homogenising machinery, the world is increasingly – despite ongoing fragmentary resistance in some parts of it – a homogeneous place. By 'homogeneity', I refer to the spread and globalisation of institutions of modernity. How the world reacts to the latter is a different question altogether. What is clear, however, is that globalisation has made our world more connected. Needless to say, this does not suggest evenness or balance. On the contrary, our world is one of unevenness and imbalance. The historical conditions that inspired change in the Western conception of culture are now compensated for by the relentless globalisation of modernity and its institutions. This perhaps justifies the call by Abbas and Erni for an internationalist paradigm of cultural studies that tackles not only local but also global and trans-local issues.[50]

The Arab world is, like the rest of the global South, subject to the dynamics of the global capitalist order and its hegemonic culture. As such, I do not see the 'historical' argument as an obstacle. As for the problem of the dominant paradigm in cultural studies, the answer lies simply in translation and re-appropriation. The hermeneutics upon which Arab cultural studies rely in the future to give meaning to the world and our experience in it should account for the 'social', the 'cultural' and the 'existential'. The last category is crucial not only to appeal to, or be inclusive of religious and other discourses, but also because its omission will make it difficult for us to think outside the 'social' and the 'cultural'. That would be limiting and go against Lalande's and Jabri's ideal of 'l'esprit critique nécessaire'. Paddy Scannell, who has no interest in propagating any type of religiosity, puts it succinctly in his critique of British cultural studies' hermeneutics.

> Is 'life' (human existence) then, coterminous with the social? Is human being more or less equivalent to social being? Is 'man' a 'social animal', and if so, is that the most fundamental thing about him? I do not want to rush to the bluntly obvious answer. Rather, to pose this question is to ask (obliquely) whether or not sociology and cultural studies have an 'outside'. More exactly, can they think outside of themselves? If there is no outside of the social/cultural 'in thought' then thought cannot imagine human being as anything other than the socio-cultural. Social being is an intimate aspect of the being that I, in each case, have. But it is not definitive of that being. 'Life' is not so much a more encompassing term than society/ culture. Rather it is earlier than such terms.[51]

ARAB CULTURAL STUDIES AND THE POSTCOLONIAL QUESTION

Even though most Arab societies are postcolonial societies, the postcolonial question is seldom posed in the Arab world today in relation to the identity and structures of feeling of Arabs. It is as if the aftermath of colonialism had washed away completely, or perhaps Albert Memmi's long-awaited 'new man' had finally arrived: 'The colonized lives for a long time before we see that really new man.'[52] Unfortunately, neither has happened. Arab society, whether in the Maghreb, the Mashreq or the Gulf, is very much a postcolonial society, and, apart from a limited amount of literary work on the topic, we still know very little about the ways in which imperialism has altered the ordinariness of culture and structures of feeling in the region.

There have been many attempts at defining the term 'postcolonialism'. The authors of the seminal work *The Empire Writes Back* used the term 'postcolonial' to cover 'all the culture affected by the imperial process from the moment of colonisation to the present day'.[53] Robert Young defines the term as a 'dialectical concept that marks the broad historical facts of decolonisation and the determined achievement of sovereignty – but also the realities of nations and peoples emerging into a new imperialistic context of economic and sometimes political domination'.[54] For Leela Gandhi it is 'a theoretical resistance to the mystifying amnesia of the colonial aftermath'.[55] What we understand from these brief definitions is that postcolonialism and the postcolonial period extend to the present, and that they ought to 'cover' and 'mark' not only the history of colonialism but the *now* and present material 'realities' of postcolonised peoples throughout the world. Postcolonial theory has been critiqued for its lack of political agency,[56] as it puts more emphasis on deconstructing the complexities of the 'post-colonial' text than on the 'post-colonial' subject per se, whose condition and material realities it ought to be representing. Rather than being a 'theory of resistance' against the 'amnesia of the aftermath of colonialism', postcolonial theory is accused of rendering 'non-western knowledge and culture as "other" in relation to the normative "self" of western epistemology and rationality'.[57] I take issue with postcolonial theory, but not principally because of its choice of methods of analysis, for I think that adhering to determination and human agency as the 'motors of history' is as important as theorising 'entrapment', 'in-betweenness', 'alienation', 'dislocation' or 'hybridity'. Rather, my own objection lies in postcolonial theory's nonchalant privileging of complex 'post-colonial' texts over the 'real' material conditions and 'realities' which govern and influence the lives of the real, living and breathing postcolonial subject. Silencing subalterns, under the pretext that they cannot speak, positions the postcolonial theorist as their immediate speaker. This role has been effected without much care for listening to what subalterns can tell us, which in turn deepens the fissure between the postcolonised and the theorist; it abstracts the field further from material realities of the postcolonial. My answer to the question 'Can the subaltern speak?'[58] is 'Yes, but have we listened to him?' To speak of the 'subaltern' in a homogeneous fashion masks material realities within postcolonial societies. There is in fact no subaltern but 'subalterns', whose consciousness and structures of feeling are not the mere product of colonialism but also the product of internal power dynamics and social relations inherent to their postcolonial societies. For us to understand, for example, the postcolonial consciousness of young Arabs today, it is imperative that we also examine power dynamics within Arab societies.

In the same vein, while postcolonial theory's preoccupation with concepts of 'hybridity, creolisation, *mestizaje*, in-betweenness, diasporas and liminality'[59] has enriched the field of cultural studies in Western academy, these concepts remain abstractions, for they never come with empirical evidence nor real points of reference to support them. As we learn from Homi Bhabha, the concept of 'hybridity' as a 'third space' has no empirical foundation to support it, for how does one purport to understand a hybrid state of consciousness if the structure of the latter has not been put to the empirical test? Using a metaphor from the African-American artist Renée Green, Bhabha remarks:

> The stairwell as liminal space, in-between the designations of identity, becomes the process of symbolic interaction, the connective tissue that constructs the difference between upper and lower, black and white. The hither and thither of the stairwell, the temporal movement and passage that it allows, prevents identities at either end of it from settling into primordial polarities. The interstitial passage between fixed identifications opens up the possibility of a cultural hybridity that entertains difference without an assumed or imposed hierarchy.[60]

If this passage means that postcolonial consciousness is complex and problematic, I have no qualms that it is. But then what? What does it tell us about the so-called 'in-between' that can further our understanding of postcolonial consciousness? What other 'identities' are prevented from 'settling into primordial polarities'? What is this 'symbolic interaction' that takes place in the liminal space? What is the nature of its dialectical mechanisms? What are the 'fixed identifications' that Bhabha talks about? I am confused by Bhabha's passage because I do not understand what it has to do with the material realities of the 'postcolonial' and its structures of feeling. It seems to be an example of the many ways in which the postcolonial 'subject' is objectified, reified, theorised and then put on display in, to borrow the words of Mohamed Gassous, the ontological museum of the different, for the consumption of the sympathetic gaze of the Western reader.[61]

THE ROAD AHEAD

Bhabha avoids tackling the 'real' nature of dynamics at play within the 'third space' or the 'in-betweenness' he is at pains to describe. Perhaps, instead of a 'third space', there is continuous struggle. If that is the case, the concept of hybridity underwrites the very injustices of imperialism by masking the many complexes from which postcolonised consciousness suffers. The ways in which Bhabha theorises hybridity mask the dialectics of imperialism. Since we can no longer afford to theorise the postcolonial in abstraction, I am hoping that, in dealing with the postcolonial question, Arab cultural studies will encourage an empirical and interdisciplinary approach. Edward Said warned that postcolonial discourse analysis risked 'falling into a premature "slumber" if it did not continue to develop'.[62] In dealing with the postcolonial question, Arab cultural studies cannot afford to ignore the latest crucially important terrain of capitalism: cultural production and the relationship between the colonisation of communication space and postcolonial identity. An understanding of the postcolonial through theory, if it is to gain any potency at all, needs to be complemented by empirical research, investigating the structures of feeling of people living in postcolonial societies. If it is to succeed, research of this kind needs to incorporate bold and innovative methodological strategies. Arab cultural studies already exist, but only as fragments without coherence or any sense of direction. The studies are there in the form of isolated journal articles, books and doctoral theses, but they are not conscious of themselves. This body of intellectual work cannot form a coherent intellectual project unless it embodies an epistemic space in which it can operate and develop paradigms, and unless it positions itself within an intellectual *raison d'être* that can define it. The intellectual challenge is threefold. Arab cultural studies must identify themselves as a coherent field of study, decide on the kind of hermeneutics that will form the basis upon which to interpret the world, and rework the idea of Arab and Islamic culture so they can take broader forms. Epistemologically (and it is to be hoped that this may save us from becoming mere native orientalists), Arab cultural studies should build bridges and linkages with Arab and Islamic thought to resuscitate what Lalande calls 'la raison constituante', and produce an intellectual repertoire that is conscious of its own cultural time. Only then can we claim to have found our present cultural tense.

NOTES

CHAPTER 1

1 See, for example, the chapter on 'Measuring cognitive impact of media', in Barrie Gunter, *Media Research Methods* (London, 2000), especially pp. 230–235.

2 Katerina Dalacoura, 'US democracy promotion in the Arab Middle East since 11 September 2001: A critique', *International Affairs* 81/5 (October 2005), p. 973.

3 Agence France-Presse (AFP) report from Paris, 9 December 2005.

4 E.g. Jenny Kitzinger, 'A sociology of media power: Key issues in audience reception research', in G. Philo (ed.), *Message Received: Glasgow Media Group Research 1993-1998* (New York, 1999), pp. 13–14.

5 W. Russell Neuman, *The Future of the Mass Audience* (Cambridge, 1991), p. 114.

6 Timothy Cole, 'The political rhetoric of sacrifice and heroism and US military intervention', in L. Artz and Y. Kamalipour (eds), *Bring 'Em On: Media and Politics in the Iraq War* (Lanham: MD, 2005), pp. 141 and 151.

7 See, for example, Lila Abu-Lughod, *Dramas of Nationhood: The Politics of Television in Egypt* (Chicago, 2005), e.g. pp. 101–108 and 236–241; Christa Salamandra, *A New Old Damascus* (Indianapolis, 2004), pp. 111–115. See also Sahar Khamis, 'Multiple literacies, multiple identities: Egyptian rural women's readings of televised literacy campaigns', in N. Sakr (ed.), *Women and Media in the Middle East: Power through Self-Expression* (London, 2004), pp. 98–102.

8 Jon Alterman, 'Arab media studies: Some methodological considerations', in M. Zayani (ed.), *The Al Jazeera Phenomenon: Critical Perspectives on New Arab Media* (London, 2005), p. 207.

9 Maha Akeel, 'Audience research is main challenge', *Arab News*, 7 December 2005.

10 Mention should be made here of Deborah Wheeler's ethnographic work on Internet use in Egypt, Jordan and Kuwait, including *The Internet in the Middle East: Global Expectations and Local Imaginations in Kuwait* (Albany: NY, 2006). For an opinion poll based on an unusually large sample but in no way specific to media use, see James J. Zogby, *What Arabs Think: Values, Beliefs and Concerns* (Utica: NY and Washington, 2002).

11 UNDP Regional Bureau for Arab States, *Arab Human Development Report 2003: Building a Knowledge Society* (New York, 2003), pp. 87 and 188.

12 UNDP Regional Bureau for Arab States, *Arab Human Development Report 2004: Towards Freedom in the Arab World* (New York, 2004), p. 98.

13 United States Institute of Peace, *Arab Media: Tools of the Governments, Tools for the People?*, released online in August 2005 at http://www.usip.org/virtualdiplomacy/publications/reports/18.html [accessed 30 December 2005].

14 Clifford Geertz, *The Interpretation of Cultures* (New York, 1973), p. 14.

15 Geertz: *The Interpretation of Cultures*, p. 14.

16 Marc Lynch, 'Assessing the democratizing power of Arab satellite TV', *Transnational Broadcasting Studies* 14 (Spring 2005), pp. 150–152.

17 Lynch: 'Assessing the democratizing power', p 155.

18 In *Voices of the New Arab Public* (New York, 2006), Lynch writes that the 'new public sphere has had an enormous effect in shaping the underlying narrative structuring how the Arab public understands events'; p. 68.

19 Piers Robinson, *The CNN Effect: The Myth of News, Foreign Policy and Intervention* (London, 2002), p. 2.

20 Mohammed el-Nawawy and Leo A. Gher, 'Al Jazeera: Bridging the East–West gap through public discourse and media diplomacy', *Transnational Broadcasting Studies* 10 (Spring/Summer 2003), http://www.tbsjournal.com/Archives/Spring03/nawawy.html.

21 Dale Eickelman, 'Bin Laden, the Arab "street", and the Middle East's democracy deficit', *Current History* 101/651 (January 2002), p. 39.

22 Naomi Sakr, *Satellite Realms: Transnational Television, Globalization and the Middle East* (London, 2001), p. 208.

23 For a comprehensive list of relevant studies in the US and UK see Goldsmiths Media Group, 'Media organizations in society: Central issues', in J. Curran (ed.), *Media Organizations in Society* (London, 2000), pp. 29–30.

24 Daniel Hallin, *We Keep America On Top of the World: Television Journalism and the Public Sphere* (London, 1994), p. 55.

25 Robinson: *The CNN Effect*, p. 15.

26 Daniel Hallin, *The Uncensored War* (Berkeley: CA, 1986).

27 Robinson: *The CNN Effect*, p. 31 and pp. 34–35.

28 Naomi Sakr, 'Media policy in the Middle East: A reappraisal', in J. Curran and M. Gurevitch (eds), *Mass Media and Society*, 4th edn (London, 2005), p. 239.

29 Nada Bakri, 'Syrian-American CNN anchor sacrifices personal life for career', *Daily Star*, 1 March 2006.

30 Bakri: 'Syrian-American CNN anchor'.

31 Naomi Sakr, 'Egyptian TV in the grip of government', in D. Ward (ed.), *Television and Public Policy* (Mahwah: NJ, 2006), pp. 439–440.

32 James Napoli and Hussein Amin, 'The good, the bad and the news: Twenty years of the Egyptian media', *Cairo Papers in Social Science* 21/4 (2001), p. 72.

33 Joshua Meyrowitz, *No Sense of Place: The Impact of Electronic Media on Social Behavior* (Oxford, 1985).

34 Meyrowitz: *No Sense of Place*, pp. 15 and 114.

35 Meyrowitz: *No Sense of Place*, p. 43.

36 Meyrowitz: *No Sense of Place*, p. 309.

37 E.g. Hans Verstraeten, 'The media and the transformation of the public sphere', *European Journal of Communication* 11/3 (September 1996), pp. 355–356.

38 Muhammad I. Ayish, *Arab World Television in the Age of Globalisation* (Hamburg, 2003), p. 30.

39 Meyrowitz: *No Sense of Place*, p. 42.

40 For a discussion of how important it is that everyone knows that everyone else has access see Meyrowitz: *No Sense of Place*, p. 91; Verstraeten: 'The media and the transformation', p. 355.

41 Frances Z. Brown, 'My students, reveling in the Cedar Revolution' (20 March 2005), http://www.washingtonpost.com.

42 Lynch: *Voices of the New Arab Public*, p. 32.

43 Dyala Hamzah, 'Is there an Arab public sphere? The Palestinian intifada, a Saudi fatwa and the Egyptian press', in A. Salvatore and M. LeVine (eds), *Religion, Social Practice, and Contested Hegemonies: Reconstructing the Public Sphere in Muslim Majority Societies* (New York and Basingstoke, 2005), p. 199.

44 Hamzah: 'Is there an Arab public sphere?', p. 181.

45 Armando Salvatore and Mark LeVine, 'Reconstructing the public sphere in Muslim majority societies', in Salvatore and LeVine (eds): *Religion, Social Practice, and Contested Hegemonies*, p. 7.

46 Armando Salvatore and Mark LeVine, 'Socio-religious movements and the transformation of "common sense" into a politics of "common good"', in Salvatore and LeVine (eds): *Religion, Social Practice, and Contested Hegemonies*, p. 30 and pp. 34–35.
47 Nicholas Garnham, *Emancipation, the Media, and Modernity* (Oxford, 2000), p. 169.
48 If other media workers are added in, the death toll in this three-year period was over 90, according to data from the Committee to Protect Journalists.

CHAPTER 2

1   E.g. Ingrid Volkmer, *News in the Global Sphere: A Study of CNN and its Impact on Global Communication* (Luton, 1999).
2   E.g. Jon W. Anderson and Dale F. Eickelman (eds), *New Media in the Muslim World: The Emerging Public Sphere* (Bloomington: IN, 1999).
3   E.g. El-Nawawy and Gher: 'Al-Jazeera'. See also Mohammed Zayani, *Arab Satellite Television and Politics in the Middle East* (Abu Dhabi, 2004), pp. 31–39.
4   See David Deacon, Peter Golding, Jim McGuigan, Heather Purdey and Sarah Rawson, 'Information/News Management, Journalism Culture(s), and (a) European Public Sphere(s) (EPS(s)): The Case of Great Britain', report delivered to the EU-funded programme on 'Adequate Information Management in Europe (AIM)' (Dortmund, 2005), http://www.aim-project.net/uploads/media/GreatBritain.pdf [accessed 15 March 2005].
5   See Hans J. Kleinsteuber, 'Der Dialog der Kulturen in der Kommunikationspolitik', in Claudia Cippitelli and Axel Schwanebeck (eds), *Nur Krisen, Kriege, Katastrophen? Auslandsberichterstattung im deutschen Fernsehen* (Munich, 2003), pp. 145–192.
6   Roland Robertson, *Globalization: Social Theory and Global Culture* (London, 1992), pp. 173–174.
7   'BBC World Service Announces "Biggest Transformation in 70 Years": BBC Arabic TV - The Complete Picture from the World's Most Respected Broadcaster', BBC press release (25 October 2005), http://www.bbc.co.uk/pressoffice/pressreleases/stories/2005/10_october/25/world_arabictv.shtml [accessed 31 October 2005].
8   Cited in Christiane Buck, 'BBC gegen al-Dschasira: Der britische Sender soll für 50 Millionen Euro jährlich einen arabischsprachigen Fernsehkanal starten', *Die Welt* (22 October 2005), http://ww.welt.de/data/2005/10/22/792172.html?s=1 [and 2] [accessed 12 November 2005].
9   'France enters "battle of the images" with "French CNN"', AFP report from Paris, 30 November 2005.
10 Oliver Hahn, *ARTE - Der Europäische Kulturkanal: Eine Fernsehsprache in vielen Sprachen* (Munich, 1997); Oliver Hahn, 'ARTE an der Kreuzung der Kommunikationskulturen: Interkultureller und multilingualer TV-Nachrichtenjournalismus beim Europäischen Kulturkanal', in Marcel Machill (ed.), *Journalistische Kultur: Rahmenbedingungen im internationalen Vergleich* (Opladen and Wiesbaden, 1997), pp. 137–153.
11 Barbara Thomaß, 'Public Service Broadcasting als Faktor einer europäischen Öffentlichkeit', in Lutz M. Hagen (ed.), *Europäische Union und mediale Öffentlichkeit: Theoretische Perspektiven und empirische Befunde zur Rolle der Medien im europäischen Einigungsprozess* (Cologne, 2004), p. 59. All direct quotations have been translated by the author.
12 See, for example, Colin Sparks, 'Is there a global public sphere?', in Daya Kishan Thussu (ed.), *Electronic Empires: Global Media and Local Resistance* (London, 1998), pp. 108–124.
13 Jürgen Habermas, *Strukturwandel der Öffentlichkeit: Untersuchungen zu einer Kategorie der bürgerlichen Gesellschaft* (Neuwied, 1962); Jürgen Habermas, *The Structural Transformation of the Public Sphere: An Inquiry into a Category of Bourgeois Society* (transl. Thomas Burger and Frederick Lawrence) (Cambridge: MA, 1989).

14 Hans J. Kleinsteuber, 'Strukturwandel der europäischen Öffentlichkeit? Der Öffentlichkeitsbegriff von Jürgen Habermas und die European Public Sphere', in Hagen (ed.): *Europäische Union und mediale Öffentlichkeit*, pp. 29–46.

15 Kleinsteuber: 'Strukturwandel der europäischen Öffentlichkeit?', p. 34.

16 Hans J. Kleinsteuber, 'Habermas and the public sphere: From a German to a European perspective', in Risto Kunelius and Colin Sparks (eds), 'The European Public Sphere: Dreams and Realities', *Javnost/The Public* (special issue) 8/1 (April 2001), pp. 95–108.

17 Peter Uwe Hohendahl (ed.), *Öffentlichkeit: Geschichte eines kritischen Begriffs* (Stuttgart, 2000), p. 1.

18 See Tatsuro Hanada, 'Toward a politics of the public sphere', in Tatsuro Hanada (ed.), 'The public sphere and communication policy in Japan and the UK', *Review of Media, Information and Society* (special issue) 4 (1999), pp. 115–134.

19 Kleinsteuber: 'Strukturwandel der europäischen Öffentlichkeit?', p. 33.

20 See Nicholas Garnham, 'The media and the public sphere', in Nicholas Garnham (ed.), *Capitalism and Communication: Global Culture and the Economics of Information* (London, 1990 [1986]), pp. 104–114; Nicholas Garnham, 'The media and the public sphere', in Craig Calhoun (ed.), *Habermas and the Public Sphere* (Cambridge: MA, 1992), pp. 359–376.

21 E.g. Craig Calhoun, 'Introduction: Habermas and the public sphere', in Calhoun: *Habermas*, pp. 1–48; Peter Golding, 'The mass media and the public sphere: The crisis of information in the "information society"', in Stephen Edgall, Sandra Walklate and Gareth Williams (eds), *Debating the Future of the Public Sphere: Transforming the Public and Private Domains in Free Market Societies* (Aldershot, 1995), pp. 25–40.

22 E.g. Kunelius and Sparks (eds): 'The European Public Sphere'.

23 E.g. Anderson and Eickelman (eds): *New Media in the Muslim World*.

24 See Oliver Hahn, Julia Lönnendonker, Karen K. Rosenwerth and Roland Schröder, 'Information/News Management, Journalism Culture(s), and (a) European Public Sphere(s) (EPS(s)): The Case of Germany', report delivered to the EU-funded programme on 'Adequate Information Management in Europe (AIM)' (Dortmund, 2005), http://www.aim-project.net/uploads/media/Germany.pdf.

25 E.g. Dieter Grimm, 'Does Europe need a constitution?', *European Law Journal* 1/3 (November 1995), pp. 282–302; Peter Graf Kielmannsegg, 'Integration und Demokratie', in Markus Jachtenfuchs and Beate Kohler-Koch (eds), *Europäische Integration* (Opladen, 1996), pp. 31–55; Fritz W. Scharpf, *Regieren in Europa* (Frankfurt/Main, 1999); Rainer M. Lepsius, 'Demokratie im neuen Europa: Neun Thesen', in Oskar Niedermayer and Bettina Westle (eds), *Demokratie und Partizipation. Festschrift für Max Kaase* (Opladen, 2000), pp. 332–340.

26 E.g. Philip R. Schlesinger, 'Changing spaces of political communication: The case of the European Union', *Political Communication* 16/3 (July 1999), pp. 263–279.

27 E.g. Gerd G. Kopper, 'Europäische Öffentlichkeit: Ansätze für ein internationales Langzeitprojekt', in Gerd G. Kopper (ed.), *Europäische Öffentlichkeit: Entwicklung von Strukturen und Theorie* (Berlin, 1997), pp. 9–16; Jürgen Gerhards, 'Europäisierung von Ökonomie und Politik und die Trägheit der Entstehung einer europäischen Öffentlichkeit', in Maurizio Bach (ed.), 'Die Europäisierung nationaler Gesellschaften', *Kölner Zeitschrift für Soziologie und Sozialpsychologie* (special issue) 40 (2000), pp. 277–305; Christoph O. Meyer, *Europäische Öffentlichkeit als Kontrollsphäre: Die Europäische Kommission, die Medien und politische Verantwortung* (Berlin, 2002).

28 E.g. Friedhelm Neidhardt, 'Öffentlichkeit, öffentliche Meinung, soziale Bewegungen', in Friedhelm Neidhardt (ed.), 'Öffentlichkeit, öffentliche Meinung, soziale Bewegungen', *Kölner Zeitschrift für Soziologie und Sozialpsychologie* (special issue) 34 (1994), pp. 7–41; Klaus Eder, 'Zur Transformation nationalstaatlicher Öffentlichkeit in Europa', *Berliner Journal Soziologie* 10/2 (May 2000), pp. 167–184; Hans-Jörg Trenz, 'Korruption und politischer Skandal in der EU: Auf dem Weg zu einer europäischen Öffentlichkeit?', in Bach: 'Die Europäisierung nationaler Gesellschaften', pp. 332–359; Hans-Jörg Trenz, *Europa in den Medien: Die europäische Integration im Spiegel nationaler Öffentlichkeit* (Frankfurt and New York, 2005);

Klaus Eder and Cathleen Kantner, 'Interdiskursivitätin der europäischen Öffentlichkeit', *Berliner Debatte Initial* 13/5–6 (October 2002), pp. 79–88; Thomas Risse, 'Zur Debatte um die (Nicht-)Existenz einer europäischen Öffentlichkeit', *Berliner Debatte Initial* 13/5–6 (October 2002), pp. 15–23; Cathleen Kantner, 'Öffentliche politische Kommunikation in der EU: Eine hermeneutisch-pragmatische Perspektive', in Ansgar Klein, Ruud Koopmanns, Hans-Jörg Trenz, Ludger Klein, Christian Lahusen and Dieter Rucht (eds), *Bürgerschaft, Öffentlichkeit und Demokratie in Europa* (Opladen, 2003), pp. 215–232; Marianne van de Steeg, 'Bedingungen für die Entstehung von Öffentlichkeit in der EU', in Klein, Koopmanns, Trenz, Klein, Lahusen and Rucht (eds): *Bürgerschaft*, pp. 169–190.

29 Hahn, Lönnendonker, Rosenwerth and Schröder: 'Information/News Management', p 14.

30 Donskis is director of the Institute of Political Science and Diplomacy at the Vytautas Magnus University of Kaunas, Lithuania.

31 Leonidas Donskis, *The European Public Sphere, Identity, Self-Perception and Self-Comprehension Gaps in Central and Eastern Europe*, authorised transcript of guest keynote address to the Second Workshop of the EU-funded programme on 'Adequate Information Management in Europe (AIM)' (Kaunas, Lithuania, April 2005).

32 Author's translation of quotation from Andrea Nüsse, 'Die Massenmedien als Kriegswaffen: Tagung in Beirut zu den Arbeitsbedingungen von Journalisten im arabischen Raum', *Stuttgarter Zeitung* 108 (11 May 2004), p. 27.

33 Oliver Hahn, 'Die tiefen Gräben der globalen Medienwelt: Interkulturelle Medienkompetenz, Krisenkommunikation und der Kampf um regionale und lokale Absatzmärkte', *Frankfurter Rundschau* 59/287 (9 December 2003), p. 9.

34 Rainer Hermann, 'Den Amerikanern ebenbürtig: Aber die arabische Kritik an Al Dschazira hat in letzter Zeit zugenommen', *Frankfurter Allgemeine Zeitung* (F.A.Z.) 106 (7 May 2004), p. 10.

35 See Edward T. Hall, *The Silent Language* (New York, London, Toronto, Sydney and Auckland, 1959); Edward T. Hall, *The Hidden Dimension* (New York, London, Toronto, Sydney and Auckland, 1966); Edward T. Hall, *Beyond Culture* (New York, London, Toronto, Sydney and Auckland, 1976). In the US Foreign Service Institute, founded in the context of the 1946 US Congress-approved Foreign Service Act to reform diplomacy, Hall taught diplomats and their trainees how to act and behave abroad properly according to the different mentalities in the hosting countries.

36 Mohammed El-Nawawy and Adel Iskandar, *Al-Jazeera: How the Free Arab News Network Scooped the World and Changed the Middle East* (Boulder: CO, 2002), pp. 27, 54 and 202.

37 Mohammed El-Nawawy and Adel Iskandar, 'The Minotaur of "contextual objectivity": War coverage and the pursuit of accuracy with appeal', *Transnational Broadcasting Studies* 9 (Fall/Winter 2002), http://www.tbsjournal.com/Archives/Fall02/Iskandar.html [accessed 19 December 2003].

38 Heike Bartholy, 'Barrieren in der interkulturellen Kommunikation', in Horst Reimann (ed.), *Transkulturelle Kommunikation und Weltgesellschaft: Zur Theorie und Pragmatik globaler Interaktion* (Opladen, 1992), pp. 174–191.

39 Oliver Hahn, 'Neues arabisches und westliches Nachrichtenfernsehen zwischen Kulturbindung und Propagandadialog', *Zeitschrift für Kommunikationsökologie* 6/1 (2004), pp. 44–47.

40 E.g. Thomas Rid, 'Die Öffentlichkeitsarbeit der USA im Mittleren Osten: Amerikanische "Public Diplomacy" als Waffe in Kriegszeiten?', *Stiftung Wissenschaft und Politik-Aktuell* 16 (April 2003), http://www4.swp-berlin.org/common/get_document.php?id=121 [accessed 30 January 2004].

41 E.g. R. S. Zaharna, 'Al Jazeera and American public diplomacy: A dance of intercultural (mis-)communication', in Mohammed Zayani (ed.), *The Al Jazeera Phenomenon: Critical Perspectives on New Arab Media* (London, 2005), pp. 183–202.

42 El-Nawawy and Gher: 'Al-Jazeera'.

43 Eytan Gilboa, 'Mass communication and diplomacy: A theoretical framework', *Communication Theory* 10/3 (August 2000), p. 295.

44 Kai Hafez, *Die politische Dimension der Auslandsberichterstattung: Theoretische Grundlagen*, vol. I (Baden-Baden, 2002), pp. 157–163.

45 Zayani: *Arab Satellite Television*, p. 24.

46 Zayani: *Arab Satellite Television*, pp. 24 and 27.

47 Zayani: *Arab Satellite Television*, p. 25.

48 Hafez: *Die politische Dimension*, pp. 56–72.

49 Eytan Gilboa, *The Global News Networks and US Policymaking in Defense and Foreign Affairs*, paper presented at The Joan Shorenstein Center on the Press, Politics, and Public Policy, John F. Kennedy School of Government, Harvard University (Cambridge: MA, Spring 2002), http://ksgwww.harvard.edu/presspol/Research_Publications/Papers/Working_Papers/2002_6.pdf [accessed 30 January 2004].

50 E.g. Volkmer: *News in the Global Sphere*.

51 E.g. El-Nawawy and Gher: 'Al-Jazeera'.

52 Gilboa: *The Global News Networks*, p. 6.

53 Jon W. Anderson, *Technology, Media, and the Next Generation in the Middle East*, paper presented to The Middle East Institute, School of International and Public Affairs, Columbia University, and to the 'Arab Information Project', Center for Contemporary Arab Studies, Edmund A. Walsh School of Foreign Service, Georgetown University (New York and Washington: DC, 28 September 1999), http://nmit.georgetown.edu/papers/jwanderson.htm [accessed 7 June 2005].

54 El-Nawawy and Iskandar: *Al-Jazeera*, p. 91.

55 Julia Gerlach, 'Live aus Tumultistan', *Die Zeit* 59/13 (18 March 2004), p. 6.

56 Carola Richter, 'Medienkampf der Kulturen: Al Jazeera und Al Arabiya laufen Gefahr, zu stark die arabische Sache zu verfolgen', *message – Internationale Fachzeitschrift für Journalismus* 3 (2004), pp. 32–35.

57 Faisal Al Kasim, '*The Opposite Direction*: A program which changed the face of Arab television', in Zayani: *The Al Jazeera Phenomenon*, pp. 93–105.

58 Andreas Dörner, *Politainment: Politik in der medialen Erlebnisgesellschaft* (Frankfurt, 2001).

59 Muhammad I. Ayish, 'Media brinkmanship in the Arab world: Al Jazeera's *The Opposite Direction* as a fighting arena', in Zayani: *The Al Jazeera Phenomenon*, pp. 106 and 124.

60 Mehdi Abedi and Michael Fischer, 'Etymologies: Thinking a public sphere in Arabic and Persian', *Public Culture* 6/1 (1993), pp. 222–224.

61 El-Nawawy and Gher: 'Al-Jazeera'.

62 Zayani: *Arab Satellite Television*, p. 38.

63 John E. Mueller, *War, Presidents, and Public Opinion* (New York, 1973).

64 Zayani: *Arab Satellite Television*, p. 38

CHAPTER 3

1 Lina Khatib would like to thank Maha Issa for her help in researching this chapter.

2 Nabil Dajani, 'Lebanese television: Caught between government and the private sector', in J. Atkins (ed.), *The Mission: Journalism, Ethics and the World* (Ames: IA, 2002), pp. 123–141.

3 Nabil Dajani, *Disoriented Media in a Fragmented Society: The Lebanese Experience* (Beirut, 1992), pp. 175–176.

4 Dajani: 'Lebanese television', p. 138.

5 Jürgen Habermas, 'The public sphere: An encyclopaedia article' *New German Critique* 3 (Fall 1974), p. 50.

6 Monroe E. Price, *Television, the Public Sphere, and National Identity* (Oxford, 1995), p. 24.

7 Price: *Television*, p. 25.

8 Eric Louw, *The Media and Cultural Production* (London, 2001).

9   Habermas: 'The public sphere', p. 49.

10 Thomas Meyer, *Media Democracy: How the Media Colonize Politics* (Cambridge, 2002).

11 Colin Sparks, 'The global, the local and the public sphere', in R. C. Allen and A. Hill (eds), *The Television Studies Reader* (London, 2004), p. 140.

12 John Keane, *The Media and Democracy* (Cambridge, 1991), p. 168.

13 John Hartley, *The Politics of Pictures: The Creation of the Public in the Age of Popular Media* (London, 1992), p. 36.

14 Hartley: *The Politics of Pictures*, p. 35.

15 Peter Dahlgren, *Television and the Public Sphere: Citizenship, Democracy and the Media* (London, 1995).

16 Michael Gurevitch and Jay G. Blumler, 'Political communication systems and democratic values', in J. Lichtenberg (ed.), *Democracy and the Mass Media* (Cambridge, 1990) pp. 269–289.

17 Kevin Robins, *Into the Image: Culture and Politics in the Field of Vision* (London, 1996).

18 Pierre Bourdieu, *On Television and Journalism* (London, 1998).

19 Bourdieu: *On Television*, p. 21.

20 Nicholas Mirzoeff, *An Introduction to Visual Culture* (London, 1999), p. 257.

21 Antonio Gramsci, *Selections from the Prison Notebooks*, edited and translated by Quintin Hoare and Geoffrey Nowell-Smith(London, 1971), p. 133.

22 Daniel Dayan and Elihu Katz, *Media Events: The Live Broadcasting of History* (Cambridge: MA, 1992).

23 Meyer: *Media Democracy*, p. 67.

24 Margaret Morse, 'News as performance: The image as event', in Allen and Hill (eds): *The Television Studies Reader*, pp. 209–225.

25 Don Slater, 'Marketing mass photography', in H. Davis and P. Walton (eds): *Language, Image, Media* (Oxford, 1983), p. 246; emphasis is in original.

26 Jean Baudrillard, *Simulacra and Simulation* (Ann Arbor: MI, 1994).

27 Meyer: *Media Democracy*, p. 65.

28 Bourdieu: *On Television*; Hartley: *The Politics of Pictures*.

29 Samer Abu Hawash, 'The image of the opposition and the allies: An exchange of roles?', *Al-Safir* (2 March 2005).

30 Zainab Yaghi, 'History is no longer told…but seen', *Al-Safir* (4 March 2005).

31 Zainab Yaghi, '"Al-balad" that he built regains its spirit', *Al-Safir* (21 February 2005).

32 Ali Al-Azir, 'Let's congregate', *Al-Balad* (10 March 2005).

33 Dajani: *Disoriented Media*.

34 Jerome Bourdon, 'Live television is still alive: On television as an unfulfilled promise', in Allen and Hill (eds): *The Television Studies Reader*, p. 193.

35 Claus-Dieter Rath, 'Live television and its audience: Challenges of media reality', in E. Seiter, H. Borchers, G. Kreutener and E. M. Warth (eds), *Remote Control: Television, Audiences, and Cultural Power* (London, 1989), p. 89.

36 Dajani: *Disoriented Media*; Dajani: 'Lebanese television'.

37 Price: *Television*, p. 29.

38 John A. Walker, and Sarah Chaplin, *Visual Culture: An Introduction* (Manchester, 1997), p. 67.

39 Hartley: *The Politics of Pictures*.

40 Meyer: *Media Democracy*.

41 John Eldridge, 'News, truth and power', in J. Eldridge (ed.), *Getting the Message: News, Truth and Power* (London, 1993), pp. 3–33.

42 Gurevitch and Blumler: 'Political communication systems', pp. 283–284.

43 Robert M. Entman, 'Framing: Toward clarification of a fractured paradigm', *Journal of Communication* 43/4 (1993), p. 52.

44 Ciaran McCullagh, *Media Power: A Sociological Introduction* (New York, 2002), p. 26.

45 Rath: 'Live television', p. 88.

46 Bourdieu: *On Television*.

47 Ghassan Rizk, 'When did the screens ever see images like these?', *Al-Safir* (1 March 2005).

48 Dalal al-Bizri, quoted in Rasha al-Atrash, 'Freedom Square: Zoom in on the Arab audience', *Al-Safir* (8 March 2005).

49 Rasha al-Atrash, 'The television day', *Al-Safir* (1 March 2005).

50 Doha Shams, 'The image', *Al-Safir* (7 March 2005).

51 Elie Frizly, 'The contagious quality of television', *Al-Safir* (10 March 2005).

52 Samir Khalis, *Heart of Beirut: Reclaiming the Bourj* (London, 2006) p. 241.

53 Hartley: *The Politics of Pictures*, p 26.

54 Khalaf: *Heart of Beirut*.

55 Hartley: *The Politics of Pictures*, p. 35, emphasis in original.

56 'National unity day in commemoration of 13 April', *Al-Safir* (13 April 2005).

57 Al-Atrash: 'The television day'.

58 Bourdieu: *On Television*, p. 19.

59 Meyer: *Media Democracy*, p. 32.

60 Hartley: *The Politics of Pictures*.

61 Judith Lichtenberg, 'Foundations and limits of freedom of the press', in J. Lichtenberg (ed.), *Democracy and the Mass Media* (Cambridge, 1990), pp. 102–135.

62 Kenneth E. Foote, *Color in Public Spaces: Toward a Communication-Based Theory of the Urban Built Environment* (Chicago, 1983).

63 Bradley Butterfield, 'The Baudrillardian symbolic, 9/11, and the war of good and evil', *Postmodern Culture* 13/1 (September 2002), http://www3.iath.virginia.edu/pmc/text-only/issue.902/13.1butterfield.txt [accessed 7 February 2006].

64 John R. Gillis, 'Memory and identity: The history of a relationship', in J. R. Gillis (ed.), *Commemorations: The Politics of National Identity* (Princeton: NJ, 1994), p. 7.

65 Khalaf: *Heart of Beirut*, p. 194.

66 Dayan and Katz: *Media Events*.

67 Dayan and Katz: *Media Events*, p. 20.

68 Dayan and Katz: *Media Events*.

69 Morse: 'News as performance', p. 218.

70 Hayden White, 'The modernist event', in V. Sobchack (ed.), *The Persistence of History: Cinema, Television, and the Modern Event* (London, 1996), pp. 17–38.

71 White: 'The modernist event', p. 24.

72 Dayan and Katz: *Media Events*.

73 Samir Khalaf, *Besieged and Silenced: The Muted Anguish of the Lebanese People* (Oxford, 1989).

74 Geoffrey Bennington, *Lyotard: Writing the Event* (Manchester, 1988), p. 108.

75 Dayan and Katz: *Media Events*, p. 211.

76 Bill Readings, *Introducing Lyotard: Art and Politics* (London, 1991), p. 57.

77 Walter Benjamin, quoted in White: 'The modernist event', p. 17.

CHAPTER 4

1   Marwan Kraidy, 'Reality television and politics in the Arab world (preliminary observations)', *Transnational Broadcasting Studies* 2/1 (Autumn 2005), pp. 7–28.

2   Liesbet van Zoonen, 'Imagining the fan democracy', *European Journal of Communication* 19/1 (March 2004), p. 42.

3   In Italy, the porn star Cicciolina was elected to parliament. In India, the televised versions of the Hindu epics, *Ramayana* and *Mahabharata* had active links with the changing political landscape; see Arvind Rajagopal, *Politics after Television: Hindu Nationalism and the Reshaping of the Public in India* (Cambridge, 2001). In Latin America, sensitive socio-economic themes are often politicised in the context of *telenovelas* and other forms of public culture; see Nestor García-Canclini, *Consumers and Citizens: Globalization and*

Multicultural Conflicts (Minneapolis, 2001) and Jesus Martín-Barbero, *Communication, Culture and Hegemony: From the Media to Mediations* (London, 1993).

4 Van Zoonen: 'Imagining the fan democracy', p. 43.

5 These include Lila Abu-Lughod, *Dramas of Nationhood: The Politics of Television in Egypt* (Chicago, 2005), for Egypt; and Marwan M. Kraidy, *Hybridity, or the Cultural Logic of Globalization* (Philadelphia, 2005), pp. 116–147, for Lebanon.

6 'Stars return to politics…a job or a search for the audience?', *Asharq Al-Awsat* (14 August 2005).

7 'Stars return to politics', *Asharq Al-Awsat*.

8 Said Yassin, 'Fifi, Abdo confronts corruption and smuggling of antiquities', *Al-Hayat* (16 September 2005).

9 'Because of their political activities, Israel considers Nancy and Maria and Haifa to pose a danger', Al-Arabiya.net (14 September 2005).

10 See van Zoonen: 'Imagining the fan democracy'. Preparations for *The American Candidate* ceased because of spiralling costs.

11 See Kraidy: 'Reality television and politics in the Arab world'.

12 For more on the regionalisation of Arab media, see Marwan M. Kraidy. 'Arab satellite television between globalization and regionalization', *Global Media Journal* 1/1 (Autumn 2002); Jon Alterman, *New Media, New Politics? From Satellite Television to the Internet in the Arab World* (Washington: DC, 1998); and Sakr: *Satellite Realms*.

13 Made possible by satellite technology, this regionalisation is driven by economic calculations. In news, regionalisation has created an 'anywhere but here' trend, whereby satellite television channels tend to criticise all governments, politicians and other powerful players except those from the country in which they are based. For example, Al-Jazeera's coverage only rarely raises questions about Qatari affairs, especially government performance. Yet its relentless criticism of Saudi Arabia's rulers creates a kind of 'asymmetrical interdependence' between Qatar and Saudi Arabia by giving more influence to the former. See Marwan M. Kraidy, 'Transnational satellite television and asymmetrical interdependence in the Arab world: A research note', *Transnational Broadcasting Studies* 5 (Autumn 2000). In that context, the creation of Al-Arabiya by the Saudis aimed at restoring full asymmetry by undermining Al-Jazeera's influence.

14 See Kraidy: *Hybridity*, pp. 97–115.

15 *Man Sa Yarbah al-Malyoun*, as it was called in Arabic, was initially produced in London. Production moved to Paris in June 2001 and then to Cairo in February 2002. The 2005 series was produced in Beirut.

16 Author interview with Roula Saad, director of Promotion and Marketing, Lebanese Broadcasting Corporation International, Adma, Lebanon, 5 July 2005. Ms Saad also played the on-screen role of director of the Academy and is LBCI's point person for the programme.

17 Kraidy: 'Reality television and politics in the Arab world'.

18 There were many articles in the Western and Arab press presenting this argument, including Carla Power's 'Look who's talking', in *Newsweek International* (8 August 2005), pp. 50–51. Many of these arguments were made about the song contest show *Super Star*, broadcast by the Lebanese channel Future Television. While this argument is worth considering, we should certainly be cautious not to exaggerate the democratising impact of reality television, or at least give some time for systematic research on the topic before we make optimistic claims.

19 Dayan and Katz: *Media Events*, p. 226.

20 Again, caution is advisable in evaluating the political *impact* of this video clip, in distinction from its political connotations.

21 At that time tensions between Syria and Lebanon reached their peak since the early 1990s, as there was a widespread suspicion that Syria contributed in one way or another to Hariri's assassination. What occurred on the *Star Academy 2* stage reflected popular

discontent with Syria in Lebanon. Contrary to the clapping and dancing that usually accompanies the exit of a losing contestant, the amphitheatre where the primes are shot was fully silent as the Syrian contestant stepped out.

22 It is significant to this analysis that LBCI decided to include a celebration of Kuwait's national day in the first prime (25 February 2005) following the killing of Hariri. By this means the producers appeared to establish a symbolic link between Kuwait's ordeal under Iraqi occupation and Lebanon's under the Syrians. In fact, the following day, 26 February, is celebrated in Kuwait as Yawm al-Tahrir (Liberation Day).

23 I will explore the full dynamics of the *Star Academy* controversy in Kuwait in future work, having recently conducted fieldwork in Kuwait (November 2005) at the time of this writing.

24 'Kuwaiti MPs to question minister over concert', *Arab News* (9 May 2004). A few days earlier an Islamist activist had filed a lawsuit against the Cabinet for allowing *Star Academy* to hold a concert in Kuwait.

25 'Kuwait bans concerts involving women entertainers', *Arab News* (25 May 2004).

26 'Kuwait minister faces grilling over "Failure to Protect Morality"', *Arab News* (22 October 2004).

27 I interviewed Moubarak al-Sahly, head of the Committee to Monitor Video Clips and director of Kuwait TV Channel 4, on 15 November 2005, at his office in the Ministry of Information in Kuwait City. My impression, which I still have to confirm from other sources, is that the committee was created to placate the Islamist bloc, as few policy-makers believe that the flow of music videos and music-oriented reality television shows can be stemmed.

28 My forthcoming book, on the social and political impact of Arab reality television, gives a fuller account of the political firestorm around *Star Academy* in Kuwait, discussing connections with events such as the struggle for women's political rights.

29 Author interview with Joumana Fehmi, director of Programming and Production at al-Rai TV, Salhiyyah, Kuwait City, 16 November 2005.

30 'Court fines Kuwaiti MP for insulting women', Deutsche Presse-Agentur (1 January 2006).

CHAPTER 5

1 This chapter is a substantially revised, updated and expanded version of the author's 'The Internet in the Arab world: playground for political liberalisation', *International Politics and Society* 3 (2005), pp. 78–96. We are grateful to IPS for permission to use the article.

2 Libyan Abd al-Raziq al-Mansuri was detained in January 2005 after publishing articles on the UK-based blog/news site akhbar-libya.com, and sentenced in November to one and a half years in prison (http://committeetoprotectbloggers.civiblog.org/blog/Libya). Iraqi engineering student and blogger Khalid Jarrar recounts his abduction by Iraqi intelligence service and subsequent ordeal at http://secretsinbaghdad.blogspot.com/2005_07_01_secretsinbaghdad_archive.html. He had been charged with visiting the well-known Iraqi blog raedinthemiddle.blogspot.com. Egyptian Abdel-Karim Nabil Sulaiman, who had been attacking Islamic fundamentalists in very strong terms on his blog (http://karam903.blogspot.com), was arrested on 26 October 2005, ostensibly to protect him from an Islamist attack; he was released 18 days later. On 5 December 2005, two days before the last round of parliamentary elections, Egyptian state security arrested Ahmed Abdallah, editor of the Islamist Baladynet.net. He was released on 22 December to await trial on hitherto unpublished charges ('Malaff i'tiqal al-Shaikh Abu Islam Ahmad Abdallah', http://www.baladynet.net/abuislam/jail.htm; 'Le directeur d'un site Internet remis en liberté après deux semaines de détention', Reporters sans frontières (26 December 2005), http://www.rsf.org/article.php3?id_article=15840).

3   'Mideast reform forum ends in confusion', *The Daily Star* (14 November 2005).

4   Elijah Zarwan/Human Rights Watch, *False Freedom: Online Censorship in the Middle East and North Africa* (New York, November 2005).

5   'Reporters sans frontières rend publique sa liste des 15 ennemis d'Internet', Reporters sans frontières (16 November 2005), http://www.rsf.org/article.php3?id_article=15611.

6   Produced by Secure Computing (http://www.securecomputing.com). Iran also uses SmartFilter. The side effects of using commercial software from the US are overblocking (due to wrong categorisation) and a tendency for English-language filters to be more comprehensive than those in other languages. This can mean that sites on religious conversion, which are not available in English to Saudi Internet users, may be accessed in Arabic.

7   http://www.isu.net.sa/saudi-internet/contenet-filtring/filtring-policy.htm [sic].

8   Etisalat's monopoly was due to be replaced by a duopoly in 2006, through the licensing of a new telecoms company under 40 per cent state ownership ('What will Etisalat's lost monopoly mean?', *AME Info*, 8 May 2005). Procrastination over ending the monopoly was criticised in the blog 'Sorry Dubai' in December 2005. A few days later the blog disappeared from the web, having reportedly been blocked by Etisalat ('Dubai blog blocked', *AME Info*, 8 December 2005).

9   *United Arab Emirates Yearbook 2004: Information and culture*, p. 254, cited in OpenNet Initiative, *Internet Filtering in the United Arab Emirates in 2004–2005: A Country Study*, 2.E., http://www.opennetinitiative.net/studies/uae/.

10   OpenNet Initiative, *Internet Filtering in Tunisia in 2005: A Country Study* (November 2005), 4.A., http://www.opennetinitiative.net/studies/tunisia/. In July 2005 the number of Internet users in Tunisia was estimated at 905,000 (http://www.ati.nat.tn/stats/).

11   Zarwan: *False Freedom*, p. 107.

12   Renaud Cornand and Vincent Geisser, 'Après le sommet de l'information, Internet dort en prison' (2 December 2005), http://www.oumma.com/article.php3?id_article=1809.

13   Zarwan: *False Freedom*, pp. 109–110. Zouhair was the nephew of former judge Mokhtar Yahyaoui, president of the Centre de Tunis pour l'Indépendance de la Justice and one of Tunisia's leading political dissidents. Mokhtar maintains a blog at http://yahyaoui.blogspot.com, opened in July 2001 with an open letter to the Tunisian president, calling for respect for the independence of the judiciary.

14   Zarwan: *False Freedom*, pp. 110–115. See also the solidarity site http://www.zarzis.org.

15   Inal Ersan, 'Syria restriction narrows broadband Internet', *Reuters* (29 January 2005).

16   Gamal Eid, *The Internet in the Arab World: A New Space of Repression?*, The Arab Network for Human Rights Information (2004), http://www.hrinfo.net/en/reports/net2004.

17   Zarwan: *False Freedom*, pp. 82–85; 'Massoud Hamid, lauréat du prix cyberliberté 2005', Reporters sans frontières (8 December 2005) http://www.rsf.org/article.php3?id_article=15865.

18   By early January 2006 SCS-Net was again blocking SMTP on the most common port 25, but alternative ports, as well as tunnelling through SSL, were still possible.

19   Al-Ayham Saleh, 'Siyadat al-wazir musta', fa-ma al-'amal?' (5 October 2005), http://www.alayham.com/modules/news/article.php?storyid=366; Al-Ayham Saleh, 'Hajb mawaqi' al-Internet al-Suriyya juz' min al-istrategiyya li'l-ma'lumatiyya' (11 May 2004), http://www.alayham.com/modules/news/article.php?storyid=366.

20   Al-Ayham Saleh and George Kadar, 'Siyasa jadida li-hajb al-mawaqi' wa'l-khidamat 'ala al-Internet al-Suriyya' (6 November 2005), http://www.alayham.com/modules/news/article.php?storyid=391. New private ISPs started to emerge, with the Computer Engineering Company launching its own service (cec.sy) in mid-November, advertising 'family-safe' computing. Tarassul.sy is next in line. The new providers are resellers to Syrian Telecom's digital Public Data Network launched in March 2005, and thus easily subject to state control of traffic. Satellite downstream connections, which cannot be monitored so easily, have been offered by Best Italia since January 2005; SCS and another

provider have obtained licences for similar services, but the expense of satellite links restricts them mainly to embassies and large companies.

21 See Adnan Malik, 'Bahrainis ask for information minister's resignation', *Associated Press* (4 May 2002); OpenNet Initiative, *Internet Filtering in Bahrain in 2004–2005: A Country Study* (February 2005), http://www.opennetinitiative.net/studies/bahrain; Mahmood Al-Yousif, 'Websites "shut without notice"', *Mahmood's Den* (24 November 2005), http://mahmood.tv/index.php/news/2034.

22 Rachid Jankari, Morocco's foremost blogger, was the first to report the blocking: 'Censure des sites de Polisario au Maroc' (23 November 2005), http://www.jankari.org/index.php?2005/11/23/595-censure-des-sites-de-polisario-au-maroc; the news then spread quickly in the blogging scene. See also 'Le site anti-censure Anonymizer.com ajouté à la liste noire du Net marocain', Reporters sans frontières (20 December 2005), http://www.rsf.org/article.php3?id_article=15808. Morocco had in 2001 blocked the site of the Islamist youth monthly *Risalat al-Futuwwa*, but unblocked it in 2002 while banning the print edition of the paper. The online edition never really came alive, however, and remains dormant to this day.

23 Zarwan: *False Freedom*, p. 34.

24 'Reporters sans frontières exprime ses condoléances à la famille de Zouhair Yahyaoui', Reporters sans frontières (14 March 2005), http://www.rsf.org/article.php3?id_article=12848.

25 Sihem Bensedrine, 'La bataille de la communication en Tunisie: un enjeu de pouvoir', *Kalima Tunisie* (13 February 2005), http://www.kalimatunisie.com/num32/Communication.htm.

26 Ammar Abdel-Hamid, 'Media reform in Syria: A door ajar?', *Arab Reform Bulletin* 2/11 (10 December 2004), p. 15, http://www.carnegieendowment.org/publications/index.cfm?fa=view&id=16242#media. Ammar – who started a blog in February 2005 at http://amarji.blogspot.com – nevertheless felt sufficiently threatened by Syrian security to go into exile in September 2005, becoming a visiting fellow at the Brookings Institution.

27 Data derived from the International Telecommunication Union (ITU), 'Internet indicators: Hosts, users and number of PCs – 2004', http://www.itu.int/ITU-D/ict/statistics. The market information company TNS has given much higher estimates, but their data collection methods are not transparent. In 2004 they put percentage Internet penetration at 36 in the UAE (ITU: 32 per cent), 28 in Lebanon (ITU: 17), 26 in Kuwait and Jordan (ITU: 24 and 11), 17 in Saudi Arabia (ITU: 6), 14 in Syria (ITU: 4) and 9 in Morocco (ITU: 12) ('Survey research over the Internet', *AME Info*, 19 September 2004).

28 'Internet penetration in the Arab world', *Madar Research Journal*, Issue 0 (October 2002).

29 For Egyptian data, see the Information and Decision Support Center (IDSC) report edited by 'Ala al-Khawaga, *Ta'thir al-Internet 'ala al-shabab fi Misr wa'l-'alam al-'Arabi: dirasa naqdiyya* (Cairo, November 2005), p. 18. For Morocco, see Rachid Jankari, 'Les indicateurs d'internet au Maroc', *Menara* (15 December 2005), http://www.menara.ma/Infos/includes/detail.asp?article_id=10987&lmodule=Technologie. Moroccan Internet space continues to be dominated by francophone content, which means less interchange with Middle Eastern cyberspace.

30 Of Egyptian families using the net, 48 per cent spend up to E£50/month (Euros 7) on access, which is roughly 7 per cent of average monthly income, while 25 per cent spend E£50–100/month. For the lower spenders, this translates into as much as 50 hours from home or approximately 20 hours in an Internet café. The IDSC found that 70 per cent of the youth surveyed access the net from home ('Istitla' ra'y al-usar hawl istikhdam al-shabab li'l-Internet' and 'Istitla' ra'y al-shabab hawl istikhdam al-Internet', 1 October 2005).

31 'Traffic rank' in this table is taken from Alexa.com. IslamOnline is not included here because its traffic rank (534 in January 2006) was largely due to the popularity of its English version. In the Alexa Arabic directory, the relative position of IslamOnline's Arabic version sank from 10 in November 2003 to 22 in January 2006. Al-Ahram, which also

offers important non-Arabic content, was included here according to its position in the Arabic directory.

32 Estimate of traffic rank based on position in Alexa directory, since it is only measured there. In December 2005 MSN Arabia was the second most-visited site from Saudi Arabia, after google.com and before google.com.sa.

33 In January 2006 8 per cent of traffic was drawn by english.aljazeera.net, down from 25 per cent in November 2003 and 10 per cent in May 2005. Traffic rank was adjusted accordingly.

34 http://www.amrkhaled.net/ar/amr/pollBooth.php?op=results&pollID=7 [accessed 23 December 2003 but no longer available]. In 2003 41 per cent of 11,123 users said they had come to know the site via the free e-mail service ForIslam.com, which offered 10MB of free web space at a time when MSN Hotmail and Yahoo! Mail were still at 4–6 MB. 34 per cent came via advertisements on satellite television, 15 per cent via friends, 8 per cent via Internet links and 2 per cent via the press (pollID=10). The significance of ForIslam.com has declined significantly subsequently.

35 Data from ISU at King Abdul-Aziz City for Science and Technology (www.isu.net.sa). This list contains, in order of popularity, sites (excluding web directories and technical sites) not listed in Table 5.1 that appear in at least 12 out of the 37 months for which the ISU has published the top 30–40 sites most visited from Saudi Arabia. For a more elaborate presentation, see Albrecht Hofheinz, 'Das Internet und sein Beitrag zum Wertewandel in arabischen Gesellschaften', in S. Faath (ed.), *Politische und gesellschaftliche Debatten in Nordafrika, Nah- und Mittelost: Inhalte, Träger, Perspektiven* (Hamburg, 2004), pp. 449–472.

36 E.g. saudistocks.com, musahim.biz, mubasher.com.sa, hawamer.com, saudishares.net, cnbca.net, hawamir.com. Dubai's dfm.ae also made a mark.

37 E.g. filbalad.com, acmilanclub.com, sport4ever.com, zamalek.tv, alzaeem.net, yallakora.com.

38 E.g. netarabic.com, arb3.com, 66n.com, q6of.com.

39 E.g. egypty.com, farfesh.com, mooga.com, lahdah.com, BosWTol.com.

40 E.g. roro44.com, arb3.com, alfrasha.com, x333x.com, 3roos.com.

41 E.g. 6rbtop.com, 6rob.com, 6rp.net.

42 E.g. 7oob.net, dardasha.net, chatrank.com.

43 E.g. syrialine.com, syrianews.com, champress.net, arabscastle.com, scs-net.org.

44 E.g. alwatanvoice.com, mahjoob.com.

45 Samar Fatany, 'Internet opens new paths for journalism', *Arab News* (15 December 2005).

46 Saudi Arabia's reformist daily *Al-Watan* is an exception.

47 Al-Hay'a al-'Alamiyya li-Nasr al-Sha'b al-'Iraqi: 'Iraq al-jihad: amal wa-akhtar', http://www.mil.no/multimedia/archive/00038/_Jihadi_Iraq__Hopes__38063a.pdf; Brynjar Lia and Thomas Hegghammer, 'FFI explains al-Qaida document', *Forsvarets Forskningsinstitutt* (19 March 2004), http://www.mil.no/felles/ffi/start/article.jhtml?articleID=71589.

48 The Israeli Internet Haganáh (haganah.org.il), which has set out to document the 'global jihad online', maintains an extensive 'database of jihad sites' and is often instrumental in their demise.

49 '25 ta'nan fi qa'imat (Jidda) al-dhahabiyya wa-jadal fi Tabuk hawl (al-Internet)', http://saudielection.com/ar/news_body.php?id=559&PHPSESSID=1524f51f0f0a73979 4ca9f8779b9e0df; 'Lajnat al-ta'un tarfa' taqriraha al-niha'i wa-tuqirr fawz al-qa'ima al-dhahabiyya', http://saudielection.com/ar/news_body.php?id=598&PHPSESSID=1524f 51f0f0a739794ca9f8779b9e0df; Qinan al-Ghamidi, 'Fawz "al-Qawa'im al-Dhahabiyya" tabi'i wa-mustahaqq: khala lak al-jaww', http://saudielection.com/ar/article_body.php? id=1026&PHPSESSID=1524f51f0f0a739794ca9f8779b9e0df.

50 Issandr El Amrani, 'The Brotherhood's media offensive', *The Arabist* (30 November 2005), http://arabist.net/archives/2005/11/30/the-brotherhoods-media-offensive/. The main Brotherhood site, ikhwanonline.com, was blocked by Egypt's most popular ISP during the campaign (in itself witnessing to its significance), but alternative

addresses were readily available. In early November the Brotherhood also launched a new English-language site, ikhwanweb.com (also reachable under ikhwan monitor.com).

51 Amira Howeidy, 'Lessons learned', *Al Ahram Weekly* 771 (1–7 December 2005).

52 Hofheinz: 'Wertewandel', pp. 468–469. For a sample of online polls, see Hofheinz, 'Tabellen zur Internetnutzung und Internetumfragen in Nordafrika, Nah- und Mittelost', pp. 11–27, http://www.menavision2010.de/dokumente/tp4-auszuege-drei.pdf.

53 http://www.aljazeera.net/gateway/vote, voteID=1024. Compare this with another poll in February 2005, in which almost 200,000 people participated, 78 per cent of whom supported an immediate Syrian withdrawal from Lebanon (voteID=1014). In September 2004 65 per cent of 62,000 had expressed their support for such a withdrawal (voteID=901).

54 http://www.aljazeera.net/gateway/vote, voteID=1160. In December 71 per cent conceded that the strong performance of the Muslim Brotherhood in the Egyptian parliamentary elections would have an effect on the political landscape (voteID=1251).

55 http://www.aljazeera.net/gateway/vote, voteID=1279.

56 As reflected by Alexa in January 2006 (http://www.alexa.com/browse?& CategoryID=16). The ratio for Arabic has been stable since at least 2003. The statistical base for Kiswahili is weak; of the 38 sites ranked by Alexa, five were Christian missionary sites, and three were Islamic. Indonesian religious sites accounted for six of the top 100 (four Islamic, two Christian). Three of the leading 81 Tatar sites were Islamic; two of the leading 100 Persian ones; one each among Azeri and Albanian sites; and none among Bangla, Hebrew and Turkish sites. Alexa did not give statistics for Urdu. The Egyptian IDSC estimated in November 2005 that 65 per cent of all Arabic content on the Internet was of a religious nature, but no data were provided to back this up (IDSC: *Ta'thir al-Internet*, p. 16). In any case, this can only refer to content creation, not to popularity.

57 'A phenomenon called Amr Khaled', *The Muslim Association of Britain*, http://www.mabonline.net/islam/personalities/articles/amrkhalid.htm [accessed 23 April 2005]. See Lindsay Wise, '*Words from the Heart': New Forms of Islamic Preaching in Egypt*, M.Phil. thesis, St Anthony's College, University of Oxford (May 2003), http://users.ox.ac.uk/%7Emetheses/Wise.html. The popularity of Amr Khaled's site has attracted people who spot an audience for Al-Qa'ida-style propaganda (cf. the thread 'Ba'd an 'arafta anna al-jihad haqq madha taf'al? ... udkhul ya akhi li-ta'rif', started on 28 July 2004 by one 'Qassamiyya 'Iraqiyya', with detailed instructions on physical training, books to read, and a discussion of the conditions of jihad (a thread since removed from the archives); but these remain a clear minority.

58 Nasrin Alavi has compiled a first anthology of Persian blogs in *We are Iran: The Persian Blogs* (Brooklyn: NY, 2005).

59 'Where is Raed?' (http://dear_raed.blogspot.com) won the 'Best African or Middle Eastern Weblog' bloggie award (http://www.bloggies.com) in 2004 and 2005. Until 2003 there had been no Middle Eastern entries. It was then partially published in book form by *The Guardian* (Salam Pax, *The Clandestine Diary of an Ordinary Iraqi*, London, 2003). Following its huge success, the first year of another English-language Iraqi blog (http://riverbendblog.blogspot.com) also appeared in print: Riverbend, *Baghdad Burning: Girl Blog from Iraq* (New York, 2005). Since August 2004 Salam Pax has been blogging at http://justzipit.blogspot.com.

60 'Hal al-muntadayat al-'arabiyya', http://www.abduh.net/wp-trackback.php/39 (20 December 2004); 'Wida'anli'l-muntadayat', http://www.serdal.com/archives/2005/01/01/farewell-forums/ (1 January 2005); 'Wa-ana aydan: wida'an li'l-muntadayat', http://osama.ae/index.php?m=200501 (18 January 2005). One of the earliest blogs in Arabic was Muharib (http://www.al7ot.net), started in December 2002 if not before, but since discontinued.

Rafedain.com, an Iraqi anti-Saddam news blog, was established in May 2003. Ishtar talking (http://ishtartalking-blogspot.com), an Iraqi woman from Basra, experimented with blogging in July and August 2003. Moodless (born 1979 in Kuwait) began blogging (Moodless.net) in November 2003 and received the 2004 Deutsche Welle International Weblog Award for Arabic, for dealing with social and political topics (http://www.thebobs.com/thebobs04/bob.php?site=winner_kat&katid=6). Ahmad Gharbeia from Egypt started his Tayy al-Muttasil (http://zamakan.gharbeia.org) in November 2003, but stopped in late 2005. Taqq Hanak (http://digressing.blogspot.com) set up his blog in December 2003, but has posted regularly only since October 2004; it was a runner-up in the 2005 Deutsche Welle International Weblog Awards. On 21 December 2003 Faiza al-Arji, mother of Raed, and Khalid Jarrar, who are known Iraqi bloggers in their own right (Raed is the eponymous friend of Salam Pax; on Khalid, see n. 2), started posting on afamilyinbaghdad.blogspot.com.

61 'Mashru' insha' niqaba li'l-mudawwinin', http://www.getphpbb.com/phpbb/viewforum.php?f=1&mforum=naqaba&sid=8068b76a5f37c38883d617920a893c83.

62 Ahmad Moghrabi, 'As'ila kathira bi-rasm mu'tamar "Sahafat al-'Arab wa-'asr al-ma'lumat"… "bloggers" al-Internet yusaddiduna darba li'l-sahafa fi "tsunami" Asia', Al-Hayat (13 January 2005), http://www.daralhayat.com/science_tech/01-2005/Item-20050112-17ee88e9-c0a8-10ed-0060-14f755eb81ea/story.html; MAP, 'Rencontre-débat sur les blogs à Rabat' (19 February 2005), http://www.emarrakech.info/php?index.action=article&id_article=122225; Jilnar Asmar, 'Mudhakkirat shakhsiyya tuhaddid al-sahafa al-maktuba: shabab "bloggers" yumidduna jisran bayn al-'Arab wa'l-'alam al-iftiradi', Al-Hayat (24 February 2005), http://www.daralhayat.com/science_tech/02-2005/Item-20050223-4063e5d5-c0a8-10ed-001c-22ff1fe0423d/story.html; Hind al-Khalifa, 'Murur akthar min 'amm 'ala zuhur awwal mudawwana 'arabiyya 'ala al-Internet', Al-Riyadh (8 March 2005), http://www.alriyadh.com/2005/03/08/article45567.html. In May the BBC Arabic Service interviewed bloggers (mainly in Jordan) for a programme on blogging in the Arab world: http://sabbah.biz/mt/archives/2005/05/29/my-bbc-arabic-world-service-interview/.

63 http://cyber.law.harvard.edu/globalvoices/author/haitham-sabbah/. See the interview with him (by the Italian news agency Lettera22), at http://sabbah.biz/mt/archives/10/062005/blogging-in-the-arab-world.

64 See, e.g., Manal and Alaa's Bit Bucket ('free speech from the bletches', http://www.manalaa.net); Al-Wa'y al-Misri (http://misrdigital.blogspirit.com); Taqq Hanaq (http://digressing.blogspot.com); Baheyya (http://digressing.blogspot.com).

65 For example, 'estr4ng3d's life' (http://estr4ng3d.blogspot.com, in English and, occasionally, colloquial Arabic). There are said to be at least two other Egyptian soldiers blogging.

66 http://www.dw-world.de/dw/article/0,2144,1783798,00.html; http://www.rsf.org/article.php3?id_article=15840.

67 Jihad el-Khazen, 'al-Internet hatamat al-quyud', Al-Hayat (5 January 2006), http://www.daralhayat.com/opinion/editorials/01-2006/Item-20060104-96ceaf15-c0a8-10ed-0025-b64d4bbd291e/story.html. 'Citizen journalism' was one of the buzzwords of 2005, and the idea was discussed at the Arab and World Media Conference held in December in Dubai (Fatany: 'Internet opens new paths for journalism').

68 'I think yes,' writes Mohammed Ibahrine, a Moroccan doctoral student of communication and political culture in Germany (http://arabblogandcommunicationpolitical.blogspot.com/2005/12/will-podcasting-bring-democracy-to.html). 'Podcast' was declared word of the year in 2005 by the New Oxford American Dictionary.

69 Blogging with an Islamically oriented agenda has started to appear (e.g. MuslimStarZ, at http://muslimz.com, since November 2005), but remains less visible so far. Among famous bloggers, MaLcoLM X of Alexandria (http://malcolmix.blogspot.com) or Baghdad's Riverbend (http://riverbendblog.blogspot.com) are pronounced practising Muslims, but with a clear anti-authority approach.

70   Participants in training workshops of NetCorps Jordan (a pilot initiative to help communities to use computers and the Internet to improve their social and economic well-being) cited these changes when describing how IT use had helped them towards better organisation, strategic thinking, creativity, and confidence in dealing with older people (of higher authority) as well as those of the other sex. Benefits of IT were also linked to new possibilities for income generation and opportunities to access information more cheaply than through international phone calls or buying books and journals. For this information I am grateful to Deborah Wheeler, who lectured on 'IT for development: lessons learned from the NetCorps Jordan initiative' at the University of Oslo on 18 April 2005.

71   For a microanalysis of the dynamics on Sudanese discussion forums, see Albrecht Hofheinz, *Kalam Sakit? Sudanese Discussing State and Society on the Internet,* presentation to the 35th Annual Meeting of the Middle East Studies Association, San Francisco, 18 November 2001.

72   'Islam NEVER said that I support a Moslem in his evil doings. At least MY Islam never said that.' 'You mentioned Sh. Qardawy's statement. Who is Sh. Qardawy? Isn't he one like many others, since we have no clergy in Islam?' ('Sameh Arab', s-arab@menanet.net, postings in *Focus on Egypt,* http://groups.yahoo.com/group/free-voice, 14 and 15 September 2001). 'Subject: THIS IS MY ISLAM !!! / what is real islam / salah we soom we zakaah? / da2n we gallabeyya we sewak? / dah el zaher bass / lakin min gowwa eeh ??? / islam to me is: - enn beta3 el fool ya3'sel eedo abl ma ya3mil akl lel nas...' etc. (Wael Abbas, waelabbas@hotmail.com, former_internet_junkies@yahoogroups.com, 25 February 2003). In February 2005 Wael Abbas established a weekly news weblog, 'al-Wa'y al-Misri / Misr Digit@l', which quickly became a highly regarded source of alternative information, publishing, for example, photos and video of the violent dispersal by Egyptian police of a demonstration of Sudanese refugees in front of the UNHCR office in Cairo (http://misrdigital.blogspirit.com/, 31 December 2005).

73   Ahmad Humeid, 'The Arabic blogging revolution: made in Jordan?', 5 January 2006, http://www.360east.com/?p=270.

74   Fatema Mernissi, *Les Sindbads marocains: Voyage dans le Maroc civique* (Rabat, 2004).

75   Zarwan: *False Freedom*, pp. 24 and 72.

CHAPTER 6

1   Uses and meanings of the terms 'young people' and 'youth' vary in different societies around the world, depending on the political, economic and sociocultural context. For the purpose of this chapter, the terms 'youth' and 'young people' are used to refer to those aged between 16 and 27.

2   Imad Karam, *Arab Satellite Broadcasting: Alienation or Integration of Arab Youth?,* paper presented to a University of Westminster workshop on 'Arab Audiences: What Do We Know About Them?' (December 2004).

3   The 'Arab world' is a geopolitical term. The term, which provides linguistic and ethnic boundaries, is widely used by Arabs to refer to the region which incorporates the Arabic-speaking counties. For the purpose of this study, the term 'Arab world' is used to refer to the Arab region, which incorporates most Arab countries except the Maghreb countries, Somalia and Mauritania. My research was conducted in Egypt, the UAE, Jordan and Palestine, among informants aged 16 to 27 who came from Bahrain, Kuwait, Lebanon, Oman, Saudi Arabia, Syria, Sudan and Yemen.

4   Young people spend much more time watching television during the summer vacation, especially in the case of females, who are less likely to spend much time outdoors. Among respondents to my questionnaire, 62 per cent said they watch television for up to six hours during the summer vacation or if they are not working or studying. Another 28.9 per cent said they watch for up to three hours. Only 7.4 per cent said they watched for less

than one hour a day, and 1.7 per cent said they hardly watched any television during the summer vacation.

5   See Peter Dahlgren, 'The public sphere and the net: Structure, space and communication', in W. L. Bennett and R. M. Entman (eds), *Mediated Politics: Communication in the Future of Democracy* (Cambridge, 2001) p. 39; Mark Poster, 'Cyberdemocracy: Internet and the public sphere', in D. Porter (ed.), *Internet Culture* (New York, 1997), p. 206.

6   Annabelle Sreberny, 'Television, gender, and democratisation in the Middle East', in J. Curran and M.Y. Park (eds), *De-Westernizing Media Studies* (London, 2000), p. 69.

7   Marc Lynch, 'Beyond the Arab street: Iraq and the Arab public sphere', *Politics and Society* 31/1 (March 2003), pp. 55–91.

8   Noha Mellor, 'Credibility gap: Until the Arab media caters to ordinary citizens, the Middle East will never be a democracy', *FT Magazine* (October 2004), p. 10.

9   Kai Hafez, *Arab Satellite Broadcasting: An Alternative to Political Parties?*, paper presented to a conference on 'Media and Political Change in the Arab World' (Cambridge, 29–30 September 2004), also available at http://www.tbsjournal.com/Archives/Fall04/camphafez.htm.

10 UNDP: *Arab Human Development Report 2004*, p. 238.

11 Middle East News Agency,' 20% increase in unemployment in Arab region' (11 July 2005), available in Arabic online at http://www.menareport.com/ar/business/231310.

12 Roel Meijer, 'Introduction', in R. Meijer (ed.), *Alienation or Integration of Arab Youth: Between Family, State and Street* (Richmond, 2000), p. 1.

13 UNDP Regional Bureau for Arab States, *Arab Human Development Report 2002: Creating Opportunities for Future Generations* (New York, 2002), p. 30.

14 UNDP: *Arab Human Development Report 2002*, p. 30.

15 UNDP: *Arab Human Development Report 2003*, p. 144.

16 Iman Bibars, 'Youth and political awareness', *Al-Ahram* (13 January 2004) [in Arabic].

17 Bibars: 'Youth and political awareness'.

18 The names of interviewees in this chapter have been changed to protect their identities.

19 Focus group interview (3), Egypt, March 2005.

20 Focus group interview (2), United Arab Emirates, January 2005.

21 Focus group interview (1), United Arab Emirates, January 2005.

22 Focus group interview (3), Egypt, March 2005.

23 Focus group interview (2), United Arab Emirates, January 2005.

24 Focus group interview (3), United Arab Emirates, January 2005.

25 Focus group interview (1), Egypt, March 2005.

26 Focus group interview (2), Egypt, August 2004.

27 Focus group interview (2), Egypt, August 2004.

28 Focus group interview (2), Egypt, August 2004.

29 Focus group interview (2), Egypt, August 2004.

30 Focus group interview with Egyptian youth (1), August 2004.

31 Focus group interview, United Arab Emirates (1), January 2005.

32 Focus group interview, United Arab Emirates (1), January 2005.

33 Focus group interview, United Arab Emirates (2), January 2005.

34 MBC2 started as a variety channel and turned later into a channel devoted exclusively to entertainment. It had news bulletins and other programmes before it turned into a 24-hour movie channel.

35 These music channels are owned by, and carry the name of, Arab music and recording companies.

36 UNDP: *Arab Human Development Report 2003*, p. 61.

37 Egypt has a package of specialised satellite channels on its Nile 1 and Nile 2 satellites, including Nile Information (1992), Nile Drama (1995), Nile News (1998), Nile Culture (1998), Nile Sport (1998), Nile Family and Kids (1998), Nile Variety (1998), Manara Scientific Research (1998), Higher Education Channel (1998) and Tanweer Channel

(2001). Egypt also has seven educational channels, including Maho Ommiya Channel (Illiteracy Eradication), Primary School Channel, Preparatory School Channel, Secondary School Channel, Vocational Channel, Languages Channel and The Knowledge Channel.

38   Focus group interview with Egyptian youth (2), August 2004.

39   Barbara Ibrahim and Hind Wassef, 'Caught between two worlds: Youth in the Egyptian hinterland', in Meijer (ed.): *Alienation or Integration of Arab Youth,* p. 163.

40   Amina Khairy, 'Egyptian teens want non-didactic programmes', *Al-Hayat* (23 December 2003) [in Arabic].

41   Focus group interview (2), Jordan, March 2005.

42   Focus group interview (1), Jordan, March 2005.

43   Focus group interview (2), Egypt, August 2004.

44   Hassan Fattah, 'Zen TV reaches out to Arab youth', *Transnational Broadcasting Studies* 9 (Autumn 2002), http://www.tbsjournal.com/Archives/Fall02/Zen.html.

45   www.balagh.com/youth.

46   Jad al-Mutawi, 'Zen TV: Openness to youth or to westernization', www.islamweb.net (22 March 2002) [in Arabic].

47   Focus group interview (2), United Arab Emirates, April 2005.

48   Focus group interview (2), United Arab Emirates, April 2005.

49   Focus group interview (1), United Arab Emirates, January 2005.

50   Focus group interview (3), Egypt, March 2005.

51   Focus group interview (1), United Arab Emirates, January 2005.

52   Focus group interview (2), United Arab Emirates, January 2005.

53   Focus group interview with Egyptian youth (1), August 2004.

54   Amina Khairy, 'Arabic video clips flirt with desires of Egyptian youth', *Transnational Broadcasting Studies* 14 (Spring/Summer 2005), http://www.tbsjournal.com/khairy.html.

CHAPTER 7

1   It is important to point out that the 2005 presidential election was presented as something of a *fait accompli*, with Hamas not putting up candidates and the Fatah candidate, according to polls, having a significant majority of support. The only other candidate polling significant public support was Mustafa Barghouti, standing as an independent.

2   Jay Blumler and Michael Gurevitch, 'Towards a comparative framework for political communication research', in S. Chaffee (ed.), *Political Communication: Issues and Strategies for Research* (Beverly Hills, 1975), pp. 165–193.

3   Hussein Amin, 'Freedom as a value in Arab media: Perceptions and attitudes among journalists', *Political Communication* 19/2 (April–June 2002), pp. 125–135.

4   Marc Lynch, 'Shattering the politics of silence: Satellite television talk shows and the transformation of Arab political culture', *Carnegie Endowment for International Peace Arab Reform Bulletin* 2/1(December 2004), p. 2.

5   United Nations, *Report on UNCTAD's Assistance to the Palestinian People,* TD/B/50/4 (Geneva, 2003)

6   Saeda Hamad, 'Palestinian media map: The clash between sovereignty and opposition', in Arab Press Freedom Watch (ed.), *State of Arab Media: Annual Report* (London, 2004), p. 138.

7   Lynch: 'Shattering the politics of silence'.

8   A core part of the research design consisted of qualitative interviews with the main stakeholders in the media sector. Unstructured interviews took place with editors-in-chief, journalists, correspondents of international and foreign media outlets, human rights activists, institutions in charge of regulating media, as well as members of the election authorities.

9   Gianni Losito, *L'Analisi del Contenuto nella Ricerca Sociale* (Milan, 1996); Earl Babbie, *The Practice of Social Research* (London, 1998).

10 Lynch: 'Shattering the politics of silence'.
11 Maxwell McCombs and Donald Shaw, 'The agenda-setting function of the mass media', *Public Opinion Quarterly* 36 (Summer 1972), p. 180.
12 Sara Bentivegna, *Al Voto con i Media* (Milan, 1997).
13 According to the results of media monitoring undertaken five days prior to the official campaign period, the incumbent candidate and his party enjoyed an evident advantage: Mahmoud Abbas was the only candidate covered during the two editions of the evening news on PBC TV, and the distribution of time among the political parties benefited Fatah, with 97 per cent of the total time. The total time amounted to two hours.
14 Al-Jazeera, 'Code of Ethics', http://english.aljazeera.net/NR/exeres/07256105-B2FC-439A-B255-D830BB238EA1.htm [accessed 2 July 2005].
15 Although they were recorded for all kinds of programmes, the statistics for the tone of coverage were analysed only for programmes within the editorial control of the broadcasters. In this regard, candidates' political broadcasts on PBC TV were excluded from the analysis as their format and content were predetermined by the Central Election Commission and were therefore beyond the editorial control of the channel. For the same reason, paid spots were not included in those statistics.
16 According to David Altheide and Robert Snow, in *Media Logic* (Beverly Hills, 1979), media logic can be defined as the whole of formats through which events are taken into account, treated and interpreted in order to achieve a final product consistent with the organisational objectives of the media enterprise as well as with the objectives and images of the public.
17 These were unstructured interviews with editors, journalists, international correspondents, human rights activists and members of regulatory bodies.
18 Interview conducted in Ramallah, December 2004.
19 Lena Jayyusi, 'The Voice of Palestine and the peace process: Paradoxes in media discourse after Oslo', in G. Giacaman and D. J. Lonning (eds), *After Oslo: New Realities, Old Problems* (London, 1998), p. 191.
20 Gianpietro Mazzoleni, *La Comunicazione Politica* (Milan, 1998).

CHAPTER 8

1 Todd Gitlin, 'Public sphere or public sphericules?', in T. Liebes and J. Curran (eds), *Media, Ritual and Identity* (London, 1998), p. 173.
2 Nancy Fraser, 'Rethinking the public sphere: A contribution to the critique of actually existing democracy', in Calhoun (ed.): *Habermas and the Public Sphere*.
3 In total, I conducted 25 interviews, some with individuals, some with households and families and some with small groups. The sample was as diverse as possible in terms of age, gender and socio-economic conditions and religious orientations and was achieved through a snowballing method. Names have been changed to protect identities.
4 Annabelle Sreberny, 'Trauma talk: Reconfiguring the inside and outside', in B. Zelizer and S. Allen (eds), *Journalism after September 11* (London and New York, 2002), p. 220.
5 Annabelle Sreberny, 'Media and diasporic consciousness: An exploration among Iranians in London', in S. Cottle (ed.), *Ethnic Minorities and the Media* (Buckingham and Philadelphia, 2000), p. 182.
6 Marie Gillespie, *Television, Ethnicity and Cultural Change* (London and New York, 1995), p. 7.
7 The 2001 UK census put the number of ethnic minority residents in the country at 4.6 million, or 7.9 per cent of the total population.
8 Afif Safiyeh, the Palestinian General Delegate to the UK until late 2005, privately estimated there to be around 20,000 Palestinians in Britain, although his office records comprised only 5000 addresses for Palestinian individuals and families around the country. The difficulty in updating these records is related to the fact that many recent arrivals,

estimated by the Shaml Centre for Palestinian Diaspora Studies in Ramallah at about 3000 in 2001, are mostly ex-refugees and political asylum seekers who do not want to officially register themselves as Palestinian for a number of reasons, including concerns over losing their refugee status and worries about being too easily identified as Palestinians.

9   Stuart Hall, 'Introduction: Who needs identity', in S. Hall and P. du Gay (eds), *Questions of Cultural Identity* (London, 1996).

10 See Stuart Hall, 'Culture, media and the ideological effect', in J. Curran, M. Gurevitch and J. Woollacott (eds), *Mass Communication and Society* (London, 1977), pp. 343–344; and Karim H. Karim, *Islamic Peril, Media and Global Violence* (Montreal, 2003).

11 This draws on Michael Billig's critique of categorisation literature in *Arguing and Thinking: A Rhetorical Approach to Social Psychology* (Cambridge, 1987). Billig sees categorisation as a cognitive imperative, thus giving only a one-sided view of human action. He suggests that human understanding always occurs in a context of argument or conflict. In this sense, even our private thoughts arise out of an internal dialogue in which we pit different positions against each other, so we take positions to counter other positions. That said, self-categorisation theory places emphasis on the cognitive aspect of social identification and collective action – that is, the point at which people begin to act as a group is the point at which they begin to identify themselves in terms of the group.

12 Gerd Baumann, *Contesting Culture: Discourses of Identity in Multi-Ethnic London* (Cambridge, 1996).

13 Baumann: *Contesting Culture*, p. 195.

14 Of course, the Palestinians concerned in this study, like other diasporas, do engage in idealised visions of the homeland and of the past. The intention, however, is to move beyond these idealisations and emphasise the tension between imagining life as having been better, purer, etc. in the past and imagining life as being better in the future.

15 Alejandro Portes, Luis E. Guarnizo and Patricia Landolt (eds), 'Transnational communities', *Ethnic and Racial Studies* (special issue) 22/2 (March 1999).

CHAPTER 9

1   See http://www.thomsonfoundation.co.uk/docs/ruby/history.htm. The Thomson Foundation offered training courses for Libyans in 1978, and then Iraqi technicians. It still manages extensive training throughout the region.

2   The Humphrey Fellows started in 1978 with the goal of training mid-career professionals from all over the world in the US for up to a year; Middle Eastern fellows have numbered over 450 to date. Since around 10 per cent of any year's group are journalists, and since 35 per cent of total Middle East numbers come from Israel, Turkey and Ethiopia, I estimate that around 30 Arab journalists have been fellows.

3   AMIDEAST in Jerusalem/Gaza sent a handful of journalists and TV technicians for short-term training during the life of their USAID-funded training project but there was no concerted effort or strategic vision regarding the end result.

4   Palestinians attending these workshops in Cyprus accused Israeli journalists of combining journalism with serving in the occupation. Israelis accused their Palestinian counterparts of being unable to separate advocacy from objectivity.

5   Herbert Kelman, 'Group processes in the resolution of international conflicts: Experiences from the Israeli–Palestinian case', *American Psychologist* 52/3 (April 1997), pp. 212–220.

6   There currently does not exist a comprehensive inventory of pre-1994 civil society interventions for peace-building in the Middle East, no matter the conflict.

7   See Robert Springborg's inaugural lecture at the School of Oriental and African Studies, *The Democratization Industry and the Middle East* at http://www.lmei.soas.ac.uk/docs/ Inaugural_lecture_printversion27april.doc. Rosamelia Andrade's Institute for Media,

Policy and Civil Society (IMPACS) Roundtable Report 'Media and the Middle East' (2002), provides a general review of media intervention, at http://www.impacs.org.

8   For a historical review of these developments, see Hugh Miall, Oliver Ramsbotham and Tom Woodhouse, *Contemporary Conflict Resolution* (Cambridge, 1999). International Alert started in 1985. Search for Common Ground was founded in 1982, added media as a component of conflict resolution in 1989 and began working in the Middle East in 1991.

9   Projects targeting the media for conflict resolution had appeared in South Africa before 1990. The Media Peace Centre and its Mediation Project for Journalists received guidance from work at Harvard that included Kelman. See 'Reporting conflict', *Track Two* 7/4 (December 1998), http://ccrweb.ccr.uct.ac.za/two/7_4/p44_reporting_conflict.html.

10   The faith-based INGOs played a role here, with the Mennonites and Quakers, for example, helping to train and support many local Palestinians in conflict resolution techniques long before 1990.

11   IMPACS is a major source of these. See Ross Howard, 'An operational framework for media and peacebuilding', IMPACS (2002), http://www.impacs.org/actions/ files/MediaPrograms/framework_apr5.pdf. See also the Canadian example: 'The media and peacebuilding, draft operational framework', http://www.impacs.org/ freemedia/mediadiscussion.htm and that of the Stiftung Wissenschaft und Politik, 'Media and Conflict Prevention', http://www.impacs.org/files/MediaPrograms/ swpandcpnseminar.pdf.

12   The European Centre for Conflict Prevention published the first major summary in 2003: Ross Howard, Francis Rolt, Hans van de Veen and Juliette Verhoeven, *The Power of the Media: A Handbook for Peacebuilders* (Utrecht, 2003). After selling out, the book was due to be reprinted. For another interesting review and teaching tool, from the Institute for Media, Peace and Security at the UN University of Peace, see Clyde Sanger and Alvaro Sierra, *The Role of Media in Conflict Prevention and Peace Building* (San Jose, 2005).

13   *Gesher* was founded in 1986 by a Palestinian academic to reach out to Israelis and to try to modify their negative stereotypes of Palestinians. See Loretta Hieber, *Lifeline Media: Reaching Populations in Crisis* (Geneva, 2001), p. 117, http://www.impacs.org/files/ MediaPrograms/lifelinemedia.pdf.

14   In his 2005 article 'Tasting Western journalism: Media Training in the Middle East' for the USC Center of Public Diplomacy, Gordon Robison carries the comment by Hassan Fattah that, during one week in December 2004 in Amman, there were four separate training workshops for Iraqi journalists run by different funders; http://www.icfj.org/files/ Tasting_Western_journalism_May05.pdf.

15   America's Development Foundation has $40 million of USAID funding for its 'Civil Society and Media Support Project' for Iraq, which makes no mention of the peace or conflict context in which the project operates; http://www.adfusa.org

16   Pernille B. Jørgensen, *The Media Situation in the Middle East: Media Support in the Context of the Danish 'Wider Middle East Initiative'* (Copenhagen, 2004), http://www.i-ms.dk/ Media/PDF/Final%20General%20report%20on%20the%20media%20situation%20in %20the%20middle.pdf.

17   See John Burton, *Conflict: Resolution and Provention* (New York, 1990), for a discussion of his alternative to traditional democratic peace theory.

18   UNESCO's 'Assistance to Media in Conflict Situations' talks of supporting media through election support activities, media development and the promotion of freedom of expression, without any clear conflict resolution framework.

19   See Jemstone reports at http://www.jemstone.net/reportdetails_print.php?id=4 and http://www.jemstone.net/jemstone_old/newsletter/news0013/index.shtml.

20   See Hans Gsanger and Christoph Feyen, 'Peace and conflict impact assessment methodology: A development practitioner's perspective', http://www.berghof-handbook.net/feyen/final.pdf, or 'Conflict analysis and response definition' http://www.

fewer.org/research/studcam401.pdf, for more information on the growing understandings emerging from PCIA evaluations of conflict interventions.

21 Miall, Ramsbotham and Woodhouse: *Contemporary Conflict Resolution*.

22 When Elise Boulding talked about the 'two-hundred-year present' required for real transformational work on conflict, she meant that present actions can be guided by an awareness of the 100 years that brought us to this conflict moment along with a vision of a strong, functioning, conflict-handling society 100 years hence.

23 Johan Galtung, *Peace by Peaceful Means: Peace and Conflict, Development and Civilization* (London, 1996).

24 Howard: 'An operational framework'.

25 http://www.ned.org/grants/02programs/grants-mena.html.

26 See Howard et al.: *The Power of the Media*, pp. 26–28, for a discussion of phases and intervention types.

27 E.g. C. R. Mitchell, *The Structure of International Conflict* (London, 1981).

28 Peter V. Jakobsen, 'Focus on the CNN effect misses the point: The real media impact on conflict management is invisible and indirect', *Journal of Peace Research* 37/2 (March 2000), p. 132. It has proved hard to overcome a general human tendency, often seen in the media, to be more concerned with violence and obvious manifestations of conflict ('war journalism') than to look at conflicts in the long term.

29 Jørgensen: *The Media Situation in the Middle East.*

30 The Conflict Resolution Network has started with the basics, providing an introductory 'Conflict resolution toolkit' for the media via the web: http://www.crnhq.org/ crmedia.html.

31 Alvin Toffler and Heidi Toffler, *War and Anti-War: Survival at the Dawn of the 21st Century* (London, 1999).

32 Johan Galtung, 'High road, low road: Charting the course of peace journalism', *Track Two* 7/4 (1998), http://ccrweb.ccr.uct.ac.za/archive/two/7_4/p07_highroad_lowroad.html.

33 http://www.crossingborder.org.

34 The SfCG series *Shape of the Future* addressed five final status issues: Jerusalem, borders, security, Israeli settlements and Palestinian refugees.

35 http://www.sfcg.org/sfcg/sfcg_toolbox.html. SfCG's current Partners in Humanity programme seeks to address mutual fear and suspicion between the Muslim world and the West, particularly the US.

36 See DfID's 2000 report *Working with the Media in Conflicts and other Emergencies*, http:// www.reliefweb.int/library/documents/2002/dfid_media.pdf.

37 http://www.panosparis.org/gb/pluralisme.php.

38 http://www.npr.org/about/nextgen/betz_morocco_12.html.

39 http://www.images-education.org/past_project.htm.

40 http://www.fordfound.org.

41 Adapted from M. Fitzduff, *Approaches to Community Relations Work*, Community Resolutions Council Pamphlet no. 1 (Belfast, 1993).

42 It is interesting to note that one of the major projects for conflict resolution intervention with Iraqi civil society post-2003, that of the Columbia University Center for International Conflict Resolution (CICR), does not include media-directed activities to support empowerment of the Iraqi media in conflict resolution; http://www. worldleaders.columbia.edu/pdf/iraq_program.pdf.

43 See 'Dialogue projects' from the International Online Training Program on Intractable Conflict for a discussion and reading list, http://www.colorado.edu/conflict/peace/ treatment/dialog2.htm, and Edward (Edy) Kaufman's chapter 'Dialogue based processes', in Edy Kaufman, Walid Salem and Juliette Verhoeven (eds), *Bridging the Divide: Peacebuilding in the Israeli–Palestinian Conflict* (Boulder: CO, 2006). See also Norbert Ropers, 'From resolution to transformation: Assessing the role and impact of dialogue projects', http://www.zef.de/download/ethnic_conflict/ropers.pdf.

44 See Miftah's 2005 report of their media monitoring supported by the EU: http://www.miftah.org/Doc/Reports/MKReports/final_monitoring_report_4_3_2005(2).pdf.

45 The Peacemakers Trust in Canada supports an annual Award for Excellence in Conflict Analysis, given by the Canadian Association of Journalists as part of its attempt to get the media to be more cognisant of conflict analysis concepts; http://www.peacemakers.ca/education/ConflictAnalysis.html.

46 Similar questions persist about the impact of the huge effort expended in Bosnia, as noted in Robison: 'Tasting Western journalism'.

47 John N. Erni, 'War, incendiary media, and international law (part I)', *Flow* 3/2 (September 2005), http://jot.communication.utexas.edu/flow/?jot=view&id=948.

48 Loretta Hieber, 'Media as intervention: A report from the field', *Track Two* 7/4 (December 1998), http://ccrweb.ccr.uct.ac.za.

49 Dennis Sandole, 'John Burton's contribution to conflict resolution theory and practice: A personal view', *International Journal of Peace Studies* 6/1 (Spring 2001), http://www.gmu.edu/academic/ijps/vol6_1/Sandole.htm; and John Burton, 'Conflict provention as a political system', *International Journal of Peace Studies* 6/1 (Spring 2001), http://www.gmu.edu/academic/ijps/vol6_1/Burton2.htm.

50 Gadi Wolfsfeld, *Media and the Path to Peace* (Cambridge, 2004), p. 38.

CHAPTER 10

1   Louis Awad, 'Contemporary Arab culture: Motivations and ends', *Journal of World History* XIV (1972), p. 757.

2   The series was organised by the University of Westminster's Communication and Media Research Institute, with funding from the Economic and Social Research Council. See 'Acknowledgements' in this volume, p. xi.

3   Ahmad Aijaz, *In Theory: Classes, Nations, Literatures* (London, 1992).

4   In the opening pages of *A Critique of Arab Reason* (Beirut, 1991), Jabri justifies using the phrase 'Arab reason' instead of 'Arab thought'. Not only does he understand that the meaning of 'thought' overlaps with that of 'ideology' but he is also aware that the word 'thought' can mean both the tool for producing thoughts and the ensemble of thoughts produced. His treatise, written in Arabic, is about thought as the tool (reason) that produces thoughts. As he later put it, in *A Critique of Arab Reason: The Structure of Arab Reason – A Critical Analytical Study of Knowledge Norms in Arab Culture* (Casablanca, 2000), p. 11, 'In this book, I am not interested in thought or thoughts as such but the tool that produces them.'

5   André Lalande, *La Raison et les Normes* (Paris, 1948).

6   Jabri: *A Critique of Arab Reason*, pp. 15–16.

7   Lalande: *La Raison et les Normes*, p. 2; author's translation from French.

8   Lalande: *La Raison et les Normes*, p. 2.

9   Jabri: *A Critique of Arab Reason*, p. 40.

10 Jabri: *A Critique of Arab Reason*, p. 44.

11 Jabri: *A Critique of Arab Reason*, pp. 38–39.

12 Jabri: *A Critique of Arab Reason*, p. 47; translated from Arabic.

13 Jabri: *A Critique of Arab Reason*, p. 47.

14 Jabri: *A Critique of Arab Reason*, p. 43.

15 Jabri: *A Critique of Arab Reason*, p. 47; translated from Arabic.

16 I use the phrase 'Islamic society' here with some reservation, as it homogenises Islamic societies into one coherent body, which is far from the truth. Islamic or Muslim societies are clearly stratified into different tastes, cultures and structures of feeling about the world. See Gholam Khiabany, 'De-Westernising media theory, or reverse Orientalism: "Islamic communication" as theorised by Hamid Mowlana', *Media, Culture*

and Society, 25/3 (May 2003), p. 416. Ayish's article appeared in Javnost 10/2, pp. 79–92.

17 Basyouni Hamada, 'Islamic culture theory, Arab media performance and public opinion', in S. Splichal (ed.), Public Opinion and Democracy: Vox Populi – Vox Dei (Cresskill: NJ, 2001), pp. 219–222.

18 George Orwell, Nineteen Eighty-Four (London, 1951), p. 5.

19 Raymond Williams, Culture and Society 1780–1950 (London, 1963), p. 276.

20 Matthew Arnold, Culture and Anarchy and Other Writings (Cambridge, 1993), p. 79.

21 'L'esthétique transcendentale ne peut compter le concept de changement au nombres de ses donnés a priori, car ce n'est pas le temps lui-même qui change, mais quelque chose qui est dans le temps. Ce concept exige donc la perception de telle ou telle existence actuelle, où se succèdent certaines déterminations; et par conséquent il suppose l'expérience' (Kant, quoted in Lalande: La Raison et les Normes, p. 26).

22 José Ortega y Gasset, The Revolt of the Masses (London, 1932).

23 Matthew Arnold, Culture and Anarchy (New Haven: CT and London, 1994 [1869]).

24 John Carey, The Intellectuals and the Masses (London, 1992).

25 Williams: Culture and Society, p. 289.

26 M. Rasem El-Gammal, Broadcasting Research in the Arab World, 1952–2002: An Overview, paper presented at the University of Westminster conference on Arab broadcasting (10 June 2003).

27 Alterman: 'Arab media studies', pp. 203–208.

28 Mohammed Abed Jabri, The Question of Identity: Arabs, Islam and the West [in Arabic] (Beirut, 1994), p. 209.

29 Jabri: The Question of Identity, p. 214.

30 Jabri: The Question of Identity, p. 223.

31 Jabri: The Question of Identity, p. 226.

32 Mehdi Manjra, The Intifada in the Age of Rule by Humiliation [in Arabic] (Kenitra, 2001); Jabri: The Question of Identity; Mohamed al-Ghazali, Cultural Imperialism Resides in our Emptiness [in Arabic] (Cairo, 1998); Samir Amin and Burhan Ghalyun, The Globalization of Culture and the Culture of Globalization [in Arabic] (Beirut, 1999); Yahya al-Yahyawi, The Arab World and Challenges of Technology, Media and Communication [in Arabic] (Kenitra, 1997).

33 Williams: Culture and Society, p. 285.

34 Jacques Berque, 'Vers une culture arabe contemporaine', Journal of World History XIV (1972), p. 739.

35 Ien Ang and David Morley, 'Mayonnaise culture and other European follies', Cultural Studies 3/2 (May 1989), p. 135.

36 Ang and Morley: 'Mayonnaise culture', p. 136.

37 We can add African and Asian cultural studies to this list, but the latter are still in their early stage of development.

38 Ang and Morley: 'Mayonnaise culture', p. 163.

39 Jon Stratton and Ien Ang, 'On the impossibility of a global cultural studies: "British" cultural studies in an international frame', in D. Morley and K-H. Chen (eds), Stuart Hall: Critical Dialogues in Cultural Studies (London, 1996), p. 362.

40 Stratton and Ang: 'On the impossibility', p. 361.

41 Kuan-Hsing Chen, 'Cultural studies and the politics of internationalization: An interview with Stuart Hall', in Morley and Chen: Stuart Hall, p. 400.

42 Stratton and Ang: 'On the impossibility', pp. 361–362.

43 Ackbar Abbas and John Nguyet Erni, 'General introduction', in A. Abbas and J. N. Erni (eds), Internationalizing Cultural Studies: An Anthology (Oxford, 2005), p. 2.

44 Abbas and Erni: 'General introduction', p. 2.

45 Stratton and Ang: 'On the impossibility'.

46 Chen: 'Cultural studies and the politics of internationalization', p. 394.

47 Ang and Morley: 'Mayonnaise culture', p. 137.
48 Ang and Morley: 'Mayonnaise culture', p. 137.
49 Chen: 'Cultural studies and the politics of internationalization', p. 395.
50 Abbas and Erni: 'General introduction'.
51 Paddy Scannell, 'Cultural Studies and the Meaning of Life', unpublished manuscript, p. 12.
52 Quoted in Leela Gandhi, *Postcolonial Theory: A Critical Introduction* (St Leonard's: NSW, 1998), p. 6.
53 Bill Ashcroft, Gareth Griffiths and Helen Tiffin, *The Empire Writes Back: Theory and Practice in Postcolonial Literatures* (London, 1989), p. 2.
54 Robert Young, *Postcolonialism: An Historical Introduction* (Oxford, 2001), p. 56.
55 Gandhi: *Postcolonial Theory*, p. 4.
56 Aijaz: *In Theory*.
57 Gandhi: *Postcolonial Theory*, pp. ix–x.
58 Gayatri Chakravorty Spivak, 'Can the subaltern speak?', in B. Ashcroft, G. Griffiths and H. Tiffin (eds), *The Postcolonial Studies Reader* (London, 1995), pp. 24–28.
59 Ania Loomba, *Colonialism/Postcolonialism* (London, 1998), p. 173.
60 Homi K. Bhabha, *The Location of Culture* (London, 1994), p. 4.
61 Mohamed Gassous, 'Observations on transformations in contemporary Moroccan popular culture', in Manshurat al-Majlis al-Baladi (ed.), *Popular Culture: A Pillar of the Arab Maghreb Union* [in Arabic] (Kenitra, 1988), pp. 33–56.
62 Quoted by Bart Moore-Gilbert in *Postcolonial Theory, Contexts, Practices, Politics* (London, 1997), p. 186.

BIBLIOGRAPHY

Abbas, Ackbar, and Erni, John Nguyet, 'General introduction', in A. Abbas and J. N. Erni
(eds), *Internationalizing Cultural Studies: An Anthology* (Oxford, 2005), pp. 1–12
Abdel-Hamid, Ammar, 'Media reform in Syria: A door ajar?', *Arab Reform Bulletin* 2/11
(December 2004)
Abedi, Mehdi, and Fischer, Michael, 'Etymologies: Thinking a public sphere in Arabic and
Persian', *Public Culture* 6/1 (Autumn 1993), pp. 219–230
Abu-Lughod, Lila, *Dramas of Nationhood: The Politics of Television in Egypt* (Chicago, 2005)
Aijaz, Ahmad, *In Theory: Classes, Nations, Literatures* (London, 1992)
Alavi, Nasrin, *We are Iran: The Persian Blogs* (Brooklyn: NY, 2005)
Al-Ghazali, Mohamed, *Cultural Imperialism Resides in our Emptiness* [in Arabic] (Cairo, 1998)
Al Kasim, Faisal, '*The Opposite Direction*: A program which changed the face of Arab television',
in M. Zayani (ed.), *The Al Jazeera Phenomenon: Critical Perspectives on New Arab Media*
(London, 2005), pp. 93–105
Al-Khawaga, Ala/Information and Decision Support Center (eds), *Ta'thir al-Internet 'ala al-
shabab fi Misr wa'l-'alam al-'Arabi: dirasa naqdiyya* [*The Internet's Impact on Youth in
Egypt and the Arab World: A Critical Study*] (Cairo, November 2005)
Alterman, Jon, *New Media, New Politics? From Satellite Television to the Internet in the Arab
World* (Washington: DC, 1998)
— 'Arab media studies: Some methodological considerations', in M. Zayani (ed.), *The Al Jazeera
Phenomenon: Critical Perspectives on New Arab Media* (London, 2005), pp. 203–208
Altheide, David, and Snow, Robert, *Media Logic* (Beverly Hills, 1997)
Al-Yahyawi, Yahya, *The Arab World and Challenges of Technology, Media and Communication*
[in Arabic] (Kenitra, 1997)
Amin, Hussein, 'Freedom as a value in Arab media: Perceptions and attitudes among
journalists', *Political Communication* 19/2 (April–June 2002), pp. 125–135
Amin, Samir, and Ghalyun, Burhan, *The Globalization of Culture and the Culture of
Globalization* [in Arabic] (Beirut, 1999)
Anderson, Jon W., and Eickelman, Dale F. (eds), *New Media in the Muslim World: The Emerging
Public Sphere* (Bloomington: IN, 1999)
Ang, Ien, and Morley, David, 'Mayonnaise culture and other European follies', *Cultural
Studies* 3/2 (May 1989), pp. 133–144
Arnold, Matthew, *Culture and Anarchy* (New Haven: CT and London, 1994 [1869])
— *Culture and Anarchy and Other Writings* (Cambridge, 1993)
Ashcroft, Bill, Griffiths, Gareth, and Tiffin, Helen, *The Empire Writes Back: Theory and Practice
in Postcolonial Literatures* (London, 1989)
Awad, Louis, 'Contemporary Arab culture: Motivations and ends', *Journal of World History* XIV
(1972), pp. 756–770
Ayish, Muhammad, 'Beyond Western-oriented communication theories: A normative Arab-
Islamic perspective', *Javnost* 10/2 (2003), pp. 79–92
— *Arab World Television in the Age of Globalisation* (Hamburg, 2003)

— 'Media brinkmanship in the Arab world: Al Jazeera's *The Opposite Direction* as a fighting arena', in M. Zayani (ed.), *The Al Jazeera Phenomenon: Critical Perspectives on New Arab Media* (London, 2005), pp. 106–126

Babbie, Earl, *The Practice of Social Research* (London, 1998)

Bahry, Louay, 'The new Arab media phenomenon: Qatar's Al-Jazeera', *Middle East Policy* 8/2 (June 2001), pp. 88–99

Bartholy, Heike, 'Barrieren in der interkulturellen Kommunikation', in M. Reimann (ed.), *Transkulturelle Kommunikation und Weltgesellschaft: Zur Theorie und Pragmatik globaler Interaktion* (Opladen, 1992), pp. 174–191

Baudrillard, Jean, *Simulacra and Simulation* (Ann Arbor: MI, 1994)

Baumann, Gerd, *Contesting Culture: Discourses of Identity in Multi-Ethnic London* (Cambridge, 1996)

Bennett, W. Lance, and Entman, R. M. (eds), *Mediated Politics: Communication in the Future of Democracy* (Cambridge, 2001)

Bennington, Geoffrey, *Lyotard: Writing the Event* (Manchester, 1988)

Bentivegna, Sara, *Al Voto con i Media* (Milan, 1997)

Berque, Jacques, 'Vers une culture Arabe contemporaine', *Journal of World History* XIV (1972), pp. 729–755

Bhabha, Homi K., *The Location of Culture* (London, 1994)

Billig, Michael, *Arguing and Thinking: A Rhetorical Approach to Social Psychology* (Cambridge, 1987)

Blumler, Jay, and Gurevitch, Michael, *Crisis of Public Communication* (London, 1995)

— 'Towards a comparative framework for political communication research', in S. Chaffee (ed.), *Political Communication: Issues and Strategies for Research* (Beverly Hills, 1975), pp. 165–193

Bourdieu, Pierre, *On Television and Journalism* (London, 1998)

Bourdon, Jerome, 'Live television is still alive: On television as an unfulfilled promise', in R. C. Allen and A. Hill (eds), *The Television Studies Reader* (London, 2004), pp. 183–195

Burton, John, *Conflict: Resolution and Provention* (New York, 1990)

— 'Conflict provention as a political system', *International Journal of Peace Studies* 6/1 (Spring 2001), http://www.gmu.edu/academic/ijps/vol6_1/Burton2.htm.

Butterfield, Bradley, 'The Baudrillardian symbolic, 9/11, and the war of good and evil', *Postmodern Culture* 13/1 (September 2002) [online], available at http://www3.iath.virginia.edu/pmc/text-only/issue.902/13.1butterfield.txt

Calhoun, Craig, 'Introduction: Habermas and the public sphere', in C. Calhoun (ed.), *Habermas and the Public Sphere* (Cambridge: MA, 1992), pp. 1–48

Carey, John, *The Intellectuals and the Masses* (London, 1992)

Chen, Kuan-Hsing, 'Cultural studies and the politics of internationalization: An interview with Stuart Hall', in D. Morley and K-H. Chen (eds), *Stuart Hall: Critical Dialogues in Cultural Studies* (London, 1996), pp. 392–408

Cole, Timothy, 'The political rhetoric of sacrifice and heroism and US military intervention', in L. Artz and Y. Kamalipour (eds), *Bring 'Em On: Media and Politics in the Iraq War* (Lanham: MD, 2005), pp. 139–154

Dahlgren, Peter, *Television and the Public Sphere: Citizenship, Democracy and the Media* (London, 1995)

— 'The public sphere and the net: Structure, space and communication', in W. L. Bennett and R. M. Entman (eds) *Mediated Politics: Communication in the Future of Democracy,* (Cambridge, 2001), pp. 33–55

Dajani, Nabil, *Disoriented Media in a Fragmented Society: The Lebanese Experience* (Beirut, 1992)

— 'Lebanese television: Caught between government and the private sector', in J. Atkins (ed.), *The Mission: Journalism, Ethics and the World* (Ames: IA, 2002), pp. 123–141

Dalacoura, Katerina, 'US democracy promotion in the Arab Middle East since 11 September 2001: A critique', *International Affairs* 81/5 (October 2005), pp. 963–979

Dayan, Daniel, and Katz, Elihu, *Media Events: The Live Broadcasting of History* (Cambridge: MA, 1992)

Deacon, David, Golding, Peter, McGuigan, Jim, Purdey, Heather, and Rawson, Sarah, 'Information/News Management, Journalism Culture(s), and (a) European Public Sphere(s) (EPS(s)): The Case of Great Britain', report to the 'Adequate Information Management in Europe (AIM)' 6th Framework Programme of the EU Commission, (Dortmund, 2005), http://www.aim-project.net/uploads/media/GreatBritain.pdf

Dörner, Andreas, *Politainment: Politik in der medialen Erlebnisgesellschaft* (Frankfurt, 2001)

Eder, Klaus, 'Zur Transformation nationalstaatlicher Öffentlichkeit in Europa', *Berliner Journal Soziologie* 10/2 (May 2000), pp. 167–184

Eder, Klaus, and Kantner, Cathleen, 'Interdiskursivität in der europäischen Öffentlichkeit', *Berliner Debatte Initial* 13/5–6 (October 2002), pp. 79–88

Eickelman, Dale, 'Bin Laden, the Arab "street", and the Middle East's democracy deficit', *Current History* 101/651 (January 2002), pp. 36–39

Eid, Gamal, *The Internet in the Arab World: A New Space of Repression?*, The Arab Network for Human Rights Information (2004), http://www.hrinfo.net/en/reports/net2004

Eldridge, John, 'News, truth and power', in J. Eldridge (ed.), *Getting the Message: News, Truth and Power* (London, 1993), pp. 3–33

El-Nawawy, Mohammed, and Gher, Leo A., 'Al-Jazeera: Bridging the East–West gap through public discourse and media diplomacy', *Transnational Broadcasting Studies* 10 (Spring/Summer 2003), http://www.tbsjournal.com/Archives/Spring03/nawawy.html

El-Nawawy, Mohammed, and Iskandar, Adel, *Al-Jazeera: How the Free Arab News Network Scooped the World and Changed the Middle East* (Boulder: CO, 2002)

— 'The Minotaur of "contextual objectivity": War coverage and the pursuit of accuracy with appeal', *Transnational Broadcasting Studies* 9 (Autumn/Winter, 2002)

Entman, Robert M., 'Framing: Toward clarification of a fractured paradigm', *Journal of Communication* 43/4 (Autumn 1993), pp. 51–58

Erni, John N. 'War, incendiary media, and international law (part I)', *Flow* 3/2 (September 2005), http://jot.communication.utexas.edu/flow/?jot=view&id=948

Fattah, Hassan, 'Zen TV reaches out to Arab youth', *Transnational Broadcasting Studies* 9 (Autumn 2002), http://www/tbsjournal.com/Archives/Fall02/zen.html

Foote, Kenneth E., *Color in Public Spaces: Toward a Communication-Based Theory of the Urban Built Environment* (Chicago, 1983)

Fraser, Nancy, 'Rethinking the public sphere: A contribution to the critique of actually existing democracy', in C. Calhoun (ed.), *Habermas and the Public Sphere* (Cambridge: MA, 1992), pp. 109–142

Galtung, Johan, *Peace by Peaceful Means: Peace and Conflict, Development and Civilization* (London, 1996)

– 'High road, low road: Charting the course of peace journalism', *Track Two* 7/4 (December 1998), http://ccrweb.ccr.uct.ac.za/archive/two/7_4/p07_highroad_lowroad.html

Gandhi, Leela, *Postcolonial Theory: A Critical Introduction* (St Leonard's: NSW, 1998)

García-Canclini, Nestor, *Consumers and Citizens: Globalization and Multicultural Conflicts* (Minneapolis, 2001)

Garnham, Nicholas, 'The media and the public sphere', in N. Garnham (ed.), *Capitalism and Communication: Global Culture and the Economics of Information* (London, 1990 [1986]), pp. 104–114

— 'The media and the public sphere', in C. Calhoun (ed.), *Habermas and the Public Sphere* (Cambridge: MA, 1992), pp. 359–376

— *Emancipation, the Media, and Modernity* (Oxford, 2000)

Gassous, Mohamed, 'Observations on transformations in contemporary Moroccan popular culture', in M. al-Majlis al-Baladi (ed.), *Popular Culture: A Pillar of the Arab Maghreb Union* [in Arabic] (Kenitra, 1988), pp. 33–56

Gerhards, Jürgen, 'Europäisierung von Ökonomie und Politik und die Trägheit der Entstehung einer europäischen Öffentlichkeit', in M. Bach (ed.), 'Die Europäisierung nationaler Gesellschaften', *Kölner Zeitschrift für Soziologie und Sozialpsychologie* (special issue) 40 (2000), pp. 277–305

Gilboa, Eytan, 'Mass communication and diplomacy: A theoretical framework', *Communication Theory* 10/3 (August 2000), pp. 275–309

Gillespie, Marie, *Television, Ethnicity and Cultural Change* (London and New York, 1995)

Gillis, John R., 'Memory and identity: The history of a relationship', in J. R. Gillis (ed.), *Commemorations: The Politics of National Identity* (Princeton: NJ, 1994), pp. 3–24

Gitlin, Todd, 'Public sphere or public sphericules?', in T. Liebes and J. Curran (eds), *Media, Ritual and Identity* (London, 1998), pp. 168–174

Golding, Peter, 'The mass media and the public sphere: The crisis of information in the "information society"', in S. Edgall, S. Walklate and G. Williams (eds), *Debating the Future of the Public Sphere: Transforming the Public and Private Domains in Free Market Societies* (Aldershot, 1995), pp. 25–40

Goldsmiths Media Group, 'Media organizations in society: Central issues', in J. Curran (ed.), *Media Organisations in Society* (London, 2000), pp. 19–65

Gramsci, Antonio, *Selections from the Prison Notebooks* (transl. Q. Hoare and G. Nowell-Smith) (London, 1971)

Grimm, Dieter, 'Does Europe need a constitution?', *European Law Journal* 1/3 (November 1995), pp. 282–302

Gunter, Barrie, *Media Research Methods* (London, 2000)

Gurevitch, Michael, and Blumler, Jay G., 'Political communication systems and democratic values', in J. Lichtenberg (ed.), *Democracy and the Mass Media* (Cambridge, 1990), pp. 269–289

Habermas, Jürgen, *Strukturwandel der Öffentlichkeit: Untersuchungen zu einer Kategorie der bürgerlichen Gesellschaft* (Neuwied, 1962)

— 'The public sphere: An encyclopaedia article', *New German Critique* 3 (Autumn 1974), pp. 49–55

— *The Structural Transformation of the Public Sphere: An Inquiry into a Category of Bourgeois Society* (transl. T. Burger and F. Lawrence) (Cambridge: MA, 1989)

Hafez, Kai, *Die politische Dimension der Auslandsberichterstattung: Theoretische Grundlagen* (vol. I) (Baden-Baden, 2002)

Hahn, Oliver, *ARTE - Der Europäische Kulturkanal: Eine Fernsehsprache in vielen Sprachen* (Munich, 1997)

— 'ARTE an der Kreuzung der Kommunikationskulturen: Interkultureller und multilingualer TV-Nachrichtenjournalismus beim Europäischen Kulturkanal', in M. Machill (ed.), *Journalistische Kultur: Rahmenbedingungen im internationalen Vergleich* (Opladen and Wiesbaden, 1997), pp. 137–153

— 'Neues arabisches und westliches Nachrichtenfernsehen zwischen Kulturbindung und Propagandadialog', *Zeitschrift für Kommunikationsökologie* 6/1 (2004), pp. 44–47

Hahn, Oliver, Lönnendonker, Julia, Rosenwerth, Karen K., and Schröder, Roland, 'Information/News Management, Journalism Culture(s), and (a) European Public Sphere(s) (EPS(s)): The Case of Germany', report delivered to the 'Adequate Information Management in Europe (AIM)' 6th Framework Programme of the EU Commission (Dortmund, 2005), http://www.aim-project.net/uploads/media/Germany.pdf

Hall, Edward T., *The Silent Language* (New York, London, Toronto, Sydney and Auckland, 1959)

— *The Hidden Dimension* (New York, London, Toronto, Sydney and Auckland, 1966)

— *Beyond Culture* (New York, London, Toronto, Sydney and Auckland, 1976)

Hall, Stuart, 'Culture, media and the ideological effect', in J. Curran, M. Gurevitch and J. Woollacott (eds), *Mass Communication and Society* (London, 1977), pp. 315–348

— 'Introduction: Who needs identity?', in S. Hall and P. du Gay (eds), *Questions of Cultural Identity* (London, 1996), pp. 1–17

Hallin, Daniel C. *The Uncensored War* (Berkeley: CA, 1986)
— *We Keep America On Top of the World: Television Journalism and the Public Sphere* (London, 1994)
Hamad, Saeda, 'Palestinian media map: The clash between sovereignty and opposition', in Arab Press Freedom Watch (ed.), *State of Arab Media: Annual Report* (London, 2004), pp. 137–141
Hamada, Basyouni, 'Islamic culture theory, Arab media performance and public opinion', in S. Splichal (ed.), *Public Opinion and Democracy: Vox Populi – Vox Dei* (Cresskill: NJ, 2001), pp. 215–239
Hamzah, Dyala, 'Is there an Arab public sphere? The Palestinian intifada, a Saudi fatwa and the Egyptian press', in A. Salvatore and M. LeVine (eds), *Religion, Social Practice, and Contested Hegemonies: Reconstructing the Public Sphere in Muslim Majority Societies* (New York and Basingstoke, 2005), pp. 181–206
Hanada, Tatsuro, 'Toward a politics of the public sphere', in T. Hanada (ed.), 'The public sphere and communication policy in Japan and the UK', *Review of Media, Information and Society* (special issue) 4 (1999), pp. 115–134
Hartley, John, *The Politics of Pictures: The Creation of the Public in the Age of Popular Media* (London, 1992)
Hieber, Loretta, 'Media as intervention: A report from the field', *Track Two* 7/4 (December 1998), http://ccrweb.ccr.uct.ac.za
Hofheinz, Albrecht, 'Das Internet und sein Beitrag zum Wertewandel in arabischen Gesellschaften', in S. Faath (ed.), *Politische und gesellschaftliche Debatten in Nordafrika, Nah- und Mittelost: Inhalte, Träger, Perspektiven* (Hamburg, 2004), pp. 449–472
Hohendahl, Peter Uwe (ed.), *Öffentlichkeit: Geschichte eines kritischen Begriffs* (Stuttgart, 2000)
Howard, Ross, Rolt, Francis, van de Veen, Hans, and Verhoeven, Juliette, *The Power of the Media: A Handbook for Peacebuilders* (Utrecht, 2003)
Ibrahim, Barbara, and Wassef, Hind, 'Caught between two worlds: Youth in the Egyptian hinterland', in R. Meijer (ed.), *Alienation or Integration of Arab Youth?* (Richmond, 2000), pp. 161–187
Jabri, Mohammed Abed, *A Critique of Arab Reason: The Composition of Arab Reason* (Beirut, 1991)
— *The Question of Identity: Arabs, Islam and the West* [in Arabic] (Beirut, 1994)
— *A Critique of Arab Reason: The Structure of Arab Reason – A Critical Analytical Study of Knowledge Norms in Arab Culture* (Casablanca, 2000)
Jakobsen, Peter V., 'Focus on the CNN effect misses the point: The real media impact on conflict management is invisible and indirect', *Journal of Peace Research* 37/2 (March 2000), pp. 131–143
Jayyusi, Lena, 'The Voice of Palestine and the peace process: Paradoxes in media discourse after Oslo', in G. Giacaman and D.J. Loning (eds), *After Oslo: New Realities, Old Problems* (London, 1998), pp. 189–211
Jørgensen, Pernille B., *The Media Situation in the Middle East: Media Support in the Context of the Danish 'Wider Middle East Initiative'* (Copenhagen, 2004)
Kantner, Cathleen, 'Öffentliche politische Kommunikation in der EU: Eine hermeneutisch-pragmatische Perspektive', in A. Klein, R. Koopmanns, H.-J. Trenz, L. Klein, C. Lahusen and D. Rucht (eds), *Bürgerschaft, Öffentlichkeit und Demokratie in Europa* (Opladen, 2003), pp. 215–232
Karim, Karim H., *Islamic Peril, Media and Global Violence* (Montreal, 2003)
Kaufman, Edy, 'Dialogue based processes', in E. Kaufman, W. Salem and J. Verhoeven (eds), *Bridging the Divide: Peacebuilding in the Israeli–Palestinian Conflict* (Boulder: CO, 2006)
Keane, John, *The Media and Democracy* (Cambridge, 1991)
Kelman, Herbert, 'Group processes in the resolution of international conflicts: Experiences from the Israeli–Palestinian case', *American Psychologist* 52/3 (April 1997), pp. 212–220

Khalaf, Samir, *Besieged and Silenced: The Muted Anguish of the Lebanese People* (Oxford, 1989)
— *Heart of Beirut: Reclaiming the Bourj* (London, 2006)
Khamis, Sahar, 'Multiple literacies, multiple identities: Egyptian rural women's readings of televised literacy campaigns', in N. Sakr (ed.), *Women and Media in the Middle East: Power through Self-Expression* (London, 2004), pp. 89–108
Khiabany, Gholam, 'De-Westernising media theory, or reverse Orientalism: "Islamic communication" as theorised by Hamid Mowlana', *Media, Culture and Society* 25/3 (May 2003), pp. 415–422
Kielmannsegg, Peter Graf, 'Integration und Demokratie', in M. Jachtenfuchs and B. Kohler-Koch (eds), *Europäische Integration* (Opladen, 1996), pp. 31–55
Kitzinger, Jenny, 'A sociology of media power: Key issues in audience reception research', in G. Philo (ed.), *Message Received: Glasgow Media Group Research 1993–1998* (New York, 1999), pp. 3–20
Kleinsteuber, Hans J., 'Habermas and the public sphere: From a German to a European perspective', in R. Kunelius and C. Sparks (eds), 'The European Public Sphere: Dreams and Realities', *Javnost/The Public* (special issue) 8/1 (April 2001), pp. 95–108
— 'Der Dialog der Kulturen in der Kommunikationspolitik', in C. Cippitelli and A. Schwanebeck (eds), *Nur Krisen, Kriege, Katastrophen? Auslandsberichterstattung im deutschen Fernsehen* (Munich, 2003), pp 145–192
— 'Strukturwandel der europäischen Öffentlichkeit? Der Öffentlichkeitsbegriff von Jürgen Habermas und die European Public Sphere', in L.M. Hagen (ed.), *Europäische Union und mediale Öffentlichkeit: Theoretische Perspektiven und empirische Befunde zur Rolle der Medien im europäischen Einigungsprozess* (Cologne, 2004), pp 29–46
Kopper, Gerd G., 'Europäische Öffentlichkeit: Ansätze für ein internationales Langzeitprojekt', in G.G. Kopper (ed.), *Europäische Öffentlichkeit: Entwicklung von Strukturen und Theorie* (Berlin 1997), pp. 9–16
Kraidy, Marwan M, 'Satellite broadcasting from Lebanon: Prospects and perils', *Transnational Broadcasting Studies* 1 (Autumn 1998)
— 'Transnational satellite television and asymmetrical interdependence in the Arab world: A research note', *Transnational Broadcasting Studies* 5 (Autumn 2000)
— 'Arab satellite television between globalization and regionalization', *Global Media Journal* 1/1 (Autumn 2002)
— *Hybridity, or the Cultural Logic of Globalization* (Philadelphia, 2005)
— 'Reality television and politics in the Arab world (preliminary observations)', *Transnational Broadcasting Studies* 2/1 (Fall 2005), pp. 7–28
Kunelius, Risto, and Sparks, Colin (eds), 'The European Public Sphere: Dreams and Realities', *Javnost/The Public* (special issue) 8/1 (2001)
Lalande, André, *La Raison et les Normes* (Paris, 1948)
Lepsius, Rainer M., 'Demokratie im neuen Europa: Neun Thesen', in O. Niedermayer and B. Westle (eds), *Demokratie und Partizipation. Festschrift für Max Kaase* (Opladen, 2000), pp. 332–340
Lichtenberg, Judith, 'Foundations and limits of freedom of the press', in J. Lichtenberg (ed.), *Democracy and the Mass Media* (Cambridge, 1990), pp. 102–135
Loomba, Ania, *Colonialism/Postcolonialism* (London, 1998)
Losito, Gianni, *L'Analisi del Contenuto nella Ricerca Sociale* (Milan, 1996)
Louw, Eric, *The Media and Cultural Production* (London, 2001)
Lynch, Marc, 'Beyond the Arab street: Iraq and the Arab public sphere', *Politics and Society* 31/1 (March 2003), pp. 55–91
— 'Assessing the democratizing power of Arab satellite TV', *Transnational Broadcasting Studies* 14 (Spring 2005), pp. 150–155
— *Voices of the New Arab Public: Iraq, Al-Jazeera, and Middle East Politics Today* (New York, 2006)

MacKenzie, Tyler, 'The best hope for democracy in the Arab world: A crooning TV "Idol"?', *Transnational Broadcasting Studies* 13 (Autumn 2004)

Manjra, Mehdi, *The Intifada in the Age of Rule by Humiliation* [in Arabic] (Kenitra, 2001)

Martín-Barbero, Jesus, *Communication, Culture and Hegemony: From the Media to Mediations* (London, 1993)

Mazzoleni, Gianpietro, *La Comunicazione Politica* (Milan, 1998)

McCombs, Maxwell, and Shaw, Donald, 'The agenda-setting function of the mass media', *Public Opinion Quarterly* 36 (Summer 1972), pp. 176–187

McCullagh, Ciaran, *Media Power: A Sociological Introduction* (New York, 2002)

Meijer, Roel, 'Introduction', in R. Meijer (ed.), *Alienation or Integration of Arab Youth: Between Family, State and Street* (Richmond, 2000), pp. 1–15

Mernissi, Fatema, *Les Sindbads marocains: Voyage dans le Maroc civique* (Rabat, 2004)

Meyer, Christoph O., *Europäische Öffentlichkeit als Kontrollsphäre: Die Europäische Kommission, die Medien und politische Verantwortung* (Berlin, 2002)

Meyer, Thomas (with Lew Hinchman), *Media Democracy: How the Media Colonize Politics* (Cambridge, 2002)

Meyrowitz, Joshua, *No Sense of Place: The Impact of Electronic Media on Social Behavior* (Oxford, 1995)

Miall, Hugh, Ramsbotham, Oliver, and Woodhouse, Tom, *Contemporary Conflict Resolution* (Cambridge, 1999)

Mirzoeff, Nicholas, *An Introduction to Visual Culture* (London, 1999)

Mitchell, C. R., *The Structure of International Conflict* (London, 1981)

Moore-Gilbert, Bart, *Postcolonial Theory, Contexts, Practices, Politics* (London, 1997)

Morse, Margaret, 'News as performance: The image as event', in R. C. Allen and A. Hill (eds), *The Television Studies Reader* (London, 2004), pp. 209–225

Mueller, John E., *War, Presidents, and Public Opinion* (New York, 1973)

Napoli, James, and Amin, Hussein, 'The good, the bad and the news: Twenty years of the Egyptian media', *Cairo Papers in Social Science* 21/4 (2001), pp. 72–85

Neidhardt, Friedhelm, 'Öffentlichkeit, öffentliche Meinung, soziale Bewegungen', in F. Neidhardt (ed.), 'Öffentlichkeit, öffentliche Meinung, soziale Bewegungen', *Kölner Zeitschrift für Soziologie und Sozialpsychologie* (special issue) 34 (1994), pp. 7–41

Neuman, W. Russell, *The Future of the Mass Audience* (Cambridge, 1991)

Nüsse, Andrea, 'Die Massenmedien als Kriegswaffen: Tagung in Beirut zu den Arbeitsbedingungen von Journalisten im arabischen Raum', *Stuttgarter Zeitung* 108 (11 May 2004), p. 27

OpenNet Initiative, *Internet Filtering in the United Arab Emirates in 2004–2005: A Country Study*, 2.E., http://www.opennetinitiative.net/studies/uae

— *Internet Filtering in Tunisia in 2005: A Country Study*, (November 2005), 4.A., http://www.opennetinitiative.net/studies/tunisia

— *Internet Filtering in Bahrain in 2004–2005: A Country Study* (February 2005), http://www.opennetinitiative.net/studies/bahrain

Ortega y Gasset, José, *The Revolt of the Masses* (London, 1932)

Portes, Alejandro, Guarnizo, Luis E., and Landolt, Patricia (eds), 'Transnational communities' *Ethnic and Racial Studies* (special issue) 22/2 (March 1999)

Poster, Mark, 'Cyberdemocracy: Internet and the public sphere', in D. Porter (ed.), *Internet Culture* (New York, 1997), pp. 201–218

Price, Monroe E., *Television, the Public Sphere, and National Identity* (Oxford, 1995)

Rajagopal, Arvind, *Politics after Television: Hindu Nationalism and the Reshaping of the Public in India* (Cambridge, 2001)

Rath, Claus-Dieter, 'Live television and its audience: Challenges of media reality', in E. Seiter, H. Borchers, G. Kreutzner and E.-M. Warth (eds), *Remote Control: Television, Audiences, and Cultural Power* (London, 1989), pp. 79–95

Readings, Bill, *Introducing Lyotard: Art and Politics* (London, 1991)

Richter, Carola, 'Medienkampf der Kulturen: Al Jazeera und Al Arabiya laufen Gefahr, zu stark die arabische Sache zu verfolgen', *message – Fachzeitschrift für Journalismus* 3 (2004), pp. 32–35

Rid, Thomas, 'Die Öffentlichkeitsarbeit der USA im Mittleren Osten: Amerikanische "Public Diplomacy" als Waffe in Kriegszeiten?', *Stiftung Wissenschaft und Politik-Aktuell* 16 (April 2003), www4.swp-berlin.org/common/get_document.php?id=121

Risse, Thomas, 'Zur Debatte um die (Nicht-)Existenz einer europäischen Öffentlichkeit', *Berliner Debatte Initial* 13/5–6 (October 2002), pp. 15–23

Riverbend, *Baghdad Burning: Girl Blog from Iraq* (New York, 2005)

Robertson, Roland, *Globalization: Social Theory and Global Culture* (London, 1992)

Robins, Kevin, *Into the Image: Culture and Politics in the Field of Vision* (London, 1996)

Robinson, Piers, *The CNN Effect: The Myth of News, Foreign Policy and Intervention* (London, 2002)

Sakr, Naomi, *Satellite Realms: Transnational Television, Globalization and the Middle East* (London, 2001)

— 'Media policy in the Middle East: A reappraisal', in J. Curran and M. Gurevitch (eds), *Mass Media and Society*, 4th edn (London, 2005), pp. 234–250

— 'Egyptian TV in the grip of government', in D. Ward (ed.), *Television and Public Policy* (Mahwah: NJ, 2006), pp. 420–443

Salamandra, Christa, *A New Old Damascus* (Indianapolis, 2004)

Salam Pax, *The Clandestine Diary of an Ordinary Iraqi* (London, 2003)

Salvatore, Armando, and LeVine, Mark, 'Reconstructing the public sphere in Muslim majority societies', in A. Salvatore and M. LeVine (eds), *Religion, Social Practice, and Contested Hegemonies* (New York and Basingstoke, 2005), pp. 1–25

— 'Socio-religious movements and the transformation of "common sense" into a politics of "common good"', in A. Salvatore and M. LeVine (eds) *Religion, Social Practice, and Contested Hegemonies* (New York and Basingstoke, 2005), pp. 29–56

Sandole, Dennis, 'John Burton's contribution to conflict resolution theory and practice: A Personal View', *International Journal of Peace Studies* 6/1 (Spring 2001), http://www.gmu.edu/academic/ijps/vol6_1/Sandole.htm.

Sanger, Clyde, and Sierra, Alvaro, *The Role of Media in Conflict Prevention and Peace Building* (San Jose, 2005)

Scharpf, Fritz W., *Regieren in Europa* (Frankfurt, 1999)

Schleifer, Abdallah S., 'The sweet and sour success of Al-Jazeera', *Transnational Broadcasting Studies* 7 (Autumn 2001)

Schlesinger, Philip R., 'Changing spaces of political communication: The case of the European Union', *Political Communication* 16/3 (July 1999), pp. 263–279

Slater, Don, 'Marketing mass photography', in H. Davis and P. Walton (eds), *Language, Image, Media* (Oxford, 1983), pp. 245–265

Sparks, Colin, 'Is there a global public sphere?', in D. K. Thussu (ed), *Electronic Empires: Global Media and Local Resistance* (London, 1998), pp. 108–124

— 'The global, the local and the public sphere', in R. C. Allen and A. Hill (eds), *The Television Studies Reader* (London, 2004), pp. 139–150

Spivak, Gayatri Chakravorty, 'Can the subaltern speak?', in B. Ashcroft, G. Griffiths and H. Tiffin (eds), *The Postcolonial Studies Reader* (London, 1995), pp. 24–28

Srebreny, Annabelle, 'Media and diasporic consciousness: An exploration among Iranians in London', in S. Cottle (ed.), *Ethnic Minorities and the Media* (Buckingham and Philadelphia, 2000), pp. 179–196

— 'Television, gender, and democratisation in the Middle East', in J. Curran and M. J. Park (eds), *De-Westernizing Media Studies* (London, 2000), pp. 63–78

— 'Trauma talk: Reconfiguring the inside and outside', in B. Zelizer and S. Allen (eds), *Journalism after September 11* (London and New York, 2002), pp. 220–234

Steeg, Marianne van de, 'Bedingungen für die Entstehung von Öffentlichkeit in der EU', in A. Klein, R. Koopmanns, H.-J. Trenz, L. Klein, C. Lahusen and D. Rucht (eds), *Bürgerschaft, Öffentlichkeit und Demokratie in Europa* (Opladen, 2003), pp. 169–190

Stratton, Jon, and Ang, Ien, 'On the impossibility of a global cultural studies: "British" cultural studies in an international frame', in D. Morley and K.-H. Chen (eds), *Stuart Hall: Critical Dialogues in Cultural Studies* (London, 1996), pp. 361–391

Street, John, *Politics and Popular Culture* (Philadelphia, 1997)

Thomaß, Barbara, 'Public Service Broadcasting als Faktor einer europäischen Öffentlichkeit', in L.M. Hagen (ed.), *Europäische Union und mediale Öffentlichkeit: Theoretische Perspektiven und empirische Befunde zur Rolle der Medien im europäischen Einigungsprozess* (Cologne, 2004), pp 47–63

Toffler, Alvin, and Toffler, Heidi, *War and Anti-War: Survival at the Dawn of the 21st Century* (London, 1999)

Trenz, Hans-Jörg, 'Korruption und politischer Skandal in der EU: Auf dem Weg zu einer europäischen Öffentlichkeit?', in M. Bach (ed.), 'Die Europäisierung nationaler Gesellschaften', *Kölner Zeitschrift für Soziologie und Sozialpsychologie* (special issue) 40 (2000), pp. 332–359

— *Europa in den Medien: Die europäische Integration im Spiegel nationaler Öffentlichkeit* (Frankfurt and New York, 2005)

United Nations, *Report on UNCTAD's Assistance to the Palestinian People*, TD/B/50/4 (Geneva, 2003)

UNDP Regional Bureau for Arab States, *Arab Human Development Report 2002: Creating Opportunities for Future Generations* (New York, 2002)

— *Arab Human Development Report 2003: Building a Knowledge Society* (New York, 2003)

— *Arab Human Development Report 2004: Towards Freedom in the Arab World* (New York, 2004)

United States Institute of Peace, *Arab Media: Tools of the Governments, Tools for the People?* (August 2005), http://www.usip.org/virtualdiplomacy/publications/reports/18.html

Van Zoonen, Liesbet, 'Imagining the fan democracy', *European Journal of Communication* 19/1 (March 2004), pp. 39–52

Verstraeten, Hans, 'The media and the transformation of the public sphere', *European Journal of Communication* 11/3 (September 1996), pp. 347–370

Volkmer, Ingrid, *News in the Global Sphere: A Study of CNN and its Impact on Global Communication* (Luton, 1999)

Walker, John A., and Chaplin, Sarah, *Visual Culture: An Introduction* (Manchester, 1997)

Wheeler, Deborah, *The Internet in the Middle East: Global Expectations and Local Imaginations in Kuwait* (Albany: NY, 2006)

White, Hayden, 'The modernist event', in V. Sobchack (ed.), *The Persistence of History: Cinema, Television, and the Modern Event* (London, 1996), pp. 17–38

Williams, Raymond, *Culture and Society 1780–1950* (London, 1963)

Wise, Lindsay, '*Words from the Heart': New Forms of Islamic Preaching in Egypt*, M.Phil. thesis, St Anthony's College, University of Oxford (May 2003)

Wolfsfeld, Gadi, *Media and the Path to Peace* (Cambridge, 2004)

Zaharna, R. S., 'Al Jazeera and American public diplomacy: A dance of intercultural (mis-) communication', in M. Zayani (ed.), *The Al Jazeera Phenomenon: Critical Perspectives on New Arab Media* (London, 2005), pp. 183–202

Zarwan, Elijah/Human Rights Watch, *False Freedom: Online Censorship in the Middle East and North Africa* (New York, November 2005)

Zayani, Mohammed, *Arab Satellite Television and Politics in the Middle East* (Abu Dhabi, 2004)

Zogby, James J., *What Arabs Think: Values, Beliefs and Concerns* (Utica: NY and Washington: DC, 2002)

INDEX